D1255993

THE SIX DAYS OF YAD MORDECHAI

MARGARET LARKIN

THE SIX DAYS
OF
YAD MORDECHAI

YAD MORDECHAI MUSEUM

First Hebrew Edition—October 1963—3.000
Second Printing—November 1963—5.000
Third Printing (Revised)—February 1964—30.000
Fourth Printing—March 1965—10.000
Fifth Printing—April 1965—10.000
Sixth Printing—April 1970—5.000
Seventh Printing—September 1971—5.000
Eighth Printing—October 1972—9.000
Ninth Printing—March 1975—8.000
Tenth Printing—January 1977—10.000

The Book was translated from the original English into:
Hebrew, Yiddish, French, German, Russian

To the people of Yad Mordechai

To those pioneers who founded it and fought for it,

To those later immigrants who helped to re-build it

To the youth who will continue it.

Foreword

The race is not to him that's got
The longest legs to run
Nor the battle to those people
That shoot the longest gun.
(Anon. 1862)

This book is about a struggle, A handful of people who tilled the soil stood against great odds and by their resistance pinned down a brigade-size force and thus took the brunt of battle from other villages.

There were several phases in the onslaught against the Jewish community in the Southern region of Mandatory Palestine — first the destruction of the system of water pipes, then the blocking of the network of roads connecting the Jewish villages, and finally the assault on the settlements themselves.

Knowingly and with the force of their conviction, the people of Yad Mordechai prepared for an unequal struggle with all the odds against them. For six days the resistance of the few continued, day in and day out, until at the end they felt that they could not continue in their village. Therefore, carrying their wounded, they withdrew to another settlement in order to seek reinforcements to retake the ground they had lost.

This is the story of Yad Mordechai and its people in the Israel War of Liberation. This is a book that recounts the valor and devotion which made the Israeli settlements so dear to the new, growing nation.

HAIM LASKOV, General
Formerly, Chief of Staff
Israel Defence Forces

Acknowledgements

When Yad Mordechai invited me to come there to write its story, a commission was appointed to aid me. Its members were Yehoshua Katzir, my interpreter; Eliahu Reicher, the gardner and librarian who told me about the battle when I first visited the kibbutz in 1959; Shaul Meirberg, who had served on the Defense Committee; Ezra Rivlis, a journalist, then the editor of the kibbutz Bulletin and the curator of the archives of the battle; and Moshe Carmi, the kibbutz secretary. I extend by gratitude to all of them; they helped me in many ways. Among them, I must single out for special mention, "Shika" Katzir. I was dealing with people of another language, another culture and another religion. I was asking them to recount memories that often were painful and sad. "Shika's" warmth and sympathy toward them and toward me helped to bridge what might have been an awkward gap. At the farewell party which the kibbutz held for me in 1960, he said, "When we began work, I was not at all sure how the book was going to turn out". If it has turned out well, much of the credit is due to him.

Miriam Bettleheim, of nearby Kibbutz Zikim, translated the narratives which the people of Yad Mordechai poured into my wire recorder, and a great number of documents besides. Her enthusiasm was a great support to me.

I want to thank my friend, Dr. Adia Frenkel, head of the Research Department of the Government Press Office, for his encouragement and help. His meticulous care in checking details is especially appreciated.

In 1962, when I returned to Israel with the first draft of my manuscript, I was fortunate to receive the advice of three military men,

General Haim Laskov (retired), formerly Chief of Staff of the Army of Israel, Colonel Shimon Avidan (retired), who commanded the Givati Brigade, and Lieutenant-Colonel Gershon Rivlin, editor and historical expert. If errors have crept into this book, it is through no fault of theirs. I am grateful to all of them for their kind and invaluable criticism.

My deepest gratitude goes to those fifty-five men and women — veterans of the battle — who so willingly shared their experiences with me. To the two commanders I give a special salute and my thanks.

It was the wish of the people of Yad Mordechai that I substitute other names for their own. Except for this, I have set down their story as they told it to me.

MARGARET LARKIN

Mexico City, May 1963

I

Beginning

Kibbutz Yad Mordechai, now in its twentieth year in that spot, lies three quarters of a mile north of the Gaza strip. An accident of geography made it a battleground. Because it is on the main road leading northward to Tel Aviv, it was the first settlement to receive the full weight of the invading Egyptian army in the War of Liberation. In the total history of that struggle, what happened there might be called a small engagement. More men were involved in other places; some settlements were under siege for longer periods; there were many other battles in that short and terrible war that matched its heroism. But the defense of Yad Mordechai had an importance that was not fully recognized at the time. Its military and political significance were profound.

Yad Mordechai did not begin its life in the Negev nor was it known by that name at first. It started as a tiny settlement on the Mediterranean shore near Natanya. Two groups of Polish pioneers — members of Hashomer Hatzair — came together to found it. One group was from Silesia; the other from Galicia. Since half of their members still were waiting in Hachshara in Poland for a chance to emigrate, neither group was strong enough to found a kibbutz by itself. They joined forces, hoping to increase in size as other members succeeded in reaching the Homeland. They called their new settlement Mitzpe Ha'yam. Looking out to the sea, they would watch for the coming of the beloved comrades they had left behind.

Every young kibbutz in that period experienced great hardships and deprivations and Mitzpe Ha'yam was no exception. At first the young people lived in tents, with an abandoned orange packing house as their dining room. The only work they could get was in the orange groves. The men picked the fruit and the girls sat on the ground and sorted it out. Such work customarily had been done by Arabs and the wage scale was low. Men received 20 grush a day and women were paid 17½ grush.

The pioneers deprived themselves of food in order to save money for tools, animals, fertilizer and all they would need to develop their four-acre plot of land. They voted themselves a food budget of 3.2 grush a day. "Eating is what keeps us poor" one of them used to joke and even today, when the food allowance has been increased more than fifty times, they like to quote him.

"Put just enough butter on the bread so that it looks as if it were sweating", Lea, the cook, used to tell her helpers. Meat was expensive; it was served once a month only and consisted of "dirty meat", i.e. butchers' trimmings. On the other hand fruit was cheap; Lea provided so much of it that the men used to grumble that the name of the settlement ought to be changed to "Kibbutz Fruit Soup". The budget did not allow for the luxury of a whole egg per person; eggs were hardboiled or scrambled, so that they could be portioned out by halves. This limited diet began to produce health problems for young people in their twenties who were working ten hours a day in the hot sun. Many broke out with terrible boils; they did not realize that undernourishment contributed to this torment. They suffered sunstroke and dysentery. Dental caries was another problem; the poor diet and the lack of money for dentists played havoc with their teeth. Sometimes it seemed that they never would get used to the climate and learn to live and work in the hot sands of Natanya. But they persisted. They had not come so far and suffered so much to give way before the difficulties.

The work chairman, Dina Gutman, was constantly on the lookout for better paying jobs. A new road was being built between Tel-Aviv and Haifa. It was hard, dirty work to break rocks and lay down asphalt, but when she suggested it, girls as well as men volunteered. Other girls went from house to house as day workers; some got jobs in laundries or as seamstresses. Still others "took nails out of wood" on a piece work basis. Wood was scarce in Palestine; the builders could not afford to discard old boards and beams.

Slowly the members learned new trades. Some of the men became expert bakers and finally founded a cooperative bakery in Natanya. Quite a number became building workers.

"When we arrived in Natanya, it was a town built of wood; we left it a town of concrete" some of the founding members told me when they took me back to the site of their early life in Palestine. They pointed out what they had helped to build — the town hall, the movie theatre, the office buildings, the homes. One could scarcely imagine the shabby, dirty little village they described as we drove around the modern town.

In the meantime the pioneers started to build up a small farm. They planted a vegetable garden; eventually they acquired chickens, cows and bees. Fania, a slight, blonde woman who had learned gardening at a Women's Training Center, was assigned to beautify the kibbutz. A scratched old picture of Mitzpe Ha'yam shows a formal arrangement of lawns, walks and shrubs in the midst of the sand dunes that surrounded the place. Since an important concept of Hashomer Hatzair was that each farm community should be a self-contained village, the kibbutz established its own sewing room, laundry, saddlery, foundry and carpenter shop. One season, when the garden had grown an overabundance of cucumbers, a primitive pickle factory was founded. It was the beginning of the fruit and vegetable processing plant which now produces over a million cans a year.

Another branch of work which the kibbutz entered upon was fishing. There were even fewer Jewish fishermen than there were farmers; therefore it was proposed that some members of Mitzpe Ha'yam should pioneer on the sea. As in every other vital matter affecting the life of the kibbutz, this enterprise was preceded by fierce debates. Tuvia Reich, who was to become one of the commanders of the battle of Yad Mordechai, told me about the struggle. As he talked, his blue eyes sparkled fiercely in his brick red face; an incident that had occurred more than twenty years before aroused him still.

Tuvia explained that fishing was such an extraordinary enterprise that the work chairman and her committee did not feel that they could assign members to it, as was the usual procedure. They asked for volunteers. Since more than enough men offered themselves, it was decided to hold an election. Tuvia's adventurous nature made him a natural candidate for the fishing crew, but he was not chosen.

"After the meeting many chaverim came to me and said that I should not be hurt by the decision — that there was nothing personal in it", Tuvia said, his voice angry with the old grievance. "They told me that it was a question of balancing things between our two groups. So many of us from the Galician side had volunteered that it was necessary to choose someone from the Lublin group, and that was why I was left out". The two groups did not yet feel themselves to be one body; the ties that stretched back to their training camps in Poland were too strong. "Not until the marriages started" were these small jealousies overcome.

However, Tuvia went fishing after all. A man from the other group resigned and begged him to take his place. "At first I said that under no circumstances would I go, for I was opposed to the whole approach", Tuvia said indignantly. "I couldn't understand that cold way of thinking. And I feel very hard about it until this day. But different chaverim came to me and begged me and finally I gave in and joined the fishing crew."

The sea was a whole new world for the land-locked Poles. The fisherman used to bring back strange underwater animals and plants to the amazed delight of their comrades, but profits were not very great. They transferred their activities to fishing grounds further to the north. A girl was detached from the kibbutz to keep house for them and to mend nets in her spare time. Finally the fishermen made a long, adventurous trip through the Suez Canal and into the Red Sea, looking for better places to fish, but somehow the sea refused to yield up its riches to them.

As time went on, living conditions were improved. The people lived in wooden huts and tents and used communal showers and toilets, but they ate and held their classes and meetings in a nicely constructed dining room. They had built it themselves. Rafael Ruder, a large, quiet man with a twinkle is his eyes, explained how hard it had been. "We were on the sea shore and no truck could get to us", he said. "We had to work at night and bring in all our materials in a human chain. One man would stand by the road with a hurricane lamp and he would pass a plank to the next man — or girl — until they came to the end of the line. Often we would work till after midnight, just bringing in the materials we needed for the next night's work."

Finally the Jewish Agency provided money and experienced workers to help construct a two-story cement house with its windows looking out to the sea. But the pioneers were not to inhabit it for long. As children were born, the nursery was set up in one of the rooms and finally the house was taken over completely by the children, while their parents went back to the huts and tents.

In spite of all of their problems, the young pioneers found time and energy for an intense cultural life. There were classes in Hebrew, in philosophy and literature, and in world problems.

A chorus was established, the forerunner of the splendid chorus of 110 voices which Yad Mordechai maintains today. There was a drama group. Everyone remembers the theatrical piece, written by members, entitled "The Kibbutz in Twenty Years". Everything that the pioneers lacked was supplied in the "future" kibbutz — an electric kitchen instead of Primus stoves, a sprinkler system instead of the irrigating hoe. The biggest laugh of all was the scene in which the secretary, ensconced in an elegant office instead of in a corner of the dining room, picked up a telephone to call one of the members. "Can you imagine it, now there really are telephones in some kibbutzim!" Chaska exclaimed in telling me of this scene. "Of course we do have an electric and gas kitchen now, and even a machine to scrub potatoes, and we do have sprinkler systems in the orchards and orange groves. And what would be so wrong if we were to have a telephone to call a mother whose baby was crying in the Babies' House? You'll see, that will come too, one day." In those early times, when they had so little, the young people could laugh at the distant possibility of a more comfortable life. They looked forward to making improvements on their little farm but they were inclined to disdain private possession as "bourgeois". As the years passed, they relaxed somewhat from this early austerity. Curtains, rugs, even an arm-chair, began to appear in their rooms, but only when such amenities could be provided for everyone.

In 1938 Mitzpe Ha'yam together with other settlements in the neighborhood, began an activity for which thousands of Israelis have reason to be thankful. In response to the Arab disturbances which had begun in 1936, Great Britain, ever sensitive to the demands of the oil-rich Arab countries, began to cut the immigration quotas. Although tens of thousands of Jews in Nazi Germany and the eastern European countries were begging to enter Palestine, Britain issued only 12,868 Immigration Certificates in 1938*. Illegal immigration to Palestine had been going on for some time under the most chaotic conditions. Any captain of a leaky coal boat could demand fantastic passage money from frantic refugees who somehow had gotten to the ports of Italy or Greece. In 1937, Mossad le Aliyah Bet had been established to organize immigration on a larger and more orderly scale. It chose the shore of Mitzpe Ha'yam as one of three places on the Palestinian coast where illegal boats would try to land their passengers.

Now the kibbutz became a real "Watch Tower on the Sea." The windows of the cement house were used to signal the immigrant runners. One pattern of lighted windows meant that British patrols were nearby; another signalled that the coast was clear.

Since there was no port and the shore was rocky, it was necessary to arrange a means of taking the immigrants from the ships as they stood out at sea. The fishing group was a natural cover for this illegal work. Tuvia and the others guided the lifeboats to the beach and men on shore received them in the surf, carrying the newcomers on their shoulders to dry land. A third group led the way up the thirty-foot bluff to the orange groves where trucks of the Hagana were waiting to spirit the "illegals" away to hiding places in other settlements until they could be provided with false papers.

The grove most often used belonged to a private owner. It was his delight to fill the newcomers' hands with the ripe fruit, crying "Eat, children eat." "They really thought that they had entered Paradise when they could have all the oranges they wanted", Lea told me. "You know what our Jewish writer, Peretz, wrote in his famous short story?" Whoever has an orange all to himself? An orange is a family affair."

* Illegal immigration more than doubled this figure — 14,675 people came illegally to Palestine in this year.

Bringing in the "illegals" was risky, since the British maintained a close watch and arrested anyone suspected of aiding them. The greatest secrecy was necessary. Leib Dorfman told me a story about how security conscious everyone was. This tall, lanky man usually had the responsibility of first aid for the incoming "illegals" but on one particular occasion he was put in charge of the group that was to guide the immigrants to the orange grove.

"It was a dark night", Leib recounted with relish. "When about half of the 'illegals' had gone up the bluff, I suddenly heard a voice that I knew very well. Someone fell upon me in the darkness, crying out 'Brother'. I had been expecting him for some months and now here he was! But I was so conscious of my duty that I hissed at him, 'Quiet. Not a word!' He couldn't understand why his own brother did not receive him with open arms and I was so flustered that it never occurred to me that I could have hidden him in the kibbutz. I sent him off with the others and it took me days to find him. He did not know where he had gotten off the boat and I did not know where he had been hidden."

Sometimes the ships did not arrive when they were expected. When that happened the whole elaborate apparatus of boats and men and waiting trucks had to be disbanded for the night. After their hard day's work and hours of fruitless watching, the disappointed, exhausted men would lie down for a few hours of rest. But on their "successful" nights, the exhilaration of actually smuggling the immigrants into the country more than made up for fatigue.

What joy there was in Mitzpe Ha'yam when members of their own kibbutzim in Poland actually jumped out of the life boats into the waiting arms of comrades! What haste to hide them in the house on the bluff until there was time for a real reunion! Shamay, Zalman and Dovik came in this way on the last day of Pesach, 1938, and for years they solemnly embraced each other at the Seder in memory of that unforgettable night. Now only Shamay and Zalman are left to carry on this little rite, for Dovik was killed in the battle.

The British knew very well that "illegals" were slipping past their guard. They made day time searches to try to uncover recently arrived immigrants without proper papers; they patrolled the shore with planes by day and with boats by night. Nevertheless, out of all the ships that approached the shores at Mitzpe Ha'yam, only two were intercepted and captured in the two years during which the kibbutz was helping to receive them.

When World War II broke out, the first men from Mitzpe Ha'yam to enlist were Zalman Shamir and Alex Biber. Although the kibbutz was proud of its soldiers, there was some criticism of their "individualistic" action. What would become of the economy of the kibbutz if all of the men went off to war? Other kibbutzim were facing the same problem. Kibbutz Artzi decided that each should offer ten per cent of its membership to the war effort, the men to serve in the Jewish Brigade, the Local Defense Forces, or the Palmach*. They would be selected by drawing lots, but men would be allowed to state their preference as to where they would serve. When the secretary of Mitzpe Ha'yam, Yael Kalman, drew the slips of paper from the bowl, the first name that she read to the meeting was that of her own husband.

Of the nine men who went to the army, all but one were sent to combat areas in Africa and Europe. The exception was Alex Biber who later became one of the two commanders of the battle. After his basic training, he was kept in Palestine as an instructor. The British officers who appointed him did not know that his marked ability as a military man came partly from his training in the illegal Hagana.

When I met him in 1960, Alex was in his early forties. A little grey showed in the stiff brush of black hair above his

* Palmach — The striking units of the Hagana.

rather square face. There was a deep groove between his heavy black eyebrows. His manner was restrained, but at times his face was lit by a quietly humorous expression. Although he knew English, he insisted on communicating with me through my interpreter. Whether this was because he was ashamed of his English, as he said later, or whether he used Hebrew because he did not fully trust a non-Jewish woman and wished to set up a barrier between us, I never knew. On my second visit he spoke to me freely in English.

Alex explained that the Arab disturbances of 1936-39 were cut short only because the war began and not because the issues had been settled; the Hagana feared their renewal at the war's end. Thus it was determined to use the opportunity afforded by large bodies of troops and big stores of arms and ammunition to provide "iron rations" for the future. Alex was one of many soldiers appointed by the Hagana to "collect" arms which the Jews would use to defend themselves should the need arise.

In his dry way, Alex told me of some of his illegal activities. Once he went to an English camp with two other soldiers of double allegiance. With a falsified order they obtained 300 rifles and turned them over to the secret arms store of the Hagana. On another occasion he took part in an exploit which was to have great significance for the future State of Israel. The Hagana had decided to begin the clandestine manufacture of arms. Learning that the British had a captured set of blue prints for German mortars and light machine guns in a certain warehouse, it organized an expedition to steal them.

"Lieutenant Mordechai Makleff, who later became a general and Chief of Staff of the Army, came for me in a British military car," Alex related. "There were two other men — one of them was Rafael Rupin, now our Ambassador in Africa. The warehouse was guarded by an international police force — a Jewish platoon, an Indian platoon and a British platoon. In the Jewish platoon, there was a young second lieutenant — Amos

Ben Gurion. Amos helped us get into the shed where the blue prints were. There we saw so many weapons that we couldn't resist taking some. It seemed a shame to leave with nothing more than some pieces of paper. So, although this was not in our orders and certainly was a bit reckless, we filled the truck with guns. We got out of the camp all right and started south to deliver the plans and the arms."

They had not gone far when they were intercepted by two men, Israel Galili, who later was to become head of the High Command of Hagana, and Jehuda Arazi who was in charge of all such operations as this one. They brought the news that the British had closed the road for one of their periodic searches of vehicles. The raiding party would have to make its way by back roads to another kibbutz. Running down a wadi without lights, the truck hit a donkey. It sputtered on a little farther but the radiator was broken and clearly it could not continue without repairs.

"We had a piece of luck", Alex said with his quiet smile. "We had stopped only about a hundred yards from a British ROAC camp which had a workshop. 'Go in and tell them that these weapons have to be sent over at once to the front in Africa', Makleff ordered. So I went in and woke up the commander and said 'I'm on special duty', and made up some kind of story as to what had happened to my truck. He ordered his men out and in an hour the truck was ready to go. We delivered the plans — and the extra bonus of a truck load of arms — to a kibbutz near Haifa. And really, though we had no right to exceed our orders, that truck load of arms was what saved us. I couldn't have asked the commander to get his men up in the middle of the night to repair an empty vehicle — empty, that is, except for the stolen blue prints!"

While the men were still at war, it came the turn of Mitzpe Ha'yam to apply to the Jewish National Fund for more land. The young pioneers had served an apprenticeship of seven years.

Beginning with nothing but their bare hands they had managed to accumulate work animals, fowls, cows and bees, trucks, tools and a second hand tractor. They had learned many different skills that would be needed on a larger farm. There now were 140 adults and 43 children in the kibbutz; four acres of ground and outside jobs could scarcely support them all.

The first step in finding a new home was to elect a commission to inspect the sites that were available. Since the kibbutz still clung to its dream of a combined fishing and agricultural kibbutz, the first places visited were on the coast. But as none was suitable for one reason or another, the commission began to consider a new home in real pioneering land — the Negev desert. It went to see a place near Beersheba, flat, sandy and hot. The man who would be in charge of growing grain was in favor of this location; he could imagine broad fields of waving wheat where now there was only desolate sand stretching to the horizon. The others joked with him: "When you turn the tractor around it will be time for you to shave again". But the members of the commission who worked in the orange groves disapproved of the Beersheba site as being inappropriate for trees.

Finally they were offered a place five miles north of the Arab town of Gaza. There were about four hundred acres of land and both grain and oranges could be grown there. Only a few miles of sand dunes separated this parcel from the Mediterranean; perhaps in the future they could find a way to continue fishing. But the feature which most attracted the members of the commission was the possibility that a beautiful home could be built there. They could envision the future meshek, nestling among the low hills that relieved the monotony of the plain. There was an Arab well on the property, a square pit lined with stones. It was not very deep but it would supply water for the time being. The commission decided to recommend this site.

This land, which the Sheik of Hirbya had sold to the Jewish National Fund, was typical of the kind of land which was available to the Jewish settlers. It consisted of worn out, unproductive fields, drifted over with sand and no longer worked. Rarely did the Jews move onto fertile land in Palestine. Nearly always they had to reclaim the soil from years or centuries of neglect. In some places they drained malarial swamps; here, sand would be the enemy.

The kibbutz said farewell to the community of Natanya, with which it had many ties, in a meeting sponsored by the trade unions of the area. On the eve of the founding of their new home, the members held their own private meeting to sum up the achievements of their first years and to hearten themselves for the future struggle. Leaders of Kibbutz Artzi were present and spoke. Meir Ya'ari pointed out that the settlers of Mitzpe Ha'yam were among the last immigrants to arrive from Poland; some of them actually had been on the high seas when the war began. "Half of your comrades are lost to you" he said. "Probably the Nazis have destroyed them and they are continuing to destroy Jews wherever they can reach them. Ours is the task to regenerate what is left of the Jewish people. You have chosen to do your part by settling in pioneer territory. In your new kibbutz you must strive to achieve the maximum, whether it be in education, in culture, in industry, or in what you take out of the ground."

The solemnity of the occasion was broken when there was a sudden stir at the door. Everyone turned to look and then joyful cries of greeting broke out all over the dining room. A small, slight figure in British uniform had walked into the room — Zalman Shamir. Determined to be present at the founding of the new settlement, he had persuaded his commanding officer in Africa to send him on a mission to Tel-Aviv. Hitching rides on planes, sometimes with priority and again without, he had managed to make this dramatic appearance in the midst of the farewell party.

After Chaska, his wife, had run to him, and after he had exchanged hearty hugs or handshakes with everyone in the room, he was brought to the platform to speak. He could not say more than that he hoped that a fine new kibbutz would be developed by the time he and the others finally came home from the war. With this the formal part of the evening ended; cake, fruit and wine were served and the young people drank toasts to their returned soldier and to the success of their future enterprise.

After a few hours sleep, the chaverim set out for the new site at four o'clock in the morning. It was December 1, 1943. As was customary, they intended to found their new kibbutz in one day. There were certain unknown factors in their situation which made this desirable. They were settling in Arab territory and it was necessary to provide protection in case of hostile action from their new neighbors. In the second place, their land had been acquired for them in defiance of the British Mandatory authorities. According to the White Paper of 1939, the areas allowed to the Jews for settlement were severely limited; the place where they meant to make their new home was one of those forbidden to Jews. Nevertheless they hoped to be able to establish themselves without interference. The application of the rules of the White Paper depended upon the local British Commissioner; the one stationed in Gaza was known to be friendly to the Jews. Besides, they were relying on an old Turkish law, still in effect, that once a roof was raised on a piece of land, the builders could not be evicted.

Shortly after dawn the caravan of six trucks arrived at the new site. Others were there before them. The founding of a kibbutz was an occasion for rejoicing and for the same kind of neighborly help that used to bring the settlers of pioneer America together for a roof raising. Volunteers from half a dozen sister kibbutzim had come to offer aid.

There were two primary tasks to be accomplished on the Founding Day. The first was to build and roof the dining room, and the second was to construct a tight wire fence for the protection of the property.

Ground had been leveled for the dining room which was to be thirty six feet long and fifteen feet wide. Foundation stones of hollow cement blocks were laid. (They had been used to conceal part of the kibbutz stock of illegal weapons when the trucks brought them). Prefabricated sides were erected and the floor was made by laying tiles directly on the sand. Then roofing with red tiles was begun.

A large crew of men and women were assigned to fence in two acres of ground. Teams of three men drove the iron stakes into the ground at intervals of six feet. Women handled the 40-pound rolls of barbed wire. Seven strands of wire had to be attached to the posts with a crossing between each two. The women took turns with the pliers and with the back breaking task of moving the rolls of wire.

While the work progressed, Efraim, the kibbutz Ghaffir,* patrolled the area. He was a small man, like so many of the Polish pioneers, but he cut a dashing figure in his uniform and "Australian" hat pinned up on one side. He was armed with one of the official rifles which the British had provided to the kibbutzim during the Arab disturbances. It was an Italian gun and bore its date of manufacture — 1911; it had been captured by the British in the World War, when the Italian troops collapsed in the Western Desert. The kibbutz had much more effective rifles among its illegal armory but on this day, when a British patrol might pass, Efraim carried his "legal" weapon. At least it would intimidate any hostile Arab who might be thinking of firing into the crowd from ambush. The other members of his little troop, who were pounding in the fence stakes, also kept their guns nearby.

At two o'clock all work was stopped for the official Founding Day ceremonies. Pressing as were their tasks, the settlers felt the need to mark this important occasion with a formal meeting.

* Ghaffir — a local name for special constables.

25

On one of the low hills a table and chairs had been set up. Over the table was an arch of greenery with a motto from the Bible fastened to it. "They shall raise up the former desolations and they shall renew the waste cities*." The red flag and the blue and white Zionist flag flew at either end of the arch. In their desire to establish friendly relations with their neighbors, the chaverim had invited representatives from the surrounding Arab villages to attend this first festival. The result was disappointing — only a few had come. They sat in a place of honor at one side of the table. After the assembly had sung Hatikvah and the International, speakers from the Jewish Agency, the Jewish National Fund, Histadruth and Kibbutz Artzi greeted the new settlement. The last thing on the program was the reading of a scroll which would be placed in the foundation of the dining room. Meilech, who had composed it, stood up to read it. With his narrow, intellectual face, his glasses and his flaming red hair, he must have been a strange sight to the visiting Arabs. After relating the history of the kibbutz up to this time, Meilech concluded his document with these words. "Against the walls of the ghetto we will erect walls of construction, labor and creation."

After the ceremony the guests sat on the hill and ate the sandwiches which the women of Mitzpe Ha'yam had prepared the day before. Trucks from distant kibbutzim began to leave. The Arab guests made their ceremonious farewells. As dusk approached, the work on the fence was finished. The crew of men and women who would stay behind to build and plant said goodbye to the wives and husbands who were returning to Mitzpe Ha'yam. The first night's guard was posted. Around a campfire, the twenty people who had remained finished the last of the picnic lunch and then began to sing. It was a comfort to sing in this lonely place. The minor strains of an ancient Hebrew melody rose in the still air of the desert. As if in answer came

* Isaiah 61:4. In Hebrew these phrases are expressed in six words.

a single, wailing voice from some Arab shepherd, returning late to his village. There was more than a little kinship between the song of the Muslim and that of the young Jews.

The pioneers had allowed themselves a year to develop the new farm before all of the members would move into it. The first task was to prepare the ground for a seven-acre vegetable garden. The tractor driver worked ten hours a day, hauling the scraper to clear the ground of its overlay of sand. Then deep plowing was done and nitrate was mixed with the soil. Humus and fertilizer, bought from the Arabs, were added. A crew of men and women set to work to plant potatoes, cucumbers, onions and tomatoes. A hundred acres were prepared for wheat. Landscaping of the meshek was started at once. Although Fania, the kibbutz gardener, had to leave her two little sons behind in Natanya, she came eagerly to the new site, her head filled with dreams of the beauty she would be able to create in this larger place. She transferred her plant nursery and put in young trees, azaleas and roses. Sometimes she had to struggle with the work chairman for the use of the tractor and grader. "Of course the work in the fields is important, but the garden is important too!" she would cry. "Why was I sent here if it is not important?" The women of the very first kibbutz in Palestine, Degania, had been laughed at by their male comrades for wanting the "bourgeois" amenity of flowers, but beauty had been accepted long since as compatible with the ideas of the kibbutz movement, so Fania had her way as often as not.

During the year, farm buildings were erected, foundations for the canning factory were laid, communal showers and toilets were constructed. Housing was the last consideration of the builders; the needs of the farm came first. The wooden houses in Mitzpe Ha'yam were taken apart and set up again in the new meshek. Part of the members would live in the houses, the rest in tents. Since living in a house obviously was more comfortable than life in a tent, the people would follow their old custom of changing places from time to time. In the name of equality, there would be a grand moving day every six months.

Finally everything was ready for the move to the Negev (south). The chickens, ducks and cows had been transferred to their new runs and barns. The work animals had gone. The tools and the guns had been sent. The little personal property of the members — their clothes, a few books, some pictures — were gotten ready. The children, who never had seen the new meshek, were excited and eager. But in some ways their elders were sorry to be leaving their first settlement. They had many ties in Natanya; these ardent young people had been active in struggles to raise wages, to strengthen the trade unions and to advance Zionism's cause. In their new home they would be pioneering again, deprived of the friends they had made, suffering some of the discomforts that they had put behind them in Mitzpe Ha'yam. But their dream had been to work on the land, to take barren ground and make it yield. For this they had left comparatively comfortable homes and the secure inheritance of their fathers' trades, shops and little businesses, to go to Hachshara. Often they had been cold, hungry or sick in those bleak training camps where they had learned to work with their hands. In pursuit of their dream — to give Palestine the farmers it needed if it ever were to become a real Homeland for the Jews — they had travelled thousands of miles by any means they could, never to return to their families and their native land. In seven hard years in Mitzpe Ha'yam they had proved themselves; now they had been entrusted with a real farm. Even though they felt some regrets at leaving Natanya, they looked forward with joy to the coming struggle with those sandy acres in the south.

2

Growth

When these young Polish Jews decided to settle in the Negev in the midst of a "sea of Arabs", they knew that they would have to pioneer in human relationship as well as upon the land. How would the local Arabs react to their presence? Would they be met with hostility and have to work their fields with their guns beside them? They had tried to show their own friendly intentions by inviting the Elders of nearby Arab villages to the Founding Day festivities. Only a few had responded. Had they come as friends or as spies?

The year of preparation had not been without its incidents. Once an Arab had managed to burrow his way under the fence. Raya woke to see the whites of his eyes and his hand under the tent flap. Her screams had sent him scurrying away into the darkness but in the morning she had no clothes. Few people in the camp had extra clothes; she had to be outfitted with men's pants and shirt, much too large for her tiny body.

On another occasion a truck coming from Mitzpe Ha'yam had a flat tire in the middle of an Arab village. Not suspecting any danger in such a normal situation, the men had gone down to change it. Immediately they had been surrounded by a group of Arabs who began to grab things off the truck. "Get on! Get back on!" the driver had yelled. "We'll lose everything we have." The

Arabs had tried to keep them from getting back on the truck — one man had lost both his shoes before he could escape. The party had driven on for three or four miles, ruining the tire, before they had felt safe to change it.

The chaverim* had had some experience with how bitter and revengeful the Arabs could be once they had been aroused against the Jews. In 1936, soon after they founded Mitzpe Ha'yam, a serious Arab revolt had broken out in the country, directed both at the British rulers and at Jewish immigration. Four hundred and sixty-one Jews had lost their lives and nearly a thousand had been wounded in the three years of disturbances. Mitzpe Ha'yam had not been attacked but its members had been affected none the less. Some had been sent for training in Jewish self-defense to the underground Hagana. Everyone in the kibbutz had been taught to handle a gun. Nightly patrols of the orange groves had been necessary. Some members, working on the roads outside the kibbutz, had been close to a bomb explosion and had seen its victims.

In spite of these experiences, these young Jews were not hostile to the Arabs. They were convinced that there was room in Palestine for both groups. As Zionists, they believed in their right to settle in the country from which their forefathers had been expelled two thousand years before. As Socialists, it was against their creed to despise any man because of his race. Furthermore, they knew that not every Arab was an enemy, even when his leaders had declared a "holy war" against the Jews. One of their members owed his life to an Arab's friendly warning. He had been waiting in an Arab village for a bus connection when a young man whispered to him, "Don't wait until after dark. Take the train. You are in danger". Shortly afterwards the Arab had been found dead — murdered by fanatics as "a friend of the Jews."

* Comrades.

There was another element in the newcomers' attitude toward the Arab question. As Socialists, they were keen students of history; therefore they understood why the Arabian nationalists felt betrayed by a plan to establish a Jewish homeland on Arab soil. Their hopes had been aroused during World War I when certain dual promises had been made by "Lawrence of Arabia" and by British officials, which seemed to guarantee them independence if they would rise against their Turkish masters. They had carried out their part of the bargain, only to find, in 1920, that they were not to be independent for many years. Palestine and Iraq had been placed under a British Mandate by the League of Nations. Syria and Lebanon were to be governed by the French. In Palestine the situation was aggravated by the fact that the aspirations of the Jews had been given a legal basis in the Mandate; it included the Balfour Declaration which had said, in 1917, "His Majesty's Government view with favor the establishment in Palestine of a national home for the Jewish people and will use their best endeavours to facilitate the achievement of this object." The Arabs felt, and quite rightly, that they had been double crossed. Jewish immigration, and British approval of it, seemed to them to be part of a world-wide Zionist plot to take over their country. In 1920-21 they had reacted with sporadic attacks in which more than a hundred Jews were killed. In 1929 there had been another explosion directed by the Grand Mufti of Jerusalem. In 1936-39 he had financed a new revolt with funds from Hitler[*].

Although the situation had been quiet since the outbreak of the war, the first concern of the new settlers had been to erect a tight fence for the protection of themselves and their property. Their attitude was an ambivalent one. They expected to live among Arabs for the rest of their lives and they hoped to be

* This fact was revealed after the war in captured documents of the German High Command.

able to live in peace with them. At the same time they took the precautions that were customary in all the isolated settlements.

If two such disparate groups are to live side by side success-fully, a common language is indispensable. Most of the Jews had picked up some Arabic in the casual relationships of market or work, but only five or six could speak it well. Within a month after their arrival, classes in Arabic began with a teacher who came especially from Jerusalem. Since Hebrew and Arabic are 'cousin' languages, the students made rapid progress.

As was usual, the settlers hired an Arab to act as a field guard and as a go-between in all sorts of dealings with their Arab neighbors. Abu Ramadan was especially useful in boundary disputes since he knew every parcel of land in the surrounding country. The fields of the new kibbutz were not contiguous, but were scattered among the holdings of poor Arab farmers. Often the settlers would find Arab sheep or cattle grazing in their fields; then Abu Ramadan would be called upon to define the boundary lines and to mediate the dispute. He had to chart a careful course; guards like him had been murdered by Arabs who felt that they had been wronged by one of their own.

The suspicion and hostility of the Arabs to the newcomers, and the ignorance of Arab customs on the part of the settlers, caused an incident within a few weeks of their coming. Every day the cart was sent to the neighboring kibbutz of Gvar 'Am for bread. One day, as it was passing a group of shepherds, an Arab boy tried to steal some loaves of bread. The driver and his helper shouted at him, other young Arabs ran up and there was a tussle. Feeling that they could not let the incident pass without re-taliation, eight or ten men went back to the scene of the attack in a pick-up truck. Words were exchanged and then blows. Unfortunately for the kibbutz, one of the shepherds was the son of the Arab Mukhtar. Abu Ramadan explained to the young Jews that the Arab village had suffered an insult, for he who hits last is guilty and there was no doubt that the Jews had attacked last. Unless peace was made and the honor of the village satisfied, a feud would develop.

There was an established ritual for settling disputes of this kind which the settlers now had to learn. The first step was to select a committee of judges to mediate between the offended village — Barbara — and the new kibbutz. Each nominated the Mukhtar* of a neighboring Arab village and a third Mukhtar was named as a neutral. Although he was illiterate, Abu Fatha, the Mukhtar of Beit Jirja, was esteemed for his knowledge of Arab history and tradition as well as for his fairness in judgement. It was known that he was not unfriendly to the Jews; his relation with earlier Jewish settlements had been amiable. In the Mafada** of his village the two sides told their stories to the judges, the settlers emphasizing that the trouble had begun with an attempted theft and the Arab village complaining of the intolerable insult to their shepherds and to the son of the Mukhtar. After hours of speeches and appeals for peace on the part of the judges, the verdict was handed down. The kibbutz would have to pay an indemnity of fifteen pounds sterling to the village. Two *sulhas,* or feasts of reconciliation, must be held, the first to be offered by the kibbutz.

Abu Fatha dropped his neutralist attitude and came to advise the kibbutz on the traditions of the *sulha.* On the appointed day all of the tables and chairs were removed from the dining room; the floor was covered with carpets and pillows borrowed from Abu Ramadan's village, Deir Suneid. About twenty Arab guests filed into this improvised *Madafah* and shook hands ceremoniously with their hosts, an equal number of men from the kibbutz. Only a few of the Jews could speak Arabic fluently as yet, but everyone knew at least how to return the ritualistic greetings

* Mukhtar — The representative of the village towards the Government.
** Guest home and the men's club.

which were spoken, not only when the men shook hands but at any moment when it seemed that there might be a lull in the conversation.

"How is your health?"

"Excellent, thanks to God."

"How is your crop?"

"Very good, thanks to God."

Your brother? Your sons? Your father? Your journey? And so on through every possible common topic.

When the men had seated themselves in opposite lines, there were ceremonial speeches of greeting. Abu Fatha spoke of the grace and beauty of peace between neighbors, as well as its necessity. The other Mukhtar-judges elaborated the theme. No mention was made of the unfortunate incident. The courtesies of the reconciliation feast were intended to wipe out all memory of it.

Finally the banquet began with the drinking of small cups of strong, sweet coffee. A bowl and a carafe of water were passed, so that each man might dip his fingers preparatory to eating with them, as the Arabs of this region did not use knives and forks. Then great platters of highly seasoned rice and mutton were set down on the floor. The women of Deir Suneid had roasted the sheep out-of-doors, had steamed the rice and provided that flat Arab bread, the *pittah*. Five or six men grouped themselves around each platter. Although they were the guests, the Arabs graciously took the lead in showing the young Jews how to form balls in the palm of the hand so that the sticky rice could be popped into the mouth. They selected choice morsels (the fat pieces) of the sheep and placed them in the section of the plate from which the novices were eating. Abu Ramadan had instructed them that some food must be left on each platter, to be consumed later by women and children, so the Jews stopped eating early. Their Arab friends urged them to continue.

"Don't you have a good appetite?"

"Yes, thanks to God."

"Perhaps you don't enjoy the food?"

"Indeed yes, the mutton is delicious."

When this ritual had been repeated twice over and the Jews were incapable of eating more, they remembered the polite way of indicating satiety. They belched loudly and repeatedly. The Arabs belched in return and the platters were taken away. Plates of grapes and figs were passed and finally cups of bitter coffee which indicated that the feast was over. A week later Barbara offered a return *sulha* and the whole affair was forgotten.

Even more important than such ceremonial occasions were the daily contacts of Jews and Arabs in the fields. The Jew with his tractor, the Arab with his wooden plough, had this in common; they both loved the land that they worked. For the Jew, this bit of land was the fulfillment of the dreams of his youth; he was tilling the very fields where Samson had fought against the Phillistines. He was happy to bring scientific farming to the exhausted land; he ploughed deep and straight with the tractor. The Arab, who would profit from this change one day, barely scratched the surface of the soil. An ox pulled his wooden plough and if he had no ox, his wife was his work animal. Yet he sang as he worked, pouring out his own verses in celebration of a productive field and a beautiful morning. He was illiterate and untutored but he knew the ways of the desert. In his field there were big stones that no tractor could cope with; in an arid land he had left them there to collect the dew.

As is always the case when the haves and the have nots settle down together, petty thievery was common. It remained a constant irritant. When a tool was missing Abu Ramadan "never knew the thief", but he would try to calm the indignation of the settlers with a folk saying, "Until he has stolen from you twice, an Arab is not your friend." Upon occasion the settlers would try themselves to get restitution and sometimes they succeeded. Shamay Wasser told me of the theft of a horse, one of the six work animals on the kibbutz. Shamay was a watchman at that time, for he was recuperating from an operation. He loved horses; when they had taken him away in an ambulance he had called to his comrades, "I'll be back — don't give away my work with the horse." Now he was unable to plough, but he could guard the fields at night and he used the horse to make the round of the scattered fields. One night he thought he heard a suspicious noise and dismounted to investigate. When he came back to where he had tied the horse, the animal was gone. This was a serious loss to the kibbutz and Shamay felt responsible. Besides he was fond of his horse. Since he could speak Arabic, he paid a call on the Sheikh of Hirbya, and after the strong, sweet coffee had been drunk, he related the incident. His appeal to friendship and honor was not in vain; within a few weeks the horse was returned. Thinking in European terms, Shamay gave the Arab five pounds. He was surprised to be summoned to the Sheikh's home a day later and even more surprised at what the Sheikh had to say. "Never reward a thief", the Sheikh admonished him. "Now it will be harder for me to control thievery since these fellows will think 'Even if I can't keep the horse, the Jews will give me five pounds'."

Little by little the two groups began to get used to each other. The Arab who cheekily put his flock to graze on a kibbutz field was not insulted when he was sent off; after all, his fellow Arabs would do the same. He learned to respect the Jew as a worker and a farmer and as a stout defender of his property.

On their side, the Jews tried hard to make friends. They grasped at every opportunity to cement good relations. In this, their children became ambassadors of good will. With the facility of children they began to pick up the language from a family of Arabs whose farm adjoined the kibbutz. Every Friday afternoon their teacher, Sevek, took them to visit some nearby Arab village or farm. Their coming always was a great occasion. The children would be offered sandwiches, figs, apricots, grapes, sugar cane. They learned each other's games and played happily together, absorbing for the future, so their elders hoped, the respect and tolerance that would be the foundation of good human relations.

The position of Mukhtar took on greater importance in the new situation. In Natanya his role had entailed few duties; here he became a sort of Foreign Minister to the Arabs. A visitor's room was established with rugs and cushions on the floor. The kibbutz provided a set of tiny coffee cups; Turkish coffee and sweets were ready at all hours for the Arab visitors. The Jews, with their bustling sense of how to get things done, had to accustom themselves to the slow Oriental rhythm. When an Arab neighbor came to visit, the Mukhtar usually could guess that he had come to request a favor. But the Arab would not be so crass as to introduce the real reason for his visit at once. While they sipped coffee he would ask the Mukhtar if he had noticed the unusual configuration of clouds at dawn that morning. Perhaps he would quote what his favorite poet had said about the exquisite blue of the Palestinian skies. Then he would mention the rising wind and what effect it might be expected to have on the weather — perhaps it would turn and bring the dreared sharav* from the desert. This would lead to reminiscences of other unseasonable hot spells. Queries as to the health of the Mukhtar's family and the Arab's family would be exchanged. Then the talk might touch on the crop prospects or on politics. Finally, at the end of an hour or so during which the Mukhtar must not fidget, the Arab visitor would come around to his request. He might want to borrow a plough or a horse for a day. Or, recognizing the superiority of kibbutz agriculture, he might ask for some tomato or wheat seeds. At times the kibbutz lent or rented its tractor or other agricultural machines to Arab farmers. It was able to give, and was glad to give, many

* Sharav — a hot wind blowing from the desert.

material advantages to the surrounding Arabs, but the first thing that each successive Mukhtar had to learn was that the manner of giving was even more important than the gift.

Ruben, who became Mukhtar shortly after the entire kibbutz moved to its new home, often visited the neighboring villages. He would ride to the outskirts on a white Arab horse, gaily decked out in an embroidered saddle blanket, with a pistol in one of its pockets. Ruben was a dry, matter of fact man; it was hard to imagine him cutting a dashing figure on "Atziel" or "Noble" as the horse was called. As he approached the Arab village the children would announce his arrival with shouts that sent all of the women indoors. In the *Madafa,* Ruben was sure to find some of the elders drinking coffee and fingering their amber prayer beads while they listened to the radio which always was turned up to full pitch. He would sit down with them for the same kind of long, slow visit that he was used to conducting in his visitor's room before he issued an invitation to a kibbutz festival or began to discuss a mutual problem.

The village of Deir Suneid, from which Abu Ramadan came, was especially friendly. It was within sight of the new kibbutz and was its closest neighbor. Whenever there was an important wedding in the village, members of the kibbutz would be invited. " 'Atziel' always was invited too," Ruben told me. "He was a very handsome horse and often was honored with an invitation to carry the bridegroom". After a private ceremony in the home of the bride, "Atziel" would lead the procession into the village square, dancing prettily on his slender legs as the Arabs shot off their guns. More than once he won the race that was the culmination of the festival, and then there might be some good natured grumbling among the Arabs that the kibbutz horse and rider had beaten them.

A service which the kibbutz offered to the area was much appreciated and used by the Arabs. This was the free medical treatment which Dr. Julius Heller began to give in 1945 when he became Yad Mordechai's doctor. He also served the neighboring kibbutz of Gvar 'Am, riding there every day on his donkey. However, he found time for a daily clinic for the Arabs and scarcely a day passed without a line of twenty or thirty women waiting with their children for attention. The children suffered from intestinal parasites, from impetigo and other skin diseases, and from trachoma. Doctor Heller was a refugee from Germany; he was a dour and taciturn man who could not forget the humiliations to which he had been subjected by his own colleagues. But he was a scrupulous and tender physician who knew how to coax and threaten the veiled Arab women into using his foreign medicines. Since he feared the spread of infectious diseases, the kibbutz built a special clinic for the Arabs outside the main gate. From this little hut there radiated new ways of thinking about hygiene and health to the whole Arab community.

During their first five years in the Negev, and until war cut short the process, the young Polish Jews continued to develop friendly relations and mutual aid between themselves and the Arabs. For the most part this was true throughout Palestine. Although some distrust remained, the two cultures, so foreign to each other, could and did exist side by side in peace. This was particularly true in the country. Although the settling of the Jews on the land might work hardships for dispossessed Arab tenants, in the long run the Arabs benefitted. Changes in agriculture and improved health always followed the coming of the Jews. Many Arabs recognized this; it was for that reason that they sent their children to the settlement doctors or asked for seeds in a kibbutz visitors' room.

However much individuals or groups might depart from it (and I have heard Jews say "Never trust an Arab") a conscious aim of the Jewish community was to foster liking and respect for the Arabs. In day to day contacts between ordinary people, this aim was realized for the most part. Troubles between Arabs and

Jews had little to do with their relations as human beings. Rather they were instigated at high political levels by the Arab Nationalist leaders.

Not all of the land which the Sheikh of Hirbya had included in his hard bargain was fit for cultivation. Some was too rocky or eroded to be worth tilling; part was occupied temporarily by a British army camp. In the first years the kibbutz put 175 acres under cultivation. A water tower was built on one of the hills and pipes were laid to the newly planted banana plantation and to the young orchards of apples, plums and olives. The settlers could not afford the sprinkler systems that now irrigate their fields. With the mules pulling the ditching machine, they dug irrigation channels. It was hard, tedious work to control the flow of the water with their irrigating hoes. Ploughing with the little tractor, spreading fertilizer with a pitchfork, planting, cultivating, weeding the vegetable gardens by hand, tending the animals — these were the daily tasks that had to be performed under the hot sun or in the rain and mud of winter.

From their Arab neighbors the young pioneers learned the cultivation of grapes. They bought canes from the village of Barbara which was famous for its large, sweet, green table grapes. The villagers showed them how to plant the canes deep in the earth so as to conserve water, how to fertilize them and how to prune the vines.

The beautifying of the new meshek went on slowly, since bushes and trees take more time to mature than a wheat crop. Fania was obsessed with planting trees. The mules brought barrels of water to a central spot so that she could water each sapling by hand. As she worked all day in the glaring sun, she longed for the beneficence of shade. With great pride she planted an ornamental Chinese tree. "It's called the Bohinia", she told her comrades, "and it will have white flowers on it all during the Spring." She planned to put in fast growing eucalyptus trees along the highway which ran close to the kibbutz and at the foot of the hill where the water tower stood. On Arbor Day the kibbutz made a ceremony of planting the ten inch trees. Under Fania's direction, the pioneers, their children and the Arab neighbors who had been invited, did the work. Since she had agitated so long for its establishment, everyone thought of the grove as "Fania's forest". They used to tease her about it. "Fania, I was walking in your enormous forest today and what do you think I saw — a bear and two wolves!" The time would come when the jokers would be grateful for the tall, thick trunks of the eucalyptus trees and the shelter they provided.

The chaverim worked terribly hard to build up their new kibbutz. Although Saturday was the day of rest, the demands of the farm often made it necessary to work on that day also. A "mobilization" would be announced to finish gathering the grape harvest or to save the fast ripening tomato crop. Mobilizations were voluntary, but few of the pioneers felt like resting at home when their comrades were out in the fields; nearly everyone volunteered. However there were many holidays when only the most urgent tasks were performed. Although they were not religious, the members of the kibbutz celebrated the Jewish festivals as part of their cultural tradition, sometimes altering the ancient rituals to give them contemporary significance. How much meaning there had been in the bower of Succoth when they had erected it for their first harvest in the land of their forefathers! In the pleasure and inspiration of the celebrations, many small irritations of communal living were forgotten as the pioneers renewed their sense of comradeship and dedication to the life they had chosen.

As part of the rhythm of agricultural life, some of the festivals were celebrated in the fields or out of doors. To these the kibbutz always invited representatives from the surrounding Arab villages. *Hag-Habikurim*, "the offering of the first fruits", was a picturesque scene. Wagons, carts and the tractor were transformed into colorful floats, each representing a branch of work. In the parade marched the workers themselves, the people from the poultry house with cockcombs on their heads, the milkmaids carrying their pails, the farmers their irrigating hoes. Now and again the parade halted while a group sang a newly composed song full of local jokes. With clapping and singing it passed by the reviewing stand on which sat a score of Arabs in their flowing white robes and headdresses.

Purim was the gayest festival of the year. All of the children were dressed in special costumes, lovingly concocted by their mothers; they were Dutch girls, gypsy boys, fairies, ballerinas. The story of Queen Esther, acted by adults, was only the beginning of the program. One year there was a political skit with the actors wearing the masks of Stalin, Roosevelt, Ben Gurion, and Churchill. Then followed a Carnival with dancing and games. There were milk drinking contests and potato pancake eating contests. A raw egg was passed from mouth to mouth until someone bit into it and was splashed by its contents. Two teams of serious young Socialists lined up to play the match box game. A small match box cover, open at both ends, was squeezed onto a man's nose. Without using his hands he transferred it to the nose next to him and so it was passed down the line while the spectators rooted for one team or the other and shouted with laughter at the ludicrous scene. The wine bottles were emptied and at this "happiest festival" a bottle of vodka made the rounds among these abstemious young people. They danced the *hora* for hours one ring of skipping people inside another, children holding hands with adults and everyone singing.

In its second year the kibbutz was able to begin the construction of better housing. The new cement houses followed the pattern recommended by the parent movement; each contained four rooms, the living space of four couples. A man and his wife would occupy one room but according to the kibbutz system, their children would live elsewhere. They would eat and sleep and go to school in The Childrens' House, seeing their parents for afternoon visits and on Saturdays and holidays.

This system had developed originally out of the necessities of pioneer life. Woman's labor power was as important as man's in the task of draining swamps, conquering sandy wastes and building good farming soil from ruined land. It made sense to have one woman look after a number of infants, thus releasing their mothers for "productive work". Later on a body of theory was added to this practical need.

Many young people decide to raise their children in some different mode from that of their parents. These pioneers had radical ideas, indeed. Just as they had tried to transform themselves into people who could share everything, so they wished to create in their children a new type of human being, capable of transforming society. In their revolt against the mores of their elders, they had rejected the traditional forms of family life. They wanted their children to be raised "scientifically" by trained people — therefore they extended the early plan of infant care to a system in which the children lived apart from their parents and were cared for by nurses.

In their view the authoritarianism of parents crippled a child's natural development and distorted a relationship that ought to be based upon mutual respect as well as love. All of them had suffered under dictatorial parents. ("When my father said a thing, it was as if God said it"). Since economic dependence upon the father was what gave him power, such dependence was abolished in their society. The child would look to the kibbutz, not to his parents, for his education and for all of his physical needs. The newborn babe did not go "home"; instead he became a member of the "Childrens' Society" and lived in his own quarters with other babies. One of the women was appointed as nurse and upon her devolved the responsibility for his physical care and the beginnings of his education. The rule was one nurse for each four or five little ones.

In my visits to Yad Mordechai, I was especially interested to see how this system, in effect for more than twenty years, had worked out. My experience with my own children, in the close intimacy of family life, made it hard for me to imagine how a mother could part from her child as soon as she came home from the hospital and see him thereafter on a visitor's basis.

The first thing I learned was that kibbutz children are viewed as belonging to the whole community as well as to their parents. My interpreter, Zalman Shamir, was telling me about some army exercises that had taken place nearby during my first days in Yad Mordechai. "Our son took the medal for sharpshooting," he reported proudly.

"Oh, have you another son?" I enquired in surprise, since I had just become acquainted with his seven-year-old boy.

"Oh, no, I mean our son of the kibbutz", he replied.

The children enjoy this situation in which every man is a loving "uncle" and every "aunt" may stop to talk to and kiss a child who has been sent on an errand. But this does not in any way modify their need to belong to their own parents. Like children everywhere, they boast to each other, "My father is driving the new tractor and it's the biggest one in all Israel and I'll get to ride on it." "I can ride on it too — it's not *his* tractor." "Yes, but I can ride on it the most". Even though they love their nurses (sometimes cause for a mother's jealousy) their parents take first place in their hearts. If a child's father and mother leave the kibbutz for some reason so that his visits to the parental room are disrupted, he may become very disturbed. Recognizing this, the kibbutz seldom permits both parents to leave at the same time. The universal need of a child to define his place in the world by identifying himself with his parents was illustrated by the only adopted child in the kibbutz. One might have thought that living with his peers in the Childrens' Society, subject to the same disciplines and rewards as all the others, would have lessened his preoccupation with his adoption, but it was not so. He fantasied endlessly, I was told, that he *really* was the child of the couple who had taken him from an orphanage.

I was able to observe the visits of the children to their parents in more than one home. In those several hours before his bedtime, the child is King. His parents play games with him, go for walks with him, read to him, give him the chocolate and cookies which they keep especially for him. An adult guest is there on sufferance and may not interfere with the attention lavished on the child. This is his exclusive play time with his parents and they all treasure it.

Few discipline problems enter the relationship; the child's socialization is the province of his nurse. Consequently the attitude of the parents is extremely permissive and loving; they do everything in their power to please and entertain their children. Yad Mordechai mothers say that they spend as much time with their children as many Western mothers do and that the quality of their attention may be superior, since they only see the children when they themselves are rested and are psychologically disposed to put their full feelings into play. Certainly there is no doubt that the fathers have closer relationships with their offspring than is possible to most working fathers.

Such a radical innovation did not take place without problems. Nurses, who had received special training in a Teachers' Institute conducted by the Movement, were not always tactful in their dealings with "untrained" mothers. Conflicts between mother love and "scientific" regulations sometimes occurred. Today the Yad Mordechai women laugh ruefully over the youthful extremism of the system. They remember the doctor, whose word was law, and who forbade the babies to sleep on mattresses. He believed in a Spartan regime for babies; it was good for their backs to sleep on boards covered only by a blanket. They remember also their struggle to be allowed to put their children to bed at night. Little by little the stern rules were relaxed; nowadays the parents are welcome in the childrens' houses.

In my limited observation, it seemed to me that this unique method of child rearing has worked very well — in this unique society. The kibbutz parents point with pride to their tall, straight-backed children and tell stories of their self-reliance and intelligent self-discipline. There seem to be few maladjusted children and none of the rebellious, destructive teenagers that dismay their elders in many parts of the world.*

In the new kibbutz, as everywhere else in Palestine, all able-bodied men and women belonged to Hagana**, the Jewish Defense organization. They had received instruction in the handling of weapons and some few among them had made work in the Hagana a sort of second career. These people had gone for special training which had to be given secretly since the Hagana was illegal, or quasi-legal, during all of its history.

Like all isolated settlements, the kibbutz possessed a stock of illegal arms besides those rifles allowed to the Ghaffir. These had to be kept hidden, since the British raided settlements from time to time, looking for forbidden weapons. Since 1939, two men had been in charge of the "slik", as the deposit of illegal weapons was called. In Mitzpe Ha'yam, they had buried ammunition in milk cans and had placed the greased guns inside an iron tank in the ground. Every six months they had changed

---

* It should be noted that not all kibbutzim subscribe to this system. In a few the children sleep in their parents' homes, although the kibbutz assumes responsibility for their support and education.

** Hagana was formed in the early 1920's for self-defense against the Arab attacks that followed the establishment of the British Mandate. Although the new Administration asserted that it would be responsible for law and order in Palestine, in practice it was unable to protect the Jewish people against Arab extremists. In the 40ties it became the underground army of the Jews in Palestine; during the War of Liberation in 1948 it became the armed forces of the new state of Israel.

its location, working at night and covering the evidence of digging even from members of the kibbutz. In their new home it became more difficult to hide the "slik" since the British began to search with mine detectors. Now the weapons had to be put in some place where there was a cover of iron, such as plumbing.

Just because the "slik" was so secret, it piqued the curiosity of the pioneers. One of its keepers, Natek, told me of an incident when a British official came to visit the kibbutz. As he was inspecting the dairy, one of the pioneers said in a low voice to another, "He's standing right on top of our "slik". "He thought it was a great joke", Natek grinned, "but the joke was on him. We had moved the "slik" from the dairy a week before. We knew that people gossiped and we had to hide the arms from our own comrades as well as from the British."

There were strict Hagana regulations regarding the care of the illegal arms. It was forbidden to keep lists. The "sliks" had to be buried at a depth of five feet and no mark of any kind could be placed over them. "Once I lost the "slik," Natek told me. "I thought I knew how many steps it was from a certain tree and from the corner of a building, but when the time came to move it, Dovik and I dug for two nights and couldn't find it. I was half crazy. I *knew* that it had to be where we were digging. Finally, on the third night, we found it a little to one side. When we struck the box, Dovik and I sat down and laughed and cried. Our treasure, our life was in that box!"

Actually, the kibbutz never was subjected to a thorough search, although the "slik" in nearby Ruchama was found and people went to jail for possession of the illegal weapons.

Two years after the pioneers had settled in the Negev, their soldiers began to come home from the war. Like soldiers everywhere they brought home little souvenirs of their service abroad. But they also presented a gift to the kibbutz. From the moment of their enlistment, they had resolved to live as chaverim. They did not consider their army pay as theirs to spend in whatever way soldiers use money to forget boredom and danger. Whatever they earned belonged to their kibbutz, just as when they had been sent to work in distant vineyards. They appointed Moshe Kalman to be their treasurer. Each man had submitted a budget of his needs — these might vary from country to country. If a man's pay did not suffice him, he was entitled to draw extra money from the common fund. On the other hand, those who were promoted were expected to contribute their higher pay. When distance prevented the actual turning over of cash to treasurer Kalman, each man had done his own careful book-keeping and had saved that part of his pay which had been agreed upon. When the men were released from service, they were proud to turn over to their kibbutz these savings, which, plus their discharge bonuses, amounted to nearly five hundred dollars. The kibbutz debated for weeks as to how to use this money. Finally it was decided that the desert heat merited a swimming pool. The soldiers' contribution paid for the materials and the men and women of the kibbutz worked on Saturdays to construct a large pool on top of the hill where the water tower stood.

Some men were discharged later than others from their army service. Zalman Shamir was employed as an interpreter in the search for Nazi war criminals. Gabriel Ramati had been sent with his unit to Holland. Like Alex, he had double duties to perform. Once the long agony in Europe came to an end, the Jewish leaders in Palestine began to plan how they could rescue the remnants of European Jewry. They would re-institute illegal immigration, if necessary, but first they would seek out those Jews who wanted to come to the Homeland. Gabriel was unofficially detached from his unit and along with others was sent to a concentration camp in Germany to work among the inmates. He went to Bergen-Belsen. Although the camp had been liberated by the English, most of the former prisoners had stayed there.

There was no other place for them to go. The British fed them, clothed them and did what they could to stop the raging epidemic of typhus in the camp. People like Gabriel began to look for those who were strong enough and who wanted to emigrate. They gave classes in Hebrew and tried to orient these abused and broken people toward a new life in Palestine. When he first arrived at Bergen-Belsen, Gabriel came upon a Polish girl who was so close to starvation that she could no longer stand upright. When the blonde soldier from Palestine came into her barrack saying, "Who speaks Polish here?" she crawled toward him on her hands and knees. She recovered and, after a concentration camp courtship, they were married. She lives in the kibbutz today, with only her nightmares to remind her of an experience which carried six million of her fellow-Jews to death.

When the kibbutz had been established in the new locale for several years, it became apparent that its future was to rest on agriculture and the idea of continuing fishing was abandoned. The members began to discuss choosing a new name since "Watch Tower on the Sea" no longer was appropriate. This was just at the time when the heroic last stand of Jews in the Warsaw Ghetto was in everyone's thoughts. The young Polish Jews were deeply sensible of the agony and the heroism of this struggle. Some of them had known Mordechai Analevicz, the twenty-two year old leader of the uprising. He was a member of Hashomer Hatzair; it was known that he could have escaped from Poland — he might even have become a member of Mitzpe Ha'yam. When it was proposed that the kibbutz take his name, the whole community began to examine its conscience.

When the Negev site was first proposed, there had been vociferous objections to it from some members. This minority now brought forward the old arguments: "True, we have built up a fine kibbutz but you could hardly call it pioneering. We were not the first to settle in this area — Gvar 'Am and Nir'am were before us. We found water on the place — we didn't have to dig a new well. And far from being isolated, we sit here on the main road between Tel-Aviv and Gaza. People can go to Tel-Aviv every week if they want to. With all these luxuries, what right have we to such a heroic name?"

In the end, however, the minority was out-voted as it had been before. It was decided that the building of any kibbutz was a difficult task and justified the use of a hero's name. The kibbutz decided to call itself "Yad Mordechai" — "Monument to Mordechai." It's time of testing was to come when the black ribbon of macadam, strung through the desert, would bring great peril, not only to its own members but to the new country of Israel.

3

The Siege

On November 29, 1947, an event took place which was to change the history of Palestine and was to deeply affect kibbutz Yad Mordechai. On this day the United Nations, which had been asked by Great Britain to take over the problem, voted to divide Palestine into two states, Jewish and Arab.

For months the people in the kibbutz had been agitated over this question. The foundation of a Jewish State had been their dream and hope since their youth. For this they had severed their ties with their families and with their native land. For this they had remade themselves, the sons and daughters of shopkeepers, into farmers. With their own sweat and energy they had extracted wealth from ruined soil; with high idealism they had created a unique way of life. And now that their efforts were about to be crowned by the establishment of their own state, it seemed that they were not to be a part of it. The new borders, as defined by a Commission of the United Nations, put Yad Mordechai in the Arab State.

They had to admit, in their endless discussions of their future, that the border made ethnographical sense. The Arab towns of Isdud and Majdal* were to the north of them, Gaza was to

* Now known as Ashdod and Ashkelon.

the south. All of these centers of Arab commerce were connected by the black macadam road on which lay Yad Mordechai. Yet they hoped against hope for a rectification of the lines so that their kibbutz would come into the boundaries of the Jewish State.

The United Nations vote was completed at 7:30 p.m. but due to the difference in time, it was not heard in Yad Mordechai until midnight. Only three people were awake to get the news, the guards for that night, Ruben and Jacob, and Shamay, the settlement's wireless operator, who listened to the Palmach's midnight newscast. A jubilant voice announced that both the United States and the Soviet Union had thrown their weight in favor of partition which had been decided upon by a vote of 33 to 13. The formation of a Jewish State was only a matter of time. The announcer finished by saying that the borders, as recommended by the Commission, would stand. Out of their need to share this great news, the men woke some of their friends, but most of the settlers read it the next morning posted in giant letters on the dining room bulletin board.

A day or so later a special meeting was convened to discuss the new situation. There were several points of view. Some people felt that their position would be impossible under Arab rule. They would be cut off from their parent movement and from their market in Tel-Aviv. The new Arab State might well resent a little island of Jewishness within its borders; the discrimination they had escaped could be their lot again. Or perhaps they even would be thrust out of the Arab State by force, losing all they had built. One speaker suggested that an exchange of population might solve the problem; Arabs from the Jewish State might move into Yad Mordechai while they took over some Arab village. The thought of such a solution was dismaying to all; they loved every yard of the soil that they had renewed and planted.

On the other side of the argument there were vociferous

speakers. These people hoped for easy border regulations which would permit them to keep their contacts in Tel-Aviv. They felt that their friendly relations with the local Arabs could be translated into something larger — a historic mission to work for peace and understanding between the two States. "We'll never give up this place", they declared.

Not everyone had a clear point of view on the question. Some people felt confused and discouraged. They sensed that forces beyond their control would decide their destiny.

It was very late when the meeting broke up and the people went back to their rooms, still arguing. However, great was their joy at the prospect of a Jewish State, and whatever their opinion about their own future, all felt that a blight had fallen on Yad Mordechai.

Thirty-six Palestinian Jews were killed by Arabs in the first week after the United Nations voted partition. The violence reflected the intransigent attitude of the Arab States toward the decision. Bands of armed Arab irregulars sprang up all over Palestine; the "Arab Front" groups were under the direction of the ex-Mufti of Jerusalem who had spent the war years as a propagandist for Hitler. The bands ruled the Arab villages by terror, defying the authority of the Mukhtars, intimidating all those of more moderate views. There were incidents on the roads as the Arabs tried to disrupt communications and isolate Jewish settlements. Ambushes on the Jerusalem — Tel-Aviv highway were so frequent that it became necessary to organize convoys. Continuing their old policy of denying arms to the Jews, the British often stopped and searched the convoys. At times they deprived the Jews of their weapons and left them to the mercy of the Arabs who murdered them in cold blood. Concerned as they were with the problems of withdrawing from the country, the British could not, or in some cases did not care to put a stop to the outrages.

At first there were no disturbances around Yad Mordechai, but small signs made the settlers uneasy. Fewer and fewer women came with their children to Dr. Heller's clinic. Friendly visits to the Mukhtar stopped. In the fields the Arabs went about their work silently, with none of the shouts of greeting or of advice that they had given before. Finally one of them said to his Jewish neighbor, "Let us harvest in peace, if Allah is willing. But there are strangers in our village and they are armed. They threaten those who are friends to the Jews." And from these farmers Yad Mordechai learned with astonishment that German and Yugoslav Nazis and Italian Fascists had joined the Arab bands stationed in the villages. They had escaped the war crimes trials by fleeing to the Middle East and now had been hired by the Arabs to stiffen the morale of the irregulars.

The black macadam road which once had seemed such a luxury now became a dreaded gauntlet. The kibbutz sold its produce and bought its necessities in Tel-Aviv; two trucks made the round trip daily. Everyone knew that sooner or later they would be attacked; as they set out each morning the question was — Will it be today? The ghaffir accompanied the trucks, armed with his old Italian rifle and fifty rounds of ammunition. Under his kibbutz cap he carried an illegal hand grenade.

From time to time drivers would receive a warning from Abu Fatha of Beit Jirga or some other Arab friend who still refused to be intimidated by the "strangers". "Don't go today; there will be trouble today." But nothing happened until a December evening when the trucks were returning from Tel-Aviv. As they approached the village of Barbara — the same village that had received the men of Yad Mordechai in a *sulha* — the ghaffir saw a group of Arab women rolling barrels onto the road. "Go to the left", he yelled to the driver, Menahem, and shot above the women's heads. They scurried away, leaving half the road open. From an orange grove on one side and from the protection of houses on the other, fire was opened on the trucks

The ghaffir replied with his ancient weapon which could not be aimed straight, but at least made a lot of noise. A bullet ripped through Menahem's cab and he heard the sharp sound of steel on metal as the milk cans in the back were struck. Motke's truck, which was following also received hits. The trucks sped on and soon were out of range. Back in the meshek the drivers examined the damage while their wives and friends crowded around. Menahem tried to conceal his nervousness with a feeble joke. "They must have had a feast in Barbara today," he said. "Their bullets missed me by a foot." But no one was fooled; it was only a question of time until there would be casualties.

In the weekly meeting the kibbutz decided to armor its trucks. The steel plates would cost as much as the trucks were worth and their weight would cut down the loads which could be carried, but there was no alternative. Yad Mordechai's small foundry put aside all other work to make the cabs of the trucks safe for the drivers.

A Palmach platoon, which included girls as well as boys, was assigned to the kibbutz to help protect the trucks. It was commanded by a tall, laughing youth named Gershon. At twenty years of age he was considered a veteran. The young people lived in tents or wooden huts, and worked half a day in the fields, to maintain themselves. It was the settlers' first experience with the gaiety and matter-of-fact bravery of Palmach youth. Affectionately they nicknamed their protectors "The kilometer Platoon — each soldier weighs a kilo and is no more than a meter tall." The girls did not wear uniforms but accompanied the trucks as "passengers". It was their duty to hide illegal guns in their dresses whenever the British approached. They were the best possible answer to the frequent searches: living "sliks" whom the British soldiers were reluctant to search.

During a routine training march of a Palmach patrol an incident occurred which ended friendly relations between Yad Mordechai and its nearest neighbor, Deir Suneid. As they passed near the village, the soldiers were fired on. The patrol returned revolver fire and threw a hand grenade. This was not an incident that could be settled by a *sulha*. The Mukhtar, Ruben, and Salek Bielski, who was field guard that year, rode over to the village, their revolvers in their saddle bags. There were no friendly shouts of greeting as they approached. The Arab Mukhtar was not at home. In other days a child would have been sent to summon him, even if he were in the fields, but now he could not be reached. Ruben spoke to his unsmiling sons. "We want peace and we believe that our people should live in friendship", he said. "It may be our fate to live under the Arab power; if so, we will be good citizens of the new state. But we will not tolerate attacks on our settlement nor upon the young soldiers who are living with us."

"Be sure we will know how to protect ourselves", Salek said firmly. "Give our warning to your father and to the elders".

They had not been invited to dismount; they turned their horses' heads and rode away. It was their last visit to an Arab village.

Soon it became too dangerous for single trucks to appear on the Negev highways and convoys were organized. The convoy system was based on a cooperative trucking arrangement that had existed for some time for the scattered Jewish villages of the Negev. Now it was enlarged by the addition of those settlements on the main highway which had not needed its services before. The headquarters were moved from Tel-Aviv to Rehovot, since intermediate points were in the hands of the Arabs. A man from Yad Mordechai, Gad Aharoni, was appointed as dispatcher. "When we had sent out a convoy, how impatiently we would wait for its return or for some news of its progress!" he exclaimed as he told me of those trying days. "We never knew when it would get back. Then, finally, the armored trucks would arrive. Each convoy had a whole history, but the drivers couldn't tell their story all at once. They wandered about the station, still burning from the heat, excited, nervous, tired. Finally I would get the details — in this village there had been only barricades, but in a new place, where it never had happened before, there had been mines. At times one or two trucks would not return. Their tires had been hit by bullets and they could not manage to run on the rims; they had been abandoned. Or the British had interfered and had confiscated a truck from which they saw shooting."

To back up his memory of those anxious times, the dispatcher showed me an account of one convoy's journey, printed in an official history*. I reproduce it here since it is typical of what was happening on the roads all over Palestine.

March 23, 1948

Route: The Main highway to Yad Mordechai and by means of secondary roads through Nir 'Am to the southern Negev.

Intelligence: The enemy is gathering in the villages and preparing mines and ambushes.

The Force of the Enemy: Not known.

Our Force: Four armored cars each carrying a squad of the Palmach with standard arms; ten trucks; two wireless outfits.

The Method: One armored car preceded the convoy, two were in the middle of it, one brought up the rear.

The Journey: We started south from Rehovot at 2:15. Two armored trucks full of gasoline joined the convoy. Near Majdal we met a patrolling squad of the British army. The commander of the squad warned the commander of the convoy not to go on that day because there were many mines and ambushes on the

---

* History of the War of Liberation, edited by the Historical Department of the Israel Army.

road. The commander of the convoy asked him if he would accompany the convoy if it waited till the next day as he advised. His answer was negative. We decided to pass. The British officer warned us not to shoot at the Arabs and told us that if we did so, his soldiers would shoot at the convoy. Beyond Majdal a mine exploded in front of the armored car preceding the convoy. No harm was done to the car. The explosion of the mine was followed immediately by a rain of bullets that came from both sides of the road. One of the radio operators was hit in the head (he had put his head out for a moment to look around.) He was killed instantly. We passed through Barbara and reached the school. There another mine exploded. Again nothing happened to the car. About fifteen yards in front of the first car, there was a ditch and the wire leading to a mine could be clearly seen. One of the soldiers jumped down to cut the wire, but before he reached it the mine exploded and again did not cause any damage. The soldier was wounded by a sniper. We came to a culvert and just as we were about to go over it a mine exploded and the car was thrown into the air. However, the dirt and pieces of the culvert fell back into the ditch and we were able to pass.

One of the gasoline trucks turned over when it was passing the culvert. The driver managed to reach one of the armored cars but he was wounded in the head. The convoy succeeded in reaching Yad Mordechai. The armored cars stayed behind and tried to pull out the gasoline truck but they did not succeed and in the end they had to burn it. The convoy waited in Yad Mordechai for the armored cars and then continued to Nir 'Am. Near Deir Suneid and Beit Hanun it was attacked with heavy shooting but succeeded in reaching Nir 'Am at seven o'clock. It stayed there for the night.

Before the convoy reached Barbara it became known to the commander of the Palmach platoon stationed in Yad Mordechai that the road near Barbara was being mined. He went out with two armored cars to interfere, but he was intercepted by a patrol of the British army that did not allow him to proceed.

Our Casualties: One dead and two wounded.

Whatever the route, Yad Mordechai was a way station; often the convoys stayed overnight in the settlement. Dr. Heller had to receive the dead and tend the wounded; two women who had been trained in first aid in the Hagana were his helpers.

Because of the tension and danger of each journey, the drivers were rotated. Each time they kissed their wives and children goodbye, it was with the unspoken thought that it might be for the last time. Each time they returned safely, they felt their luck running out and wondered what would happen on the next trip.

As in any war, periods of intense action alternated with long, boring days in which there was nothing to do but wait. A new route had to be found or some trucks had been delayed in reaching the assembly point. The kibbutz men loved books but after a month or so they found themselves too nervous to read. "I never had played cards", Motke told me, "but finally I learned in order to pass the time. And of course it is more interesting if you bet. Naturally, none of us had any money so we used to 'gamble' with our loads. I remember once I 'lost' every barrel of gasoline on my trucks, but another time I 'won' a truck load of flour." When the convoys were organized at Nir 'Am which was within sight of Yad Mordechai, Motke, who knew Morse, sent messages by flashlight to his wife and friends. "We leave tomorrow — don't worry" or "No escort — will be here three more days." Sometimes he could report that a group of entertainers from Tel-Aviv had made their way along the dangerous route to bring "culture" to the bored, nervous drivers.

"The mines were our principal terror", Motke recounted. "We had gotten used to the shooting and unless someone was careless, like poor Betzalel, we were fairly safe inside the armored cabs.

But the mines were like a blind fate — they could blow up our trucks at any moment. At first the Arabs used contact mines which they had to put in place just before we passed. Often we could see the wires and someone would risk his life to jump down and cut them. But then the Arabs at Barbara began to use electric mines. With those they could let the British and Arab traffic pass and set them off just as we arrived. That was when we had to find another route — Barbara closed the main road to us. Bad as it was on the road, it was almost worse to be waiting and 'resting' in the kibbutz. Then we would wonder about the drivers who had taken our places. Yes, those were terrible times", Motke ruminated. "But through the worst of them we knew that people thought about us and worried about us. Not only our comrades in the meshek. I remember that whenever we left Rehovot we would see a little group of old women standing by the road. They had their prayer books in their hands and they were praying for our safety."

While the drivers in the Negev fought their battles on the roads, the situation throughout the country deteriorated into a state of undeclared war. The Arab nations were unwilling to leave Palestinian affairs to the Palestinians. They announced openly that they would not accept the decision of the United Nations and began to intervene even before the British Mandate ended. Part of Trans-Jordan's Arab Legion already was in Palestine; it had been used by the British for auxiliary guard duty during World War II and some units never had left. In December the six member nations of the Arab League began the formation of the "Arab Liberation Army." On January 20th its first battalion moved into Palestine and soon was followed by other battalions. Headquarters were established near Nablus in the center of the country, not twenty miles from British headquarters. Besides these organized armies, various irregular units were formed. "National Committees" and "Arab Front" groups sprang up all over the country under the leadership of the Ex-Mufti of Jerusalem. "The Moslem Brothers" from Egypt infiltrated the Negev. It was obvious that the British could have prevented this open defiance of their own sovereignty and of the United Nations if they had cared to. Since the build-up of forces went unchallenged, the Arabs initiated various actions against the Jews. They continued to attack Jewish transport. They harassed isolated settlements. In spite of the vigilance of the Palmach, they occasionally succeeded in blowing up water pipe lines.

From time to time the British interfered with these activities but they did nothing to send the Arab volunteers back across the borders. Meanwhile they continued arms searches in the settlements and convoys of the Jews.

Finally the Palmach abandoned its policy of restraint and began retaliatory actions. In some part of the country these included engagements with the invaders, but in the Negev, where transport was the chief problem, the Palmach punished the villages that were attacking the convoys with midnight raids, or in attacks on Arab traffic in the same spot where a convoy had been bombed. Several Yad Mordechai men were called to active duty with the Palmach to accompany the convoys or take part in the raids.

Nevertheless, the irregulars succeeded in closing all roads to the Negev for as much as two weeks at a time. During these periods Yad Mordechai was cut off from Tel-Aviv and Rehovot. The only communication with the outside world was by means of a little wireless set, issued by the Hagana and illegally operated by Shamay.

This isolation caused other hardships than the obvious material ones. There were several pregnant women in the kibbutz; two were within a few weeks of giving birth. After one difficult delivery in his little clinic, Dr. Heller insisted that they must be gotten to a hospital. Would a convoy get through in time and ought they to be exposed to the danger and fright of such a journey? One of the women was Tova, Shamay's wife. With his characteristic energy Shamay took the matter into his own hands. He had a passing acquaintance with a British Major who was stationed in the area and decided to try to enlist his help. One day he waited on the road until a British patrol came by, told his story to an officer, and asked to be put in touch with Major Brown. A few hours later the Major arrived at the meshek gate in a Sherman tank. "Of course I'll take your wife to Rehovot", he told Shamay. "Don't worry, man, she'll be safer with me than in an ambulance. I'll watch her as if she were my own wife." When Shamay brought Tova to the tank, they were accompanied by another pregnant woman. "Have you got two wives?" Major Brown joked, but he generously allowed the other woman to squeeze in through the top of the tank.

Shamay kept in touch with his wife through the wireless operator in Rehovot. "We were like a family of Morse men", he explained. "When someone tapped out our private code number — it was 6666 every Morse operator listened in. So when my son was born, I received congratulations from all over — from people I only knew by wireless and from others that I had met in the Morse school."

Finally Shamay received instructions for the building of a small air strip inside the fence of the meshek. Now and then a small sport plane — a Piper Cub — would land with mail, newspapers and machine parts. Other pregnant women were sent out by air and now and then a Palmach officer would be flown in for consultation. But the field was dangerous; it was very short and the only way for the pilot to gain altitude was to pass over the nearby villages of Deir Suneid and Breir, where he could expect to be fired on.

The guerrillas increased the pressure on the kibbutz by random shooting. Sometimes seemingly purposeless shots were fired nearby, but often they were directed into the kibbutz. There were many narrow escapes. "I was sitting on my bed reading when a bullet passed through my room just above my head." The greatest fears were for the children whose activities had to be limited to the safe spots behind the low hills.

To add to the tension and discomfort of the settlers, the guerrillas cut the main power line again and again. Until a repairman of the electric company was killed, the power failures were of short duration; after that, the company refused to make repairs. The motor of an old, second hand generator, which the kibbutz used to pump water from the well, broke down under the extra burden of supplying light. The Piper Cub brought in parts to repair it; it broke down again. The tractor motor was substituted. A special Tractor Commission was set up to decide when it might go to the fields and when it must be used to pump water from the well, give light, or supply the radio for the nightly news broadcast. Jacob, whose work in the vegetable garden had to be done at night when water was flowing listened to the eleven o'clock broadcast and wrote out a little bulletin of news which he posted on the dining room bulletin board before he went to sleep at dawn.

Within this distorted pattern, life in the kibbutz went on as best it could. The men cultivated the fields and worked in the orchards with their rifles beside them. They came home to shower and change their clothes as they always had. Every afternoon the parents received their children and, concealing their anxiety, went with them for walks or played with them. In the evenings, the classes in literature and languages went on as usual. However when it came to celebrating their traditional festivals, the settlers felt heavy hearted. Purim was approaching, the Feast of Esther. This always was the happiest holiday of the year, with jokes and games and skits that satirized the life of the kibbutz. But this year many people felt that the gaiety of

Purim would be out of place.
eating contest?"

"Can we dance and sing when Betzalel had been brought to us dead? Can we celebrate when Jerusalem is cut off from the rest of the country and we face such dangers here?" some people asked. "Who will have the heart to enter the pancake
The counter argument had a melancholy tone. "Who knows what the fate of our children will be? Who knows if they will be able to celebrate a festival with their parents again? Let them at least have this happy memory, whatever the future brings." So they held the festival, but left out the potato pancakes and some of the sillier games. There was no shooting that day, and in spite of the general anxiety their hearts were lightened by the festivities.

When Passover came in April, the kibbutz had been cut off for over a month. It was known that a convoy had started out from Rehovot but had been forced to unload its goods at a kibbutz en route and return to headquarters since escort was lacking. There was no Matza, no wine, no bitter herbs for the Seder. Impossible to conduct the Passover service without them.

On the afternoon before the Seder, Shamay held a conversation by wireless with Gershon at Palmach headquarters in Nir 'Am. This twenty-year-old fighter, who had been in command of the "Kilometer Platoon", recently had been advanced to area commander. Gershon informed Shamay that the convoy finally had arrived in Nir 'Am and that he would try to bring the Yad Mordechai trucks home. He had three "butterflies"* under his command. These were improvised armored cars — small trucks completely covered with steel plates and with an opening at the top. They would form an escort and start out at once.

* Armored cars — of local production, with "wings" on the roof.

64

The danger point was the Arab village of Breir. A band of the Moslem Brothers, German and Yugoslav Nazis, and a few British deserters had quartered themselves on this village with the intention of interrupting Jewish traffic in that part of the Negev. The road ran between tall cactus plants through the middle of the village, no Jewish convoy had been able to pass it without being fired upon. Nevertheless Gershon decided to risk it, since there was no other available road through the sandy fields.

As soon as the little column entered the village, firing began from both sides. The leading butterfly was hit. Motke, the driver of the following truck, saw it fly up in the air and fall back again. The rule of the convoys was that the trucks must push on, no matter what happened to the Palmach escort. The men were armed with pistols but they were unable to use them since the only opening in their steel-plated cabs was a slit in front of the driver. As Motke went on followed by the second truck, he could hear the sounds of battle behind him; the rearguard butterflies were replying to the Arab fire. Bullets rattled on the sides and roof of his cab. Just as he got clear of the village he saw two vehicles coming down the road toward him. "It's an ambush!" he cried to his companions, thinking that they were Arab trucks coming to join the battle. But as he came up to them, Motke saw that they were filled with British soldiers. A British platoon on patrol had stopped to observe the battle but would do nothing to interfere, although it was clear that the Arabs had been the aggressors.

Meanwhile the rear-guard butterflies were in difficulties. While the two trucks passed on through the firing, they had stayed behind to fire at the Arab positions. One of them received a direct hit in its motor. The driver of the remaining car pushed the other in front of him. When they came up to the wrecked butterfly that had been leading the little column, they managed to shove it ahead of them into the protection of a wadi. Just as they reached - the wadi, bullets hit a rear tire of the one operating butterfly. As the driver got out he was wounded in the leg. Nevertheless he managed to change the tire and push the damaged butterflies on toward the kibbutz.

When the trucks finally arrived, all of the people of Yad Mordechai were at the gate. With anxious hearts they had watched the battle from their hill tops without being able to give any aid.

The drivers jumped down from the trucks and with them the dispatcher and the treasurer, who often had to do his work outside in the town. Nobody had expected them to get home for the holiday. Wives and children rushed forward to welcome them. Over the babel of greetings and excited talk came Leah's voice, "Have you brought Matza, have you brought horse-radish?"

"We've brought everything you need", Motke said gleefully. "And something more important. Look under the boxes there. We've brought seven Czech rifles!"

"Czech rifles!" the people exulted. They had not known before that of all the countries that had supported partition and the formation of the Jewish State, only Czechoslovakia had been found willing to back up the vote with arms. Even the United States, whose influence had been so important in gaining partition, had refused to help the new country to protect itself by selling it arms.

Everyone was present at the Seder except for the men and women assigned to guard duty. The "Kilometer Platoon" was there and so were Gershon and the crews of the butterflies. Two groups of young people were celebrating their first Passover in the Homeland, one group between the ages of fourteen and seventeen, the other from eighteen years into their early twenties. Most wore tattooed numbers on their arms; they had been rescued from concentration camps. In Yad Mordechai they were studying Hebrew and learning to work on the land.

66

Outwardly everything seemed as usual. The tables were decorated and the Passover food never had been more abundant; chickens could not be sent to market so there were more than enough for the feast. But tension was in the air. When a group of young children asked the three questions in the traditional way, many of their elders thought, "This night is different from all other nights because I am sitting here at the Seder with a rifle between my knees." When the people chanted "Bring back the exiles, back to Zion", their hearts were weighed down with presentiments of things to come. They were celebrating their forefathers' release from slavery in Egypt. When they said the next Seder, would they again be aliens in a foreign land? As they began to sing their Zionist song, Hatikvah, shots were fired into the kibbutz. What a bad omen for their future! The singers faltered, but Zalman, who as secretary was leading the Seder, gestured to them to continue. Those who had been designated as emergency guards quietly left the dining room, the rest of the men relaxed their hold on their rifles and the Seder went on.

There were only twenty-two kibbutzim scattered throughout the northern Negev; the Jews were outnumbered a hundred to one. Members of the Moslem Brotherhood were crossing the Egyptian border in ever increasing numbers and it was clear that there would be fighting once the British withdrew. Since Arab leaders had announced that they would not respect the United Nations decision, it would make no difference whether a Jewish settlement was supposed to be part of the Arab or the Jewish State. All were likely to be attacked. Ther was no question of evacuating the settlements under threat. When actual hostilities began, where would the front be and where the rear? With its limited forces and equipment, far smaller than the Arabs believed, the Hagana expected every Jew to stand and fight. The settlements must provide centers of resistance, must hold out until partition could be enforced and the borders stabilized. Then perhaps they could expect to resume normal relations with their Arab neighbors. The Hagana undertook to assist them with their defense preparations.

In Yad Mordechai these preparations were under the general supervision of the Kibbutz Defense Committee. This Committee now took precedence over every other Committee of the kibbutz, even over the work chairman. It had five members, Alex Biber, who was given the responsibility of maintaining contact with the Hagana on questions of defense, Tuvia Reich, who was in charge of physical preparations and training, Zalman, the kibbutz secretary, Ruben, who was in charge of supplies, and a woman who usually served on the Educational Committee. She became a member of the Security Committee "accidentally", as she told me. At the beginning of each new year a special Commission interviewed kibbutz members to ascertain their wishes before job assignments were made. "The Educational Committee has too many meetings", Dina had complained to the Commission. "I feel tired — give me a light job this year". So she had been placed on the Defense Committee with the job of assigning nightly guard duty to members of the kibbutz. She also was in charge of first aid.

The two leading members of the Committee, were Alex Biber, the Hagana commander of Yad Mordechai, and Tuvia Reich, a Palmach captain who, instead of being assigned to outside duty, had been detailed to the kibbutz to share the tasks of command. They had been appointed by the Hagana in consultation with the kibbutz, which had taken personalities as well as military training into account in making its nominations. Alex, whose exploits in stealing arms and plans for the illegal arms industry have been recounted, was a man of middle height with a dark, controlled face. The deep groove between his heavy black eyebrows gave a hint of his thoughtful, introspective nature. "He's a man who always says exactly what he thinks", one of the kibbutz members told me, and added, "That is good in a commander." Tuvia was a small man, not much over five feet tall, but his big torso, thick neck and powerful arms gave him the appearance of a larger man. His blue eyes were set close above pronounced cheekbones which angled down to a sharp chin. His face always looked as if he had a fresh sunburn.

These two men, such contrasting physical types, also were temperamentally as unlike as two men could be. Tuvia was a fighting cock, intense, passionate, overflowing with energy. He was a hard driver who used tools or guns or people to get things done, each having value according to the job in hand. Alex, a less monolithic personality, was more sensitive to the hopes and despairs of people. All of his reactions were slower. No less courageous than Tuvia, he had to think twice before he could come to a decision. These differing human qualities were destined to interact in significant ways in the coming struggle.

Preparations for strengthening the defense of Yad Mordechai were to include reinforcing the fence, preparing proper look-out and firing posts and digging trenches. The area of the meshek, now grown to a hundred acres, already was surrounded by a tight wire fence. Barbed wire entanglements were placed at strategic points. The eight lookout posts were deepened and enlarged and covered with iron roofs supported on posts. The Hagana sent in a trench digger. "They're tearing up my lawns, they've cut into my rose garden!" wailed Fania as soon as it began its work. But although she carried on a fierce argument in defense of her plantings, the military mind was not impressed. She was not the only one to be upset. Benio was about to consummate his long cherished plan for a new banana plantation. The Defense Committee pointed out that it could be used as a cover from which to fire into the kibbutz. Benio argued that the trees would be too small to afford cover and insisted that the orderly development of the kibbutz was important to morale. As in any such policy disagreement, the matter was referred to the weekly meeting. To the dismay of the Defense Committee,

Benio found many supporters there. The banana plantation somehow became a symbol of the comfortable ways of peace, of the kibbutz dream of its future and the members clung to it stubbornly. The two points of view were irreconcilable and finally Alex was asked to present the dispute to the Hagana. This body vetoed the banana plantation. Fruits and flowers had to be relegated to second place; security must come before everything.

Fania lost more of her gardens when it was decided to build four underground shelters. They were six by nine feet and nearly eight feet deep. When the excavator had scarred the landscape with ugly holes, men of the kibbutz constructed wooden frames for walls and roof and covered these with iron sheets from the foundry. Two feet of earth were piled on top of each shelter and everyone took a turn at filling sandbags to go on top of that. Even the children helped. A smaller shelter was built for the command post. It housed the wireless outfit and a primitive telephone exchange which had a connection to every post on the perimeter of the settlement.

The pride of the defense system was the pill box which was placed south of the meshek about 270 yards beyond the fence. It was on a slight rise and commanded both the main road and the short side road to the kibbutz. Most of it lay underground. All that showed above the surface was its concrete roof and a space of wall large enough for firing slits though which its defenders could watch or shoot on all four sides. It was furnished with bunks and a supply of food. From the middle of April on it was occupied every night by two or three men of a special force of eight.

There were between fifty-five and sixty male members of the kibbutz at this time (no one remembers the exact figures now). Of the thirty-seven young refugees living in the kibbutz, about two thirds were boys and young men. To add to the fighting manpower there was the "Kilometer Platoon" of thirty youths. This, then, was the basic force that would have to defend Yad

Mordechai against Arab attacks: a little over a hundred men and boys.

The members of the kibbutz were not without some military experience. All of them, men and women had learned how to handle arms while they lived in Natanya. Fifteen of the men had undergone additional training in the illegal courses of the Hagana. Nine men had served in the British army. In addition to these there were a number of recent arrivals in the kibbutz who had trained or fought in one or another of the armies of World War II — Polish, Russian, or the Polish army-in-exile of General Anders. A few had fought as partisans. Out of these diverse elements, Tuvia began to shape a military organization. Post commanders were appointed, among them one woman, Miriam. She had gone for intensive training in the Hagana and was considered as good a soldier as any man. Tuvia gave her the task of instructing the new immigrants, the 'teen-age students and some of the women of the kibbutz in rifle practice. Each was allowed to fire five bullets.

Sevek, a veteran of Hagana, formed a group with the picturesque name of "The Tank Hunters". The members were the fourteen to sixteen-year old refugee boys. They learned to make and use Molotov cocktails. Since materials were short they were allowed only one throw apiece of real cocktails; the rest of the time they practised throwing with stones or with the eggs that were piling up in the storeroom.

The "Kilometer Platoon" was set to planting "shoe mines" in front of the defense posts. Fearful, lest some wandering Arab herder should set them off, the Palmach lads surrounded their mine fields with little chicken-wire fences and put up warning signs.

Dina supervised the posting of the nightly guard. Women took their turn with the men, but it was understood that in case of real trouble the women would remain in the shelters.

The greatest problem was arms. Ever since their Natanya

days the settlers had been acquiring and hiding illegal arms. Some had been bought from British soldiers, some had been stolen from army camps, some had been turned over to the kibbutz by the Hagana. The kibbutz looked continually for new sources. Dovik, who was a tall, handsome man given to jokes and laughter, often visited a nearby British camp where units of the Auxiliary Territorial Service were stationed. There were a number of pretty Jewish girls in the A.T.S. who acted as secretaries, worked in communications, or were officers' chauffeurs. Dovik became a fixture at the camp, "dating" first one girl and then another. Besides the memory of a pleasant evening he usually brought back a revolver, a few hand grenades or a sack of bullets which the obliging girls had passed on.

Ruben, who was Mukhtar that year, found another source. One of the sons of the Arab family that lived on the edge of the kibbutz was willing to buy ammunition in Gaza. It had taken much delicate negotiation to enlist him in this dangerous work. Perhaps he would not have been willing to do it if money had not been involved, but on the other hand neither would he have taken the risk if not for his genuine feelings of friendship for the kibbutz and the Mukhtar. The two would meet in the orchard for the surreptitious delivery of a market basket half full of bullets that were covered with vegetables. In spite of the precautions they took, however, the transactions became known. The young Arab was caught and badly beaten by a guerrilla band. Nevertheless, he still continued to bring ammunition to the Mukhtar and when they chanced to meet after the war, he expressed his strong feeling by kissing him on both cheeks.

Natek, who with Dovik was responsible for the "slik" gave me a precise inventory of the kibbutz armory from the records which he has kept all these years. It was as follows:

12 Italian rifles issued by the British for defense purposes. These were the "legal" weapons.

25 illegal rifles from five countries. Ammunition for the German and Polish Mausers could be interchanged, as could ammo for the British and Canadian rifles.

3,000 rounds of ammunition for the rifles.

1 British Tommy gun. (sub machine gun).

2 British Sten guns (sub machine guns) with 150 rounds of ammunition for each.

1 German Schmeiser (similar to a Sten gun).

1 German Spandau (a light machine gun which shot three times as many bullets a minute as a Sten gun); very little ammunition.

1 American Browning machine gun; 10,000 rounds of ammunition.

1 Piat anti-tank gun with three shells.

2 two-inch mortars with 50 shells.

400 hand grenades.

The Palmach unit had its own rifles and two Bren guns. It also brought shoe mines and a hundred pounds of explosives for blowing up vehicles.

"We weren't supposed to have the Schmeiser", Natek grinned. "At one time the Palmach demanded that each kibbutz give up some its arms for the general defense and I sent our contribution with Salek Bielski. I had included the Schmeiser since we had the Sten guns, but Salek had been trained to use the Schmeiser and he couldn't bear to give it up. He hid it in his truck and came back with it. You might say he made a double 'slik' for the Schmeiser."

Part of the ammunition also was "doubly" illegal. For some years Yad Mordechai had been a temporary deposit for arms and ammunition that had been smuggled across the border from Egypt by the Hagana. Natek was in charge of them; he was forever burying illegal arms that he could not keep. "I really shouldn't tell you this", he confided, "but I used to take a few bullets out of each box. The Hagana gave out ammunition according to its budget and whoever didn't worry about his own kibbutz didn't have enough. When the fighting started we certainly didn't have enough, but at least I knew that I had added a thousand bullets to our store."

Every morning the settlers of Yad Mordechai crowded around the improvised newspaper on the dining room bulletin board to learn what was happening in the rest of the country. All during March the news was discouraging. Many Jewish settlements were cut off and besieged. The road to Jerusalem was closed and there was hunger in the city. In April the British began to evacuate their troops. As they departed they left a military vacuum behind them; both Jews and Arabs rushed to fill it. There were struggles for the occupation of abandoned British camps, for the Teggart Forts* and other strong points.

In some places, on the theory that the Trans-Jordanian Arab Legion had been a war-time ally and so should be considered part of its army, the British handed over strategic points to this most belligerent of all of the anti-Jewish forces. Such decisions often were left to local officers whose private prejudices determined the outcome.

The people of Yad Mordechai were deeply concerned for the fate of their friends in kibbutz Mishmar Ha'emek, the mother colony of Hashomer Hatzair. On April 4th it was attacked by a thousand men of the Arab Liberation Army under the command of their chief leader, Fawzi El Kaukje. Shelling from heavy guns partially destroyed the settlement and inflicted casualties. On the second day the Palmach managed to evacuate the women and children during a short truce which had been arranged by the British. It was the only British intervention in the siege which

---

* The Teggart Forts, named for the British expert who suggested and supervised their building, were police strongholds which were intended to aid the British in suppressing the Arab revolt of 1936-39. They were sixty-three in number; when the British left, a great many of them were turned over to the Arabs.

74

developed into the biggest battle so far in this undeclared war. The Palmach sent in reinforcements and after nine days of attacks and counter-attacks, the invaders were defeated. Yad Mordechai rejoiced.

In May, as the British withdrew from the borders of the country, heavy fighting broke out in Galilee. Near Ramot Naftali, a small settlement close to the Lebanese border, the Teggart Fort was given to the Arabs. From the Fort and from a neighboring Arab village the settlement was attacked by Lebanese irregulars. The water supply was cut. Women and children were evacuated in a midnight operation down a precipitous gully which passed close to the Fort. Day after day the radio proclaimed "Ramot Naftali is holding fast." Other northern settlements were under similar attacks. Not one of them surrendered.

In Safed, the largest town in Galilee, a colony of 1500 Jews living in the midst of 12,000 Arabs, had been besieged for months. There, too, the large Teggart Fort and two other strong points had been given to the Arabs. In a daring operation Palmach Commander Yigal Alon relieved the colony and defeated the Arabs. Since Safed always had been the undeclared capitol of the Galilean Arabs, the Jewish victory sowed panic among them. The entire Arab population of Safed fled, as did thousands of Arabs in the surrounding territory.

The Palmach and other Hagana units went over to the offensive in many places. After repeated Arab attacks upon Jewish quarters, which the British could not, or at any rate did not, prevent, the cities of Haifa, Tiberias and Jaffa were taken over. Jewish Jerusalem, however, still was under siege and was suffering an acute water shortage, since Arab forces had blown up sections of the pipelines bringing water from the plain.

In the first weeks of May Yad Mordechai also went on the

offensive. In order to prevent the entrance of more bands of the Moslem Brotherhood, and as a measure of retaliation, the Palmach asked the settlement to try to stop Arab traffic. Salek Bielski was chosen to fire from ambush at the northbound Arab bus which passed daily.

Salek was a small man with a wiry, muscular body. He had an adventurous, intrepid nature; during the "troubles" with the Arabs in 1936-39, he had volunteered for the most dangerous front. In Galilee he had joined the "Special Night Squads" — the first Jewish commando units which were organized by the British Captain Orde Wingate to stop Arab raids on settlements and to guard the Iraq pipeline. On the appointed day Salek took his favorite weapon with him to the vineyards. It was the German Schmeiser, which the kibbutz had purchased from a British soldier who had picked it up in Africa. A little ravine ran down toward the road from the vineyards. Salek crept down this ravine and concealed himself behind a rock near the road. British traffic and British patrols were passing; he had the hope that the Arab bus would not be closely followed and that he could hide the Schmeiser and slip back to the vineyards before the attack could be investigated.

As usual, the bus was late. Salek waited calmly but the men watching in the vineyard above could scarcely contain their nervousness. "Keep on working", Zalman admonished them. "Everything must look normal." No one liked this attack on an unarmed bus but they accepted it as a necessity of the undeclared war and their whole concern was for their comrade. Finally the bus was seen approaching. As if he were expecting trouble, the driver speeded up. Salek rose from behind his rock and fired a burst just as the bus passed. Fortunately no other vehicle was in sight. He ran up the ravine, hid the Schmeiser and was quietly at work pruning the grape vines when the British patrol arrived. Salek never knew whether or not his shots had taken effect. But in other attacks upon Arab traffic, Yad Mordechai inflicted casualties. On one occasion it set off a mine which wounded several passengers and killed two men, one of them the commander of the "Arab Youth League" of Hirbya, whose members had been harassing the meshek. The Arabs tried to counter these attacks by placing their vehicles in the midst of the British columns which were being evacuated from this part of the Negev. Yad Mordechai's sharpshooters would have to aim between two British trucks going at full speed in order to hit the tires of an Arab vehicle.

From time to time a British patrol would force the settlers to discontinue these activities; as soon as the patrol was out of sight they resumed them. Zalman concocted an impudent sign, imitating the style and colors of British road markers. "Tommy, Don't Mix With The Arab Traffic If You Want To Go Home Safely!" This attempt to propagandize his troops was too much for a British lieutenant. "Don't you know that it is against the law to imitate His Majesty's traffic signs?" he scolded. "You could be arrested for this."

"It was just a suggestion," Zalman replied laconically.

The lieutenant, more concerned with moving his command out of the area than in enforcing the regulations, contented himself with taking the sign as a souvenir. This little incident illustrated the lack of any planned take-over of power from the British by the two newly created states. The U.N. suggestion that Arab and Jewish militia be formed to keep order as they withdrew had been vetoed by the British. The result was that for weeks there was no civil or military control in many areas. Zalman had known that he was safe in flouting the authority of the British officer. The kibbutz continued to halt Arab traffic and even set up a barricaded check point. In effect, it became the military authority on its portion of the road.

Arab refugees began to appear in increasing numbers, fleeing toward Egypt from Jaffa and surrounding villages. Tacitly acknowledging his inability to control the situation, the British

Area Commander asked the settlement's permission for them to pass. Zalman checked passports and assured himself that none of the southward bound refugees were disguised fighters. His egalitarian convictions were outraged and he shuddered when Arab women fell on their knees before him and kissed his hands.

Day after day, to the wonderment of the kibbutz, the refugees streamed down the road from the north. None of the local Arabs were leaving; the settlers were puzzled by this mass exodus. Not until later did they learn of the instructions that were being broadcast from Arabian capitols: "Leave your homes now. After our victory you will return and take over the lands and possessions of the Jews."

Propaganda like this was a principle factor in the creation of the grievous Arab refugee problem. The motive in inducing whole populations to flee, often against their wishes and in spite of the urgings of the Jews that they remain, seems to have been a military one — to get them out of the line of fire. Perhaps the leaders feared also that some Arabs would side with the Jews as they had done all during the undeclared war that preceded the invasion*.

The passing of the refugees created even greater uneasiness. The question was inescapable — what will our neighbors — our former friends — do when the British have left? Will they join the murdering bands of outsiders who have harrassed us all these months? Will they fall upon us in force and will we have to

---

* A tragic factor, although certainly not the most important one, that induced the Arabs to leave their homes was the terror engendered by events at the Arab village of Deir Yassin on April 12th. Units of the dissident organizations, the Irgun and the Stern group, claiming that foreign Arab volunteers were using the village as a base for attacks upon Jerusalem traffic, massacred hundred of villagers, including women and children and paraded the survivors through the streets of Jerusalem. Although the Jewish Agency and the Hagana High Command expressed their deep regret and disapproval of the deed, it became a weapon in the hands of the Arab leaders.

use our weapons to drive back Arabs with whom we once feasted?

The fear of a general Arab uprising was felt in the Palmach also. The one battalion that was assigned to the Negev began to concentrate its forces, calling in the men that were stationed in various settlements. Yad Mordechai lost the "Kilometer Platoon". The Defense Committee began to carry on a determined argument by wireless and finally an officer was flown into the kibbutz in a Piper Cub to discuss the matter. Tuvia pointed out the strategic importance of Yad Mordechai. "Here we sit on the main road between Cairo and Tel-Aviv. We are a barrier. You see how we have been able to cut off Arab traffic. If this place is captured, the Egyptian army can go straight north to the center of the country."

The officer replied that it was not likely that the kibbutz would have to face the Egyptian army. Egypt's opposition to the invasion plans of the other Arab countries was known. "You will have to hold out against Arab bands of irregulars" he told the Committee. "The Palmach can help you most if it is strong and mobile, so that we can hit them from the rear." However he agreed to leave a squad of fourteen men in the kibbutz.

In these last anxious days before the deadline of May 15th when the Mandate was to end, all farm work was abandoned in Yad Mordechai except for the necessary care of animals and poultry. Everyone, even the boys and girls, worked at some part of the defense preparations. Food was put underground — canned meat, fruit and jam from the factory; butter, sour cream and *leben* (soured milk) from the dairy. Drums of kerosene were buried. Everywhere in the meshek people were digging, dispersing the stores. Barrels of water were placed near each post. The swimming pool, which had been built with so much hope and love, received a new connection directly to the well. The settlers could not be sure that their water tower would stand against attack.

On the night of May 12th, war came closer when Gershon's men attacked the village of Breir, within sight of Yad Mordechai. The object of the attack was to open the inner road which connected southerly settlements with Negba and points north. A long section of the main coast road would lie in territory assigned to the Arabs, therefore control of this inner road would be essential to the new Jewish State. Breir was the main obstacle to its use. More than once the people of Yad Mordechai had gathered on the heights to watch as the Palmach butterflies and the men in armored trucks had fought to pass this village. Finally, after the battle on the eve of the Seder, the road had been cut altogether by deep trenches dug across it.

Four men of Yad Mordechai were called to take part in the action — the crew of the Browning Medium machine gun. Tuvia had been delighted with the addition of this gun to his "heavy" armor. It had been captured by the Palmach from an Arab band shortly before, and had been turned over to Yad Mordechai with the understanding that it could be called upon for any local action of the Palmach. No one in Yad Mordechai had had experience with a Browning. Tuvia had picked three men besides himself who were familiar with other machine guns — Shimon, Benio and Nahum. Together they had learned how to operate it.

The attack began at midnight. As soon as the first shots were heard the villagers fled to the sand dunes — like many Arab farmers, they wanted no part in the fighting. The irregulars fought stubbornly; they had been well trained by the European Nazis who had joined them. In this instance, however, they were outnumbered as well as out-generaled. Before morning they, too, had fled.

The villagers never returned to Breir. Possibly they feared further reprisals from the Jews, or perhaps they were as unhappy at the idea of remaining in a Jewish State as the people of Yad Mordechai were in being shut out of it. In any case, they joined those thousands of deluded refugees whose fate it was to be unwilling pawns in the struggle between the Arab States and the new State of Israel.

After the battle everything was quiet around Yad Mordechai. The road, which had been humming with traffic as the British went one way and the Arab refugees the other, was uncannily empty. The Arab family that had lived for years at the edge of the meshek had disappeared. Under the hot sun the whole countryside seemed to drowse, peaceful and lazy. To the people of Yad Mordechai, frantically preparing to defend their homes, the quiet seemed ominous. What would happen when it was broken?

4

On the Eve of Battle

On May 14th 1948, the people of Yad Mordechai gathered early in their dining room. An event which they had longed for all of their adult lives was taking place: the State of Israel was being born. In Hebrew, the ancient tongue of the Prophets, which living men had revived and made the common speech, David Ben-Gurion proclaimed the right of the Jews to their nationhood.

"The Land of Israel was the birthplace of the Jewish people. Here their spiritual, religious and national identity was formed. Here they achieved independence and created a culture of national and universal significance. Here they wrote and gave the Bible to the world.

"...It is the natural right of the Jewish people to lead as do all other nations, an independent existence as a sovereign State.

"Accordingly we, as the members of the National Council, representing the Jewish people in Palestine and the World Zionist Movement, are met together in solemn assembly today, the day of the termination of the British Mandate for Palestine; and by virtue of the natural and historic right of the Jewish people and of the Resolution of the General Assembly of the United Nations.

We hereby proclaim the establishment of the Jewish State in Palestine, to be called Medinath Israel (The State of Israel)".

Some people wept, some kissed each other, some explained the event to the older children who were present. Solemnly they sang Hatikvah. Underneath their rejoicing was the sorrow with which they had lived for months — we ourselves shall not be part of the new State. More than once they thought back to the fate of Moses who saw the Promised Land from afar, but after all his years in the desert could not enter it.

That very night attacks on the new State began. Settlements on the Trans-Jordanian and Syrian borders were shelled. And, ending all hope that Egypt would stay out of the war, Egyptian planes dropped bombs on Tel-Aviv. Almost up to the last moment some Jewish leaders had hoped and believed that Egypt would not join the other Arab States in an assault on Israel. She had not been a member of the Arab Military Committee which had recruited, trained and armed the Arab Liberation Army. In a meeting of the Arab League as late as April 30th, the Egyptians had refused to commit themselves to the use of their army. Egypt's Minister of Defense had declared to an enquirer, "We shall never even contemplate entering an official war", and knowing the unprepared state of his army for actual combat he had added, "We are not mad. We shall allow our men and officers to volunteer for service in Palestine and we shall give them weapons, but no more." A few days later his government reversed him. The fears of the politicians that a triumphant Trans-Jordan, engorged with the lands of Palestine, would emerge as the leading power in the Middle East proved stronger than caution.

On May 15th Israel, only a little bigger than the state of New Jersey, was invaded by the armies of five countries. In the north the Lebanese got ready to enter. They numbered 3,000 including 2,000 soldiers of the Arab Liberation Army. From the east came the Syrians, also with 3,000 soldiers. The best trained and best led army, the Arab Legion of Trans-Jordan, drove into the center of the country and northward toward Jerusalem. Its 4,500 men were commanded by Glubb Pasha and other British officers. They knew the terrain, since the Legion had been stationed in Palestine during World War II and indeed, some units never had left it. The Israel army of 3,000 men was used to augment the forces of the Trans-Jordanians. In the south the Egyptians sent 10,000 men across the border. (The Saudi Arabians fought with them later on.) The total strength of the invading armies was 23,500.

The one-day-old State had no regular army. At the beginning of the war there were only the semi-legal organizations, formed in defiance of the British authorities, to withstand the shocks of invasion. The Palmach numbered 3,000 men and girls. There were 9,500 men in Hagana field units. In addition, military training had been received by about 3,000 members of two dissident groups which did not accept the discipline of the central Jewish authorities. The settlements, many of which lay on the borders, could count on 32,500 men and women who had received basic training in the Hagana. (Every settlement that had to fight was stiffened with soldiers from one of the above units.)

Not until May 26th was a national army founded. It was organized only with great difficulty. There was no draft law. Recruiting was hampered by the fact that no provision was made for families and that a man could not even be sure that his job would be held open for him upon his return. Nevertheless, thousands of men, among them many new immigrants just off the boat, joined the new army. Many were so hastily trained that they were barely familiar with their rifles when they were thrown into battle and had to learn under fire how to dig a foxhole. There never were enough guns or supplies for any operation. "In order to send out a company, I had to steal shoes and blankets and even food", General Shimon Avidan, one of the great commanders of the war, told me.

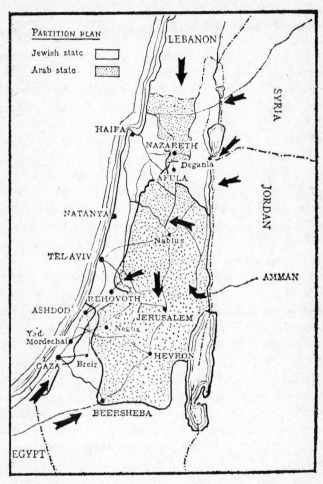

Directions of the invasion by Arab forces, May 1948

Invaluable help came later on from 2,500 Jewish volunteers from overseas. They were highly trained men, for the most part, and were used in the new Air Force and the tiny Navy.

The invading armies were fully equipped with British and French planes, tanks, heavy guns and plenty of ammunition. The Israelis, on the other hand, had no tanks and only four ancient cannons. In the beginning their Air Force consisted of a few sport planes — Piper Cubs — from which co-pilots "bombed" by dropping clusters of hand grenades over the side. When the war began there were only 10,000 rifles at the disposal of the Israeli forces. They had 3,600 sub machine guns, mostly the home-produced Sten guns for which Alex had stolen the plans. There were 700 light machine guns and 200 medium machine guns. Mortars were in short supply. There were 700 2-inchers and one hundred 3-inchers, only three of which were in the Negev. The "Davidka" mortar which the Israelis invented themselves has received much publicity. It was an unreliable gun but it made a frightening amount of noise. Since some of the Arabs believed that it was an atomic weapon, its effectiveness was out of all proportion to the damage it did. However, only sixteen Davidka's existed at the beginning of the war. Against tanks, the country had 19 Piats. There was far too little ammunition — about 50 rounds for each rifle and 700 rounds for each machine gun.

In Yad Mordechai, the quiet ended abruptly. On the morning of May 16th Egyptian planes bombed the neighboring kibbutz of Nir 'Am where Palmach headquarters were located. It was only five miles away. The people in Yad Mordechai watched anxiously as the three planes circled the settlement. They could hear explosions and see rising columns of smoke and dust where the bombs hit.

"Maybe they won't bomb us," the settlers said, trying to reassure one another. "They must know that the Palmach is in Nir 'Am — that's why they attacked there."

Those who had gone to the fields were called back and

extra men were detailed to the lookout posts. The children, who had been sleeping in the shelters for some time, were sent to spend the day there. Some of their teachers were on guard; the nurses tried to carry on the classes. Since visits with their parents were so important to them, they were allowed to take a short walk in the afternoon with their worried mothers, but when shots were heard near the meshek, they were hurried back to safety.

There still was work to do on the defenses. One of the members who had been serving with the Palmach came back with the suggestion that special positions for throwing hand grenades be dug near each post; since the posts themselves were covered with iron roofs, they could not be used for this purpose. The suggestion was adopted by the Defense Committee and men were detailed to dig the positions and protect them with sandbags.

A new generator had been brought in from Tel-Aviv during the quiet days to replace the one that had broken down. The settlers put it partially underground and protected it with sand bags.

A defense measure that had not been completed was the system of electric lights shining outward from the kibbutz. The Hagana had sent the materials for the ring of lights to every exposed kibbutz; they had arrived late at Yad Mordechai. Yehudi Rosen was the kibbutz electrician; he worked around the clock to put up the poles and rig the lights in front of their reflectors. "Now a stone has been lifted from my heart", he told his wife when he finished the work on the night of May 18th. "I have accomplished this one thing for the kibbutz, and now that it's done, I hope that it won't be destroyed."

His anxiety was shared by many. Shamay's wireless was bringing news of the Egyptian advance. Two Jewish settlements lying deep in the Negev below Gaza had been shelled. There even had been a half-hearted infantry attack against one of them, Kfar Darom, which the settlers had beaten off with machine gun fire. What would Yad Mordechai's fate be?

Some argued that the very fact that it had been assigned to the Arab State would protect it; perhaps Yad Mordechai, also, would be by-passed by the main column after a token attack. Tuvia and Alex were less optimistic. They recognized the strategic importance of their kibbutz. If, as seemed certain, the Egyptians intended to push up the main road toward Tel-Aviv, they could not afford to leave Yad Mordechai in their rear to harass their comunications.

The Palmach shared these apprehensions. On the night of May 17th it sent a detachment of sappers to blow up a bridge on the main road near the kibbutz. It was under the command of a handsome blonde boy named Dani who had just finished a course in mine laying and explosives. Gideon, as commander of the pillbox, went with the party. The men in the pill box watched expectantly. It seemed to them that the explosion was great enough to have blown up a half dozen bridges but it was not so. The heavy stone work held; although there were cracks running through it, the bridge probably remained safe for traffic. There was not enough dynamite for a second attempt.

Early the next morning a Red Cross ambulance arrived at Yad Mordechai bound for Kfar Darom. The ambulance was accompanied by a private car in which rode the Swedish doctor who headed the team and Dr. Arie Harel* who was observing the mission for the Hagana. The ambulance driver and the corps-men were Arabs. The party intended to evacuate wounded settlers from Kfar Darom and needed a local guide. After a little discussion the Defense Committee decided that Alex should go, with the double purpose of leading the ambulance safely and of discovering the exact position of the Egyptians.

"Although I agreed, it may have been a little reckless for me, as a commander of Yad Mordechai, to have gone on this

* Later Ambassador to the Soviet Union.

expedition," Alex told me in his deliberate way. "Today I would say that it was not the correct thing to do. However it was decided and I went."

Alex wanted to see for himself what was going on in the Arab villages. Therefore he told a lie; he said that the main road had been heavily mined by the Arabs, the Jews and even the Egyptians, and took the party by way of Deir Suneid and other villages where no one from Yad Mordechai had entered for many months.

"In Deir Suneid I saw that things were quiet", Alex continued. "The Arabs had their rifles but no extra equipment. I recognized a few men who, as our neighbours, used to come to the kibbutz, but fortunately no one recognized me. The ambulance was flying the flag of the Red Cross and that helped us to go on our way in peace. We passed through two more villages and then came out to the main road where we were stopped by an Egyptian patrol of three armored cars. Dr. Harel explained that we were going to Gaza to seek permission to proceed to Kfar Darom. The commander of the patrol said that he would accompany us. Dr. Harel immediately told me to put on one of the white uniforms since, as a Jew, I might be in danger. From this time on I had to pretend to be a Swede, even though I had been too busy to shave and didn't give a very good impression as a member of the Red Cross."

The party arrived at the railway station in Gaza and the doctors went off to ask for passes. Alex looked around him. "And naturally I felt very badly about what I saw", he told me in his restrained manner. "All around were cannons, armored cars, Bren carriers, soldiers, and every now and then a motor cyclist from the air-force who seemed to be coming up to give reports to the central command. Anyone with military experience could see that this was an army preparing to move."

Standing by the ambulance, Alex got into conversation with an Egyptian Major who spoke English.

"Where will you go next?", Alex asked.

The Major, who apparently found this expedition exhilarating after the monotony of barracks life, replied readily, "One column is on its way to Beersheba and Jerusalem and my brigade will go to Tel-Aviv. Tomorrow we intend to surround the village of Deir Suneid."*

Alex understood at once. There was no military necessity for this Arab army to surround an Arab village; the Major meant that the Egyptians intended to attack Yad Mordechai.

About two hours passed during which Alex felt that he had been a fool to leave the kibbutz and began to worry about how he could get back quickly. Dr. Harel and the others finally returned with the information that the Egyptians would not give a pass to the team because "they had conquered Kfar Darom** and would behave according to the Geneva Convention with the prisoners." However, headquarters had promised to ask Cairo for orders. Suddenly, while they were discussing what to do next, they were herded by soldiers into a closed room.

"We weren't certain whether this was imprisonment or not", Alex said. "It wasn't the usual sort of imprisonment because we were free to talk to each other and to move about the room. Still there was a guard at the door, so we weren't exactly free either."

Alex began to press for an immediate return. Wise in the ways of army bureaucracy he argued that the Egyptian Command had had plenty of time to receive an answer from Cairo in

---

* Official Egyptian accounts refer to the battle of Yad Mordechai as the battle of Deir Suneid. This confusion has entered a number of books about the Arab-Israeli War.

** Kfar Darom never was captured. After an unsuccessful attack upon it by the Moslem Brotherhood under the command of an Egyptian army officer, it was by-passed but kept under siege by the Irregulars. It was evacuated on July 7th by orders of the Hagana.

the more than two hours of negotiation and waiting. If they were
being held up now, it probably meant that the officers intended
to forget them and let them cool their heels in detention. That
must be the meaning of their arrest, he argued. "I have to get
back to the kibbutz, I absolutely must get back to the kibbutz",
he kept repeating. The others looked at him in wonder and
pointed out that they were prisoners in the center of an army
camp. How was it possible for them to leave until their situation
was resolved?

The guard moved away from the door for a few moments.
Alex, who had learned in his years of illegal work that nerve
and aplomb could get a man out of many a tight spot, took
command. "This is our chance, let's go!" he said. "Follow me
and walk slowly". They strolled over to the ambulance — the
driver was nowhere to be seen. "We'll have to leave it". Alex
decided. They got into the Swedish doctor's car and quite simply,
in the midst of all the confusion of the Egyptian camp, they
drove away. This time Alex directed the car down the main road.
The doctors protested that he had told them it was heavily mined.
"Don't worry — I know the road well", he reassured them.
And he sent them first to the left, then to the right in any
pattern that occurred to him, "saving" them from danger. They
passed all barricades with their Red Cross flag flying and finally
got back to Deir Suneid.

The village had changed since the morning. No women or
children were to be seen. The few village men who were about
were heavily armed. Squads of Egyptian soldiers were camped
under the big trees that screened the place from Yad Mordechai's
view. On the sand dunes near by, machine guns and mortars
were being emplaced. The statement of the Egyptian Major was
confirmed.

The party drove into Yad Mordechai at six o'clock. Alex ran
to the post nearest the gate and commanded, "Telepone Tuvia
at once and tell him to put our defense plan into action." He

asked Dr. Harel to go to the High Command with a report of what they had seen and what was about to happen.

At this hour the children had been taking their afternoon walk with their parents. They were rushed back to the shelters. No sooner were they there than two English Spitfires, marked with the signs of the Egyptian Air Force, flew low over the kibbutz, firing machine guns and dropping bombs. Although they could hear the bullets hitting the tops of the shelters, the nurses read stories or led the children in singing to distract their attention. One of the five-year-olds cried out hysterically. "I ordered him to stop," his nurse told me. "I said to him, 'You will see what our boys will do to those airplanes'."

Outside in the trenches the men were horrified to see a bomb drop in the yard of the Babies' House where the two year olds had been playing only minutes before. Some of them could not resist firing at the departing planes even though this waste of bullets had been forbidden. When the planes had disappeared over the sand dunes, they ran to put out several fires that had been started near the poultry houses.

The problem of the children had been under discussion for months. Alex had applied to the Hagana many times for their evacuation. The answer always had been no. The basic factor in this decision seems to have been the belief that Egypt would not join the war. All of the advance physical preparations reflected this thinking. Yad Mordechai and the other settlements were expected to withstand four or five months of sporadic attacks by Arab irregulars armed with rifles and machine guns. Women, who were necessary to the economic life of the settlements, would remain at their posts and their children with them. "Nothing lowers the spirit of a fighter so much as when he sees first steps in evacuation," a Palmach commander wrote later on the problem.

Now, with the reality before them, the Defense Committee

decided to evacuate the children without waiting for permission. Shamay was ordered to communicate this decision to Gershon, the local Palmach Commander, in his headquarters in Nir 'Am. Gershon did not wait for orders either. He agreed to come to Yad Mordechai with three armored cars and an armored bus. He would arrive about midnight.

The Education Committee held a hasty meeting; it had to decide who should go out with the children. Their nurses of course, but who else? It was impossible to send all of the mothers. Not enough transportation was available and, besides, the kibbutz idea still was that work somehow would go forward in the meshek and the women would be needed for the poultry, the cows, the kitchen. Finally it was decided to send out the nursing mothers "and a few other women who were more sensitive than most."

Everyone in the kibbutz, except those on guard, was called to help with the evacuation. Men loaded beds and mattresses on the kibbutz trucks. The nurses packed the children's clothes. Parents went to their rooms to bring a loved toy for the journey. No one knew what to expect. Some felt that the children were leaving forever and that this hasty parting would be the last time that they would set eyes on them. Others believed that the danger would pass and the children would return in a week or so. One of the women told me how she and her husband had argued these points of view in hurried moments before the children left. Yael Kalman was a childrens' nurse and was going out with the convoy, Moshe, her husband, was staying to fight. Their two children would go with her.

"Take our photograph albums for the children", he said.

"Why? What's the need? They will only be in the way", she answered sharply.

"Take them," he repeated.

She understood very well what was behind his insistence. They had known each other since their scouting days when they were eleven years old; she could read his thought that she must take the albums for the children to remember him by. But this thought was intolerable to her and she pushed it away. "I'll have enough to do without worrying about our albums" she retorted, her anxiety for him translating itself into anger.

He spoke to her of the dangers to come. He saw them clearly for he had known war. She herself had sent him to the British army when, as secretary of the kibbutz, she had drawn his name from the bowl. "It will not be so easy to come out of this" he told her. "An army brigade does not surround a point for nothing. It is good that you are going out, for if one of us has to fall, the children need you more. And you will know how to carry the burden."

She rejected this thought, although she remembers every word of it now, but she did take the albums.

At eleven o'clock the cars arrived and were hidden in the eucalyptus grove. Four people of Yad Mordechai returned with them. One was Yurek, the bee-keeper, who had moved his hives to a distant place in order to protect them from Arab sabotage. Another was the factory manager, Nachman Katz. The other two were Wolf and Vered, newcomers to the kibbutz. Those who met the cars were shocked to see them, for they knew that Vered had given birth to a still born child only a few days before. "What are you doing here!" they exclaimed. "Why didn't Vered stay in Rehovot to rest and recuperate? Don't you know that we are in great danger here?"

"Should we stay in safety in Rehovot while all of you and even outsiders defend our kibbutz?" Wolf replied. "Whatever your fate will be, ours will be the same."

The children were awakened. They were sleepy, cross, half-ill from the days of confinement and there was much crying. The tiny children took it best. To them it seemed like an adventure to see their parents so unexpectedly in the middle of the night and to be carried through the darkness to the waiting vehicles.

"Car! Car!" the little son of Miriam, the woman commander, kept saying. He sat by his nurse smiling, Miriam remembers, with the happiness of a secure baby who could not understand that anyone or anything might want to hurt him. "It was easier for me then, in spite of the pain in my heart and the lump in my throat", Miriam told me. "I refused to think of the dangers of the journey, of mines and shells. I kissed the child and stood for one moment to look at his face so that I would remember it well."

It was hard to tell where grief lay heaviest, on the mothers who were giving over their children to the nurses or on the nurses who were receiving the terrible responsibility of taking ninety-two children to safety. "What will happen to my child if I should die here?" one of the women asked a nurse as she handed over her two-year-old. "Then I shall take him as my own", the nurse answered simply and the mother was comforted, for she knew the loving heart of the other woman and in her few sincere words felt assured of her baby's future. Another parted from her only child with half-strangled sobs, then seeing tall young Gershon standing nearby she said to him solemnly "I am giving over to you the dearest thing in my life". One of the women watching the parents hurrying through the night with their children and carrying their belongings in all sorts of bundles and boxes, thought of the Arab refugees who had crowded the roads only a few days before. "Now we are refugees, too", she said to herself and felt that sudden, sharp disbelief that comes to people in such abnormal situations: "This can't be happening to me."

Finally the cars were loaded. Naftali, the kibbutz treasurer, who was being sent with the children much against his will, made the final count. Husbands and wives, ordinarily undemonstrative, clasped each other for the third or fourth time. Some of the parents ran beside the cars to the gate, waving and throwing kisses to children who could not see them. Then everyone went back to his task for the night. Gershon had suggested that the proud row of trees which the settlers had planted beside the road would make an excellent road block. A crew was set to work cutting it down. Dani and the Palmach squad continued to plant land mines outside the fence. Many men were assigned to dig trenches deeper or to place sandbags. In the armory, Dovik and Natek and their wives cleaned guns and sent out ammunition to the posts. This last was a meticulous task. They had to know just where each of their precious 37 rifles was located in order to supply the proper ammunition.

In between jobs the fathers and mothers besieged the headquarters for news of the children's progress. "Shamay, no word yet? Have you tried Gvar 'Am? Maybe they went to Dorot? No news yet, no news?"

When the convoy with the children left Yad Mordechai, Gershon could not be sure where he would take them. Armed men were everywhere — Egyptian patrols, Arab guerrillas and men of the Palmach were reconnoitering in the countryside. They had to proceed slowly, without light, sending scouts ahead. They dared not travel on the roads but bumped along in the fields. Thy would ride for ten or fifteen minutes and then wait while scouts searched for mines or made contact with local people who could guide them. Once they were surrounded by men holding flaring torches; for a few tense moments the women did not know whether they were enemies or friends. Although they turned out to be Palmach men, their terror was intensified, if anything, when the women learned that they had been heading into enemy territory and had been stopped just in time. Again the word came back through the convoy, "Mines ahead!" and there was a long wait while Gershon and the scouts made sure of a safe way. There were no wadis or sheltering trees where they had to stop; the six vehicles stood exposed under the pitiless light of a full moon. Before the word came to move on, Gershon

Settling on the land

The first
days of
Yad Mordechai

Opposite tanks and armor

Destruction of
Yad Mordechai

The liberators

Returning home

Home again

Graves

The Banner of Independence

Yad Mordechai today — General vi

visited all of the cars. His handsome, cheerful face and his air of competence encouraged the frightened women.

Inside the armored trucks the children sat swaying and nodding on the benches that lined the sides or lay on the floor, a group around each nurse. The older children, who understood the reason for the perilous journey, were wakeful and tense but they tried to behave with the casual gallantry of the "Kilometer Platoon". The younger ones attacked their nurses with questions. "Are we going to visit my Aunt Hanna? Are we going to the circus? Why didn't my Mommy come, too?" Others were cross when they were awakened to give another child a place on the floor. "Why do I have to sit on the bench? I want to sleep. There's too much noise, I can't sleep." The nurses took crying children in their arms, gave others cookies and cold drinks. "But the children were so tired and nervous," one of the nurses told me. "You never would have known that these were the good, disciplined youngsters of Yad Mordechai."

The hours of waiting in the fields for the convoy to move were the hardest to bear. They felt safer, somehow, when they were in motion. Hagar, who as a girl of seventeen had gone out with twenty-nine boys to found a training camp in Poland, gave me an account of her intense emotions that night.

"I sat with my charges around me and thought, 'now I have to be as a mother to these five babies, and the responsibility frightened me. I knew that I had the duty to stand in their parents' place, and not only for this flight but perhaps for their whole lives. At the same time as I understood my duty, I grieved for my husband and wished that I could have stayed with him. He had a heart condition and yet he was staying to fight and I had forgotten to give him his pills before I left. 'What am I doing here?' I would say to myself. 'I should be by my husband's side.' And I felt terribly ashamed that I was going out to safety and leaving him to his fate — to the bullets or to a heart attack. I did not believe that he would survive and I had deserted him.

Of course I knew that each of us was doing what we had been assigned to do, yet I had this wild desire to jump out of the car and run back to him."

Another woman told of her anxiety for her children who were travelling in other cars with other nurses. Like any mother, she longed to have them close to her in a moment of danger. "Tears came to my eyes as I thought of them, but then I was embarrassed in front of the babies who were in my care. 'I have been given a very hard and responsible task', I told myself. 'My children are being taken care of by other nurses who are as responsible as I am', and I got the better of my feelings."

It was dawn when the convoy finally arrived at Kibbutz Ruchama. Gershon had not been able to take it northward to safety, but at least he had gotten the children out of immediate danger. Ruchama is southeast of Yad Mordechai, ten miles to the east of the main road on which the Egyptians had advanced.

The children of Ruchama were taken from their beds to their parents' rooms and the exhausted children of Yad Mordechai were put to bed in their places. Scarcely had they fallen asleep when there was an air raid alarm. The Ruchama children were sent into their shelters but there was no room for the visitors. They had to cower in the trenches. "Why did you bring us to this terrible place?" the children cried. "It was better at home. At least we could go into the shelters". And they blamed their nurses for all of the terrifying hours in the armored cars and for subjecting them, helpless and uncovered, to the Egyptian planes. To this day they remember Ruchama as "the kibbutz of the sirens". No bombs were dropped; the planes were on some other mission, but the nurses did not dare to take the children out of the trenches.

At seven o'clock came the terrible sound for which Alex had prepared them — the rumble and roar of heavy guns. The attack on Yad Mordechai had begun. The women sat, ashen-faced, trying to feed the children while their nerves leapt with the cannonade

They guessed that the planes which had sent them to the trenches must be discharging their bomb loads of death on the husbands and friends they had left behind. With their whole souls they longed to be back there. The children clamored to know about the noise. With the urgency of children they demanded an answer. "Just a few Arabs shooting somewhere", the distracted women said, but the older children were not to be put off. They had filled sand bags, they had seen the beauty of the kibbutz marred by the excavator, they had known why they had to leave their homes in the middle of the night. They understood that the shelling was directed at their kibbutz.

When breakfast was over, one of the women said, "I can't stand it any longer. I'm going to try to see what is happening."

Like all of the settlements in that area, Ruchama had a tall water tower with a ladder leading to the top. Leaving their charges with other women, two of the nurses climbed it. "And there we saw our tragedy", one of them told me. "We saw the puffs of smoke from the cannons, we saw the explosions in the settlement. And worst of all, we saw the flames. It looked as if the whole meshek were burning. When we came down from the tower, we thought that we who had escaped to Ruchama were the only survivors. We could not imagine that anyone was left alive in Yad Mordechai."

5

May 19th, 1948

South of the meshek, about 270 yards distant, was its strongest defense point, the pill box. All during the night while their children bumped over the fields to Ruchama, the men posted in the pill box had been digging a zig-zag trench on its western side. The work was heavy, for it was hard to cope with the shifting sandy soil. They had taken turns resting on the wooden bunks inside.

With the dawn came an abrupt change in the weather. The winds shifted and the lovely spring morning turned suffocatingly hot as a *sharav* swept in from the desert. Its stifling heat and gritty air would last for three days or even longer. The men in the trench worked with the sweat pouring off their bodies.

Although they had been toughened by years of outdoor work in all kinds of weather, they suffered in this heat. No one ever gets used to the relentless, hot breath of the *sharav*.

About 6 o'clock the men began to go in pairs to the dining room. At 6:30 the field telephone rang and headquarters informed the men who remained that tanks and armored cars had entered Deir Suneid and were taking up positions near the railway line. Salek Bielski was stationed on top of the two storey house of the northern hill and was keeping track of their movements.

One of the pill box force, Faivel, did not return to his post after breakfast. He was a tractor driver and had been ordered by Alex to scrape earth over a supply of gasoline which had been only half buried the day before.

While the men in the trench watched Faivel driving back and forth, three dots appeared in the southern sky.

"Planes!" someone shouted. "Get into the pill box!"

Within seconds the planes were over Yad Mordechai — the same planes that had frightened the children in Ruchama. Dozens of small, black bombs fell out of their bellies; as each one hit, it burst into flames.

"Incendiaries!" one of the men screamed over the roar of the explosions. There were many wooden buildings in the meshek; fires sprang up everywhere. The barn began to burn. It was hit again and again until it was a mass of flames. The animals burst out of their stables and pens — riding horses, mules, a herd of sheep, cows and beef steers — over a hundred of them. The men in the pill box could see them running wildly around the meshek, some wounded, some on fire. The fuel for the kitchen stoves was hit and flames enveloped the dining room. Hay that was stored in the new dairy was set on fire. Bombs fell on the poultry houses; some ducks and hundreds of white Leghorns that had escaped the flames poured out in the meshek.

The only man in sight was Faivel who was racing his tractor toward the eucalyptus grove. With relief the men in the pill box saw him disappear between the trees, just before the planes circled low and began raking the settlement with their machine guns. There were screams and bellows as more animals were hit. Finally the planes flew off to the south. Within fifteen minutes they had destroyed much of what had taken the settlers years to build.

There were a few moments of shocked silence. The men gazed toward their homes for some sign of life. Finally they saw men running toward a shed next to the barn. "They're trying to save the combine", someone guessed. "It won't do much good if the planes come back," Zalman said grimly. Now they could see

Faivel coming through the wheat field between the pill box and the meshek. Yurek, the bee-keeper, was running with him. The two men arrived breathless. Faivel's ruddy face was white with fear; he told what it was like to be exposed and alone on top of a tractor in the midst of a bombing raid. "They were aiming at me — they wanted to get the tractor", he insisted. It had not occurred to him to abandon the machine and take cover. He had hidden it in the eucalyptus grove before he had dropped, trembling, to the earth.

Yurek explained that he had been sent as a replacement for Naftali who had gone out with the children the night before. When everyone had calmed down a little, Gideon, the commander of the pill box, set about instructing him in his duties. Yurek was a sweet, simple man who was devoted to his bees and to his hobby of photography. Although, like everyone else in the kibbutz, he had received basic instruction in how to handle a rifle, he was far from being a military man. Gideon assigned him to one of the windows and gave him the target sheet which had been plotted in advance to show the range of effective fire. Yurek did not understand it, but as he did not want to hurt anyone's feelings, he "made out as though he did". He did not comprehend the seriousness of their position in the pill box and was disturbed by the tension that he felt. In order to cheer up his fellows he began to tell them about the bees. "This will be the best year I ever had" he reported. "There never was so much honey".

Menahem, a veteran of the kibbutz, also was a replacement for a man who had been sent out with the children. He was a driver, toughened by the tensions and dangers of the battle of the roads, but he had had no military experience beyond his basic training in the Hagana. All of the other men were war veterans or had received advanced military training in Palestine. Zalman was a veteran of the African and Italian campaigns in World War II. Gelman had fought against the Nazis in the Polish army, had been captured, had escaped, had been imprisoned by the Russians, had escaped again and finally had arrived in Palestine with General Anders' Polish army from which he had deserted. Max and Ishay were among the first refugees to be taken into Yad Mordechai after the war. Both were about twenty-five years old; both had served with Jewish partisan groups in the forests of Poland. Gideon, the commander, had gone for advanced courses in the illegal Hagana. Faivel was a member of the Palmach.

Less than fifteen minutes after the planes had disappeared, an artillery bombardment of the meshek began. It was terrible in its intensity. From behind the sand dunes near Deir Suneid, mortars were firing; the men could see the hits in the meshek. Within a few minutes the water tower was pierced and water streamed out of the holes. The lookout on the northern hill was struck repeatedly; great holes were opened in its second storey. The Egyptians began to lay down their shells over the whole meshek in a methodical pattern; a spotter plane was directing them from above. One after the other the firing posts around the perimeter were destroyed; their roofs fell in and great clouds of brown dust rose over the trenches where the defenders were lying. The water tower was pierced again and again. More wooden structures went up in flames. From every part of the meshek dozens of white Leghorn chickens flew up into the air like confetti tossed against the dark and burning background. The men could not look at each other, could not speak. Their throats were dry with fear and anguish as they watched the destruction.

Gideon tried to reach headquarters with the field telephone; there was no answer. He guessed that the wires had been cut by the shelling, but still the question arose in his mind — and everyone else's — "Has headquarters been hit? — are they all dead?" The only creatures moving in the meshek were the animals and the fluttering chickens. They could hear the screams of wounded cows and horses.

The three planes reappeared. This time they stayed high as their two hundred pound bombs crashed down. Geysers of smoke and sand spurted violently into the sky and settled slowly. Dusk seemed to have fallen in the meshek while the pill box remained in full sunlight. Menahem suggested that they ought to take turns resting in the bunks — "That way we can stand it better". The others agreed, but no one lay down. They could not leave the firing slits and the awful sight before them.

Suddenly a "refugee" from the meshek appeared, one of the young Doberman Pinscher dogs which the men had been training to guard the fields. He ran around and around the pill box, whimpering to be let in to safety. Some of the defenders were filled with pity for the frantic animal and wanted to let him in. Others objected; the dog might go mad with fright and begin to bite. Gideon decided that the dog must be shot; he ordered Menahem to carry out his decision. Although he wanted to obey like a good soldier, Menahem's rifle fell away from his shoulder each time he tried to aim. Others tried, but no one could bear to kill the dog. Finally Gideon shot him. Even in dying the poor, wretched animal tried to stay close to them; he crawled up to one of the windows. They had to push his body down the slope with a rifle barrel. The incident had a profound effect upon all of them. What was happening in the kibbutz had turned their hearts to ice; the tragedy was too great and too terrible for comprehension. But the death of the dog unstopped their grief and rage. All understood when Ishay sobbed aloud.

There was a sandy road running from the village of Deir Suneid toward the sea. When the bombardment had been going on for about an hour, the men in the pill box saw armored cars moving down this road. They stopped in a row of carob trees about 700 yards from the pill box. Through binoculars Gideon could see that small cannons had been mounted on the cars; he watched their muzzles wheeling around and pointing toward the pill box. "It's our turn now", he cried and ordered every man

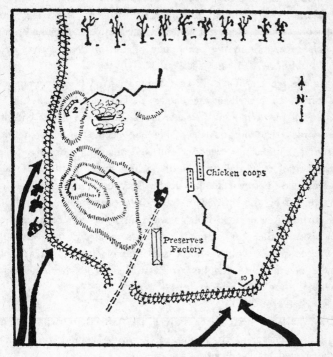

Positions in Yad Mordechai

to his place. Max stood ready with the Bren gun which was loaded with a magazine of armor piercing bullets. The men felt excited and confident. They were conscious of the importance of their outpost and they believed that it was impregnable. They saw the first shell fired from a cannon; it fell a hundred yards short of them. Max replied with the Bren gun but his bullets did not reach far enough. The Egyptians corrected their aim; the second shell dropped only fifty yards from the pill box. Max fired again. "Ha, ha! You hit the radiator!" Gideon cried exultantly. Then he reverted to Yiddish. "We have got you now! We've got you on the ground!" At that moment the third shell struck the pill box. It hit between the slits where Gideon and Max were standing and pierced the low wall. Dust and pieces of cement flew through the air. Blood streamed down Gideon's face and on the other side of the pill box Faivel cried out, "I'm blinded — I can't see !"

"Into the trench! Take all the ammunition", Gideon commanded and started to crawl to the entrance. Two men picked him up and carried him out and Yurek brought the first aid kit. Gideon's wound was large but not deep. He had been struck in the face by flying chunks of cement. Yurek bandaged the wound and Gideon began to crawl through the wheat field to the meshek.

Faivel was not wounded, but he was in shock and he had been blinded by the dust. The water in the uncovered barrel was dirty so that it was impossible to wash his eyes. Not realizing how upset he was, the others urged him to go to Dr. Heller. Although his eyelids were swollen almost shut Faivel started out. With a grenade in one hand and his rifle strapped to his back he began crawling through the wheat.

About half an hour after Faivel had left, there was a shout from the tomato patch about forty yards behind the trench. Zalman poked his head out.

A messenger was lying among the plants; obviously he did not want to crawl closer to the exposed trench. "Are you all right?" he yelled.

"Two wounded. We've sent them in."

As well as he could over the noise of the shelling, Zalman reported on the damage to the pill box. He sent word to Alex that they needed more grenades and some Molotov cocktails in case the Egyptians should send tanks against them. He asked also for someone to replace Gideon. Although most of the men in the trench were experienced fighters, none felt able to assume responsibility for this important point.

The messenger crawled away.

In the meantime Faivel had gotten lost. Confused and nearly blind he had travelled in a circle. The pungent odor of bruised plants told him that he had entered the tomato patch again. Suddenly he heard the rustling noise of someone approaching. An Egyptian? ...should he throw the hand grenade? Even in his shocked state some glimmer of good sense stayed his hand — he realized that the Egyptians had not yet issued out from behind their big guns.

"Who's there?" he cried in a cracked voice.

"It's me — Sevek. I'm on my way to the pill box."

"Here I am, over here — Faivel. I can't see. I can't find my way home."

"Carry on straight and you'll reach the fence," Sevek assured him. "There are men there who will take you to the doctor."

"I was hit in the pill box. I can't see. Show me the way."

"I can't go back with you, Faivel. I have to replace Gideon. Go ahead — straight on. You'll get there all right."

They parted, almost formally, Sevek saying "Give my regards at home" and Faivel replying "Give my regards to the fellows in the pill box." They crawled away from each other through the ripening tomatoes.

When Sevek arrived at his new post he found the six remaining defenders of the pill box plastered against the walls of the deep trench, well spread out. They looked very different from the men he had seen at breakfast. Their faces and bare arms were covered with sand and sweat, their eyes were rimmed with dust, their clothes were dirty. They all began to talk at once, shouting over the noise of the guns, asking for news. Sevek told of meeting Faivel in the tomato patch. He did not know of other casualties.

Sevek was a teacher in the kibbutz. In the early days he had been a member of the fishing crew that had made the adventurous journey through the Suez Canal into the Red, Sea, looking for better fishing grounds. He had served in the Palmach during the war, with the rank of commander. Because of this, Alex and Tuvia had picked him to replace the wounded Gideon.

With his customary thoroughness, Sevek began to inspect the position. First he dodged into the ruined pill box. It had been hit repeatedly. The wooden bunks had been tourned; there were puddles of water on the floor from the burst water barrels; a smell of gun-powder hung over everything. He saw, however, that it still was necessary to use the pill box as a lookout, for there was no other way to watch the movements of the enemy of the eastern side. He decided to send someone every ten minutes to watch this blind spot.

From the pill box, Sevek had a clear view of the terrain. To the left was the bridge on the main road which the Palmach sappers had failed to destroy two nights before. Under it passed a deep wadi which ran in front of the pill box at a distance of about 250 yards. It angled off from the road until it reached the sandy side road which was more or less on Sevek's right. There it was surmounted by a small bridge. Still further to the right and in front of the sandy track was a young banana plantation belonging to Yad Mordechai. It was about 170 yards distant. Sevek could see troops moving about in this plantation. Somewhat south of it he could see the armored cars still standing on the sandy road, the cannons firing intermittently. As he watched, soldiers began to move through the big wadi, at least half a company, he thought. There was no doubt in his mind that the Egyptians were preparing for an infantry attack, possibly against posts 1 and 2 which faced the sandy road, but more probably against the southern bastion, the pill box. It was necessary to re-group the men in accord with the changed situation. To meet an attack coming from the wadi, he would remain near the pill box with Gelman, Menahem and Ishay. They were armed with rifles and he with a Tommy gun. Max, with the Bren gun, and Zalman and Yurek with rifles, would defend the trench against troops approaching from the banana plantation. A man was kept on watch for movements from this side.

Someone was seen wriggling toward them through the wheat field. It was one of the Palmach boys; in the haversack strapped to his back were the extra hand grenades and Molotov cocktails that Zalman had asked for. The men in the trench watched his progress fearfully. Shells were falling around him; with that load on his back he must arrive unscratched or not at all. He crawled closer and closer and finally fell panting into the trench. The men gave him a few mouthfuls of their precious water and a swallow of wine while they placed the extra weapons on the sand bank in front of the trench. As he crawled back to the meshek, they settled down in the trench to wait for whatever was to come.

During these critical hours many things had been happening in the meshek. When the planes appeared over Yad Mordechai at 7:15, the dining room was half full. The tables had been laid with plenty of bread, butter, marmalade, cheese, eggs, potato salad and coffee. Nothing could get to market anyway and the women knew that after the night of tension, a hearty breakfast would help to take the place of rest. At the first alarm the people jumped up from the tables and the men ran to their posts. There were between fifty and fifty-five women; they crowded into the shelters.

As soon as the air raid was over, Alex sent a group of men to rescue the combine from the burning barn. He was in charge of headquarters and of the disposition of manpower and arms while Tuvia was in direct command of the trenches. Tuvia made a last minute check of the defenses. He warned the men to spread out in the zig-zag trenches and to leave only one man on watch in each post. The Spandau machine gun with a crew of three and the two mortars with crews of four men each were stationed in a trench behind the hill where the water tower stood. They had been placed there so as to be near headquarters; they would be sent wherever needed. In one of the shelters Dr. Heller waited with his nurse and his crew of stretcher bearers.

No one was prepared for the violence of the artillery bombardment when it came. The women sat in the shelters with their heads pressed down upon their knees, enduring their fear and the suffocating heat. The men in the trenches felt as if the roaring, screaming inferno were flattening them into the earth. They could not lift their heads to see what was happening to their homes; they only could guess at the destruction from the smashing noise of the hits. Within the first few minutes all telephone communication was cut off. The small shelter of the headquarters received a direct hit and had to be abandoned. Scuttling through the trenches, Alex, Shamay and the two women wireless operators, Fania and Rachel, entered the shelter where the arms store was kept.

In Post Number 6 Sasha Ivri was in the lookout. He was a handsome boy with straight black hair, dark eyes and a shy smile. Nothing in his appearance suggested the bitterness and tragedy of his youth, unless it was a worried frown that sometimes marred his good looks. His parents had been killed in a concentration camp in Czechoslovakia; he and his younger brother had lived in the forests with a group of Jewish partisans until the end of the war. Coming to Palestine as an illegal immigrant, he had been received into Yad Mordechai as one of the group that was in training there. His energy and intelligence had made him the natural choice for secretary of the group. At nine o'clock a three-inch mortar shell smashed into Post Number 6 and Sacha's headless body fell back into the trench. He was the first casualty of the battle; he was twenty years old when he died.

At about the same time Yehudi Rosen was joking wryly with the other members of the mortar crew about the electric light system which ringed the kibbutz. He had finished it early that morning. "There they go", he said as the shells shrieked over-head. "Every one of those two hundred bulbs must be smashed by now." It was like him to propose a toast at such a moment. He took out a bottle of wine from the niche in the trench where supplies had been placed and pulled the cork with his teeth. "For every lamp one Egyptian — let's drink to it!" he exclaimed, taking the first gulp from the bottle. Then he added the classic Jewish toast, "L'chaim — To life!" Those were his last words. The Egyptians had gotten the range of the water tower; mortar shells pierced it, dropped over the top of the hill and landed in the trench. Yehudi was killed. Shymek, mortally wounded or already dead, was buried under the sliding sand. Five others were wounded.

Somehow the wounded men crawled to Dr. Heller's shelter. No proper clinic had been prepared underground; the settlers had assumed that the doctor would be able to use his own well-equipped clinic in case of emergency. There was not even a table. The wounded had to be laid on a low bench while Dr. Heller on his knees tended them. He had two people to help him, Dora, who had received training as a nurse in the Hagana, and Leib Dorfman a first aid man who was in charge of the stretcher bearers.

Of these first wounded, one man had suffered severe head injuries; he would survive but with only one eye. Another, Leon Blau, did not seem badly wounded at first, yet after Dr. Heller had bandaged the small hole in his back, he could not lie down. A shell splinter had pierced his lung and lodged in one of his ribs and the resulting hemorrhage caused intense pain whenever he lay prone. He had to remain standing. He stood for two days and nights until the pain in his swollen legs was too much to bear. Then Dr. Heller gave him the last of the morphine and forced him to lie down.

Since the telephone system had been destroyed in the first

few minutes of shelling, Alex was faced with the problem of establishing communication with the posts. He would have to use runners. This possibility had been foreseen and three young women had volunteered. All had been members of Hashomer Hatzair since early youth. Raya had pioneered in Natanya; she knew Morse and so could be used for flashlight signalling should this become necessary. Leika had gotten to Palestine on the very day that World War II had broken out. Shula had waited out the war years in Siberia, arriving only recently. All three were unmarried.

Alex called the runners to him. "The men are wasting ammunition firing at the planes", he said. "My orders are to stop this. No one has permission to fire at the planes. You must go to the posts and give the order."

Although his voice was quiet and firm, the deepened furrow between his brows betrayed the anxiety he felt in sending the women into the hell of the bombardment. "You will be fairly safe in the trenches", he told them. "If you have to cross an open place, run fast and fling yourselves down if you think you hear a shell coming. That's all I can tell you, comrades. Good luck!"

Raya was given a special mission. Alex wanted a report on the movements of the Egyptians from Salek, who was watching from the cement house. With fast beating heart Raya ran through the trenches to the foot of the hill. There she paused for breath. She looked up the trench that led to the house. It ran straight without even one zig-zag. Shells were falling near it as the Egyptians concentrated their fire on the lookout. She sat down in a sheltered spot; she could not go on. Her flabby knees could not support even her small weight, her chest seemed emptied of air and every breath was painful. All of her kibbutz training in self-abnegation, all of the fierce desire to serve, which had made her volunteer for this dangerous task, seemed to have deserted her. "I can't, I can't" her rebellious body protested. "I must, I must", her conscience asserted. "What if I'm killed here or wounded far away from everybody?" she enquired of her weakness. "Who will bring Alex the report if you don't go?" she answered herself. Finally she got up. It seemed that there was a little lull in the firing or perhaps she only comforted herself by thinking so. She ran up the trench as fast as she could. When she was nearly at the top she saw a human hand, bloody at the wrist, lying on the embankment. With a sob she ran on and flung herself into the deep trench on the safe side of the lookout. She was so breathless that she could not speak.

"Take your time," Salek said. "Here, sip a little wine."

"A hand! I saw a hand", she gasped finally. "Who was wounded? Killed?"

He told her of Sasha Ivri's death. "Oh, that dear boy", she grieved. She knew him well for she was the temporary "mother" of the group of young immigrants who were receiving training in the kibbutz. It had been her duty to supply their physical needs, to explain kibbutz life to them, to listen to their troubles, to comfort their loneliness.

"What's the message?" Salek asked her, his abrupt manner concealing his own dismay at the death of the young man.

Raya asked for the report that Alex wanted. She memorized what he had to say and repeated it to him. Then she clasped his hand in farewell.

"Let me tell you something that will help you", Salek said. "At first the bombardment seems like one great noise, but you must learn to listen for the shells. There, did you hear that boom? That was a shell leaving the mouth of the gun — they've put the guns so close that we can hear them fire. When you hear that sound, fall to the ground. Then will come the noise of the explosion when the shell hits. After that get up and run. Now listen again. Hear it?" So he gave her a lesson in survival; she learned it quickly under the stress of the dangers she faced.

He watched her anxiously as she ran down the exposed trench practicing what he had taught her, falling too often, perhaps but getting the feel of how to run through shellfire. Safely back in headquarters, less breathless this time, she gave her report to Alex and told him of the death of Sasha Ivri. She and the other runners soon learned to report casualties to Alex, but never to tell the posts they visited what horrifying sights they might have seen on the way.

Post number 1 was dug into the top of a small hill facing south. Four men and the first aid nurse, Pola, were stationed there; the commander was Hershel Grinspan. In the days before the battle, Hershel had worried continually about his post. The ground there was very hard and the trenches were shallower than they should have been. He had asked the Defense Committee to have them deepened, but with so many urgent tasks to finish, this had not been done. During the bombardment four of the people lay in the trenches while the fifth stayed on watch in the hole that had been dug for throwing hand grenades. Every half hour the watch was changed, Pola taking her turn with the others. At eleven o'clock it would be Hershel's watch. He still was lying in the trench with his rifle across his legs when a two pound shell burst above him. "I'm hit!" he cried. Motke, who had been one of the drivers during the Battle of the Roads, was nearest to him. He saw at once that Hershel was badly wounded. The broken rifle had sliced into his legs like a knife blood was pouring from the wounds. He yelled for Pola.

"Tourniquets!" he cried as she ran crouched over into the angle where they were.

"I haven't got enough gauze", Pola said, kneeling beside the wounded man. "Give me your shirt."

Quickly they tore the shirt and bound the bleeding legs thrusting parts of the broken rifle into the knots to tighten the tourniquets.

114

"His feet are bleeding, too", Pola said. "Help me take off his shoes." Then she made a sudden, restraining gesture. As she was fumbling with the bloody laces, Hershel's feet had started to come off with the shoes.

"Motke, you take command", Hershel said, "Relieve Wolf in the lookout. Let Alex know. And don't worry about me," he added, seeming to notice their stricken faces. "I'll be all right. Just get me to Dr. Heller."

Motke sent Sioma to the lookout and he himself ran down through the trench to the factory where he knew there should be stretcher bearers. They were not there; they had carried the wounded Gideon to the shelter. There was no help for it, he would have to go for aid. He dodged through the trenches, every now and then having to jump out into the open where a trench had not been finished. Twenty minutes later he got back to the post with Leib Dorfman and his helper. Hershel still was conscious but he could hardly speak. It took another fifteen minutes to get him to Dr. Heller. They laid him on the narrow bench and cut off his clothes. He had abdominal wounds as well as the terrible wounds on his legs. After Dr. Heller had finished bandaging, had loosened and then tightened the tourniquets again as the blood gushed out, he took up a pair of large scissors. The half unconscious man noticed them. "What are you doing with the scissors?" he mumbled. The doctor did not answer. All that was holding Hershel's feet to his legs was a little untorn skin. Dr. Heller snipped this skin with the scissors and Leib caught the feet in his hands. Later, when the firing lessened, he took them outside and buried them.

The bombardment went on and on and on. The Egyptians had plenty of ammunition and they used it lavishly, hitting the same targets again and again. Some of the veterans say that 2500 shells were fired into the meshek that first day, some say 4,000. Before the battle was over the ground was covered with iron;

twelve years later I picked up shell fragments wherever walked.

Men reacted in various ways to the danger of death, to th terrifying noise of the bombardment, to their helplessness. Th veterans told me frankly that not all of them had stood it wel Some broke down and cried, some fainted, some returned humi liatingly to the incontinence of their childhood. But others kep up their courage with jokes and laughter. They laughed at th Egyptians for wasting shells on the water tower. In Miriam' post they laughed at the man who found a jar of jam among the food stores and opened it with pleasure, scooping it out with his gritty fingers. "Have some jam" became the catchword o the post. Whenever a shell would land nearby the defender would acknowledge it with "Have some jam."

Around Post number 8 the firing was especially heavy since it was in a direct line with the cement house on the hill which the Egyptians seemed determined to knock down. "It was no worse even in Stalingrad", Adek Weinfeld said, trying to encourage his fellows. Adek, who had been a member of th early kibbutz back in Poland, had escaped to the Soviet zone when the war began and had been taken into the Soviet army He had been one of the defenders of Stalingrad. After the war he had returned to Poland, anxious to join his comrades in Palestine. But there was work to be done in Poland before he could leave. He was put in charge of a home for orphaned Jewish children — "my children" he always called them, for he had no others. During the critical March days he finally had come home to Yad Mordechai. "I couldn't be among the founders of the kibbutz but I will be among its defenders", he said. When it was his turn to go into the ruined post as a lookout, he jumped up eagerly. A shell fell short of the cement house and ended his life.

Two of the four shelters were filled with women. Perhaps

fifteen of them would fulfill some necessary function during the battle. The rest had nothing to do but sit in the hot, crowded shelters. Their physical discomfort was less hard to bear than a terrible inner trembling of uncertainty and fear. What was happening outside? Who had been lost in the bombardment? How was the battle going? What would be the end?

Shelter number 2 was occupied almost entirely by young women and girls who had come to Yad Mordechai two months earlier for training. About half of them were girls between fourteen and seventeen years of age who had come out of German concentration camps. Gabriel Ramati had selected most of them from Bergen-Belsen. Bracha, one of the kibbutz pioneers, was in charge. Although she was pregnant and so could have been evacuated with the children, she had elected to stay because she thought that she would be needed in the dairy.

During the bombardment, the shelter received a direct hit. The whole structure heaved as if it were going to be thrust out of the ground. The wooden shelves rattled and smoke and dust filled the entrances. Panic swept through the shelter. Not only the younger girls but older women too, shrieked with fear. "Let's get out", someone yelled. "It's going to fall in on us."

Bracha was as frightened as anyone but she walked quietly down the aisle between the two rows of shelves saying "Quiet! Quiet! You see the shelter held. We're safe. Quiet now!" She slapped a little girl who was in hysterics. She soothed another with a motherly hug. Gradually calm was restored but it was a false calm, full of tension. The Children's House in front of their shelter was being pounded to pieces. As they heard the smashing hits each one thought, "Will the next shell fall on us? After the miseries of Bergen-Belsen will I die here in this hole?"

As the morning dragged on they suffered from a feeling of isolation. They felt completely cut off from the battle. In the other women's shelter, where some of the wounded had been sent, there was movement in and out. A runner would bring Dr. Heller if he was needed, friends would come in to visit the wounded when there was a lull in the firing. But no one came to Shelter 2. There was nothing to do but endure the stifling heat and to wait — wait for the next shell burst — wait for the cup of rationed water — wait until nightfall to go to the toilet — wait for news.

When the bombardment had been going for about three hours it stopped as suddenly as it had begun. A single airplane appeared above the kibbutz and released hundreds of leaflets. They came fluttering down to the men in the trenches. Printed in poor Hebrew they read as follows:

> In the name of Moses and in the name of Allah, the prophets of the true God who has mercy on us; God has said that if your enemy wants peace, be at peace with him. God listens and God knows the truth.
>
> With these holy words from the Koran we approach you, the inhabitants of this settlement. Our aim is to bring peace among you on condition that you act peacefully toward us. Thus you will be able to save your lives, your property and your children.
>
> It was not our intention to start a war. It is your resistance which has causd us to attack you, but your resistance will be of short duration and in vain.
>
> Therefore we ask all inhabitants to lay down your weapons peacefully, to give up your weapons, your mine and all your battle equipment, to raise a white flag, t destroy no property and to gather into one place to awai us. You are commanded to put these orders into effec

within one hour after this proclamation has reached you. After this time, if you do not obey our orders, you will be considered an aggressor and will have proven to us that you wish to fight.

God said, "If you are attacked, answer with attack" and know well that God is on the side of the righteous.

The Almighty God always speaks the truth.

This pious bit of propaganda obviously had been intended for distribution to settlements *before* a bombardment such as Yad Mordechai had suffered. Coming as it did after the destruction in the meshek, it caused grim laughter. The men set to work to tighten their defenses. Alex and Tuvia visited all of the posts. They found the men already busy repairing the trenches wherever they had been ruined by the shell-fire. Although they were shocked by the fierceness of the attack, their morale was good. Years before they had chosen to live on the frontier; now they saw themselves as the front line defenders of the new nation. "We have to hold out no matter what comes", was their attitude.

Everyone was anxious for news of the other posts. The commanders told the men that forty shells a minute had been fired into the kibbutz; considering this the losses had not been heavy. Half of the mortar crew of eight had been put out of action; this meant that only two men now were available for each mortar. Four fighters had been killed and ten wounded. There would have been fewer casualties if the men of the mortar crew had not bunched up in their trench. The commanders begged the men to remember this costly lesson.

Back in headquarters, Alex dictated a message to the Palmach commander in Nir 'Am.

12 noon. Since morning we have had heavy attacks from the air and shelling by 6 and 25 pounders. There are fires

in the meshek and the property has been greatly damaged. The pill box south of the kibbutz has been bombed. The water tower has been hit and has burst.

Shamay's hand trembled on the key as he started to send the message. With his left hand he held his arm steady. He would be given many other messages to send, each with its bitter story, but none would affect him more deeply than this first laconic account of the destruction in the meshek.

Tuvia and Alex consulted together on what arrangements would be necessary to fit the new situation. The communications system would have to be strengthened. Dina, of the Defense Committee, volunteered as a headquarters runner. Messengers also would be needed at the various posts. The commanders decided to disband the "Tank Hunters" and use the boys for this work.

No plans had been made for a kitchen underground. The members of the Defense Commission had believed that in case of attack it still would be possible for the women to use the kitchen at night, but now it was seen that this would not be feasible. Not only was the kitchen half destroyed, but it might be hit again; besides, the commanders were of the opinion that shelling would continue throughout the night. The chief cook that year, Leah, and a number of other women, searched in the wreckage for the means with which to set up a kitchen in one of the shelters. They found two Primus stoves, both damaged, pots and pans, some food supplies and the coffee that had been prepared for the uneaten breakfast. From the refrigerator in the milk shed they brought cooked meat, butter and milk. There was not time, in the hour's truce promised by the leaflet, to take food to the trenches; the men would have to use the rations that were stored in each post. In the meantime the women prepared food for the wounded.

Tuvia and Alex visited the shelter where the wounded were. After they had spoken to each man, Dr. Heller went outside with them. "We must call for the Red Cross to come in and evacuate these men", he said. "I cannot treat them properly under these conditions. There is not even enough room to lay them down."

"We are surrounded", Alex told him. "The bombardment will begin again any minute now and· we have to expect infantry attacks. Maybe it will be possible to-night, although I doubt it."

"But in every war they evacuate the wounded!", cried the doctor who had served in a German hospital in World War I. "Hershel must be operated at once — it's his only chance. If you don't get him to a hospital I won't be responsible for his life."

"Do what you can, doctor," Alex answered patiently. "We'll try, we'll try, but we're cut off."

As they returned to headquarters the two men exchanged opinions. "We need much more than Red Cross ambulances if we're to hold out here", Alex said. "We've got to have reinforcements and more ammunition. But do you think they can send us more than one platoon? The Palmach is spread out so thin. I don't see how we can hold out if we get only thirty men."

"I'm not worried," Tuvia replied. "All of this shelling... I have an idea that their morale is bad. Our boys will beat them back — you'll see."

The men in the pill box trench also made good use of the hour of quiet promised by the Arab leaflet. They cleaned the rifles and oiled the bolts; then they stood the guns against the wall of the trench with pieces of cloth over their muzzles to keep out the blowing sand. They ate a little and rationed out the remaining water. They felt that their turn would come soon. Their exposed position on the southern flank made it almost certain that the Egyptians would have to try to capture the pill box before they could send infantry against the meshek itself. The men were concerned with Faivel who had lost his way again after his meeting with Sevek and had crawled back to them.

"Listen, Faivel, it's going to be hot here in another hour. Do you hear, Faivel? You'd better try again to get home. It will be easier for you now."

This time Faivel succeeded in reaching the meshek.

The hour of truce came to an end and the shelling began again, heavier than before. The ground around the pill box trembled with explosions.

Suddenly there was a cry from the men on watch. "They're coming! They're coming!"

Zalman stuck his head above the trench to see for himself. "Look at them!" he exclaimed. "You'd think they were on parade."

Whether from inexperience in battle or from a belief that the defenders of the pill box were dead, the Egyptians were not taking the usual precautions of advancing troops. Instead of crouching, they were advancing fully erect. With the binoculars Sevek could see their smartly dressed officers, marching behind their men and waving their revolvers. *"Aleihum!* Onto them!" they were shouting.

The pill box was still under heavy fire. Its defenders waited while the Egyptians came within three hundred yards — two hundred yards — a hundred yards. Finally the cover fire ceased and the tiny force in the trench sub-divided and went into action. The three men facing the bananas lay on the mound of sand to shoot. At the other end, Sevek and Menahem jumped into the pill box to fire from the slits. The other two men flung themselves out of the deep trench onto the sand bank above. It was slippery and soft; they had nowhere to brace their feet. Nevertheless their fire was effective. There were screams of terror and pain as the attack on this side dissolved in confusion. The Egyptians ran back to the shelter of a small hill that lay between the pill box and the wadi.

"Get ready! They're coming back", Sevek yelled. Gelman and Ishay looked for a better firing position.

"Let's use the roof", Gelman shouted. The roof of the pill box, only a few feet above ground level, sloped downward from its center. There was just room for the two men to lie along the edges, partially protected by the rise.

"Fire at the officers. They'll run if they lose their officers," Gelman called to Ishay.

This time the Egyptians ran forward bent over. A few got to the bottom of the slope on which lay the pill box. Sevek swept the line with the Tommy gun. Some men fell and the others turned and fled. On top of the pill box Gelman and Ishay were yelling with excitement. "I got one! I got that big officer!" Ishay screamed. "Ya-a-ah!" Gelman shouted in the automatic rage of battle. Below them all order was lost as the enemy soldiers ran back in panic toward the wadi.

At the other end of the trench, meanwhile, the three defenders had held their fire until the Egyptians got within reach of the Bren gun. While the two riflemen aimed at the officers, Max sent careful bursts of fire into the ranks. Suddenly, he cried out, "The Bren gun — it's only firing single shots — single shots!"

"Use it like a rifle", Zalman called. "Anyhow they're retreating."

The ground in front of the banana trees was flat; there was no cover for the frightened Egyptians. They ran past the threatening pistols of their officers to the safety of the planation, leaving their wounded behind.

Now the artillery took up the battle as if it meant to avenge the triple defeat of the infantry. Every gun seemed to be trained on the pill box. It was hit again and again; exploding shells shook the earth around the trench. Flames sprang up between the trench and the meshek as the ripe wheat still standing in the field was set on fire.

The men rested in the trench, sweaty, grimed with dust, feverish with excitement. There was no shade; the noon sun

123

stood overhead and the pitiless *sharav* parched their throats. Most were jubilant at their success in routing the enemy, but others were oppressed with varying degrees of fear and guilt. For the first time in their lives they had killed other human beings. Visions of wounded, screaming, dying men tormented them. They knew that there would be another attack. It seemed impossible that they could sustain it without casualties; how could they be so lucky? They set about cleaning their guns.

"I didn't think of anything", said Yurek the beekeeper in telling me of this interlude. "I didn't care any more. I knew one thing, that I never would get out of that trench. I was a hundred per cent certain of it. I didn't even think of my family. I just cleaned my gun when Sevek told me to."

"Did you see the black men?" Ishay asked as they worked. "I never saw such black men in my life."

"They must be Sudanese"*, Gelman suggested. "I hit one but he kept right on coming. Then I guess Sevek got him."

"I think I've fixed the Bren gun" Max announced. "It was full of sand. May I fire a burst to test it, Sevek?" Sevek gave permission and Max proved to his satisfaction that the gun was working again.

The men tried to estimate what the Egyptian casualties had been. Everyone had a different opinion but they finally decided that about thirty had fallen. Under cover of the bombardment, stretchers were brought up and seven or eight men were carried off the field. "They must be officers," Sevek guessed.

All of the veterans insisted to me that the Egyptians made no attempt to rescue enlisted men, not even at night. The wounded lay where they fell, tormented by thirst, and unless they could

---

* These black soldiers actually were not from the Sudan but belonged to a war-like tribe not far from the Sudanese border. Since the veterans of the battle referred to them as Sudanese. I have done the same.

crawl back to their own lines, they died from lack of medical attention*.

The watch reported great activity in the Egyptian lines. Tanks were moving near the damaged bridge to the left of the pill box. In the big wadi, soldiers seemed to be arranging themselves in lines. To the right there was movement in the banana plantation. The tension mounted in the zig-zag trench. What would the new tactic be? Presently firing began from Post 1. That would mean that the enemy was advancing against it. A few moments later they themselves were under attack. Troops were coming at them from two directions, from the wadi and from the banana plantation.

"To your places!" shouted Sevek. "Let them come close — close! Use the grenades first! Take out the pins and wait for the order!"

It seemed to the defenders that the Egyptians were coming upon them more quickly this time. The seven men, flattened against the earth, felt helpless and vulnerable. Nevertheless they had to wait until the enemy was almost upon them before they could begin to defend themselves. The effective range of a hand grenade is about thirty yards — the length of a tennis court. It took discipline and nerve to wait and wait while the enemy advanced. Finally Sevek gave the order. "Throw." Seven grenades were lobbed into the advancing lines and then the men began to fire. The Egyptian lines wavered. The advance stopped. Some men took cover behind dead comrades, others started to run back. But the defenders were in trouble also. In front of them were tanks that might emerge from the wadi at any moment. Behind them and somewhat to their right, Egyptian soldiers appeared; they had come around the bottom of the hill on which stood Post 1 and were cutting wire. The pill box defenders were

* This class distinction in caring for the wounded may have been due to inexperience or disorganization in the Egyptian army. In later battles, observers reported that their wounded were collected by stretcher parties.

three quarters surrounded. And to add to their desperate position, their two automatic weapons had failed them. The Bren gun was firing single shots again and there was no more ammunition for the Tommy gun. All of the rifles were overheated and they had few grenades left. Sevek had to make an instant decision.

"Run!" he shouted, "Take all the ammo, Scatter out! Run toward the fence!"

The men at the far end of the sand bank did not hear the order. Yurek jumped toward them.

"Run! We're retreating!"

"There's been no order."

"Yes! Yes!" Yurek screamed. "Sevek gave it. Come on!"

"We're beating them back — I won't go," Max shouted.

"Fool! Imbecile!" shouted the usually mild Yurek. "I'll leave you then".

"The others are retreating — let's go", Zalman shouted. They all ran, bent over, through 50 yards of burning wheat. Bullets whistled over their heads. They were singed by the flames but at least they were protected from sight. They passed the burned-out baling machine and the pile of baled hay that was one great bonfire. They fell into the tomato patch and wriggled along the ground. Finally they came to the fence. As they reached it they saw a squad of Egyptians lying close to the little bluff where Post 1 stood, protected from sight from above. The two groups were not twenty yards apart. The sudden apparition of the blackened, panting men must have startled the Egyptians. Neither side fired a shot. Some of the seven climbed over the tank trap that had been set up by the gate, others wriggled through a culvert under the wire. They all ran to the shelter of the factory wall and flung themselves down to rest.

In the meantime the Egyptians, who were almost upon the pill box and its trench, turned and fled back to the banana plantation. What had happened to cause them to retreat when they were within a few yards of their objective? Zalman gave me his theory — that they were afraid of mines. It was known to the local Arabs that the Palmach had placed mines around the meshek. Zalman believed that when the attackers saw the precipitate retreat of the pill box defenders, one of them concluded that the position was about to be blown up. Possibly it took no more than a single shout of warning to send them all into panicky retreat.

When the seven men had gotten their breath, Sevek sent Ishay to report to headquarters. Without waiting for orders, however, the men took up new positions. Zalman and two others stayed near the factory, hiding behind some cement water tanks and firing at the Egyptians who lay by the fence. Sevek, Yurek and Gelman entered the trench which angled down the hill from Post 1.

In the meantime Ishay had gone to the old headquarters. When he saw the smashed roof, he knew that Alex must have moved to one of the shelters. As he was dodging through the trenches that connected various points within the meshek, he met a small, thin woman.

"Leika! What are you doing out here?"

"I'm a runner for Alex", she panted. "The telephone system was destroyed."

"I have a message for headquarters, but I can't find it. We had to retreat from the pill box — we were almost surrounded. But everyone got through safe."

"I'm going back there now — I'll take the message". Ishay knew that nothing would stop Leika from fulfilling any task given to her. She was known for her faithful devotion to duty. It was with good reason that the commanders had appointed her to the responsible task of headquarters runner.

"You take the message then", Ishay said. "I'll go back to the others. Tell Alex we were almost out of ammunition. Tell him we stayed as long as we could."

"Don't worry. I'll remember everything."

"Good luck!" "Be careful!" and they separated.

As Ishay reached the factory he met Tuvia running with the crew of the Browning machine gun. Ishay tried to report his news but Tuvia already knew of the retreat from the pill box.

"They'll attack Post 1 again any minute now" he cried. "They're gathering on the White Hill."

The White Hill was a low mound to the right of the banana plantation and about a hundred yards in front of Posts 1 and 2. It took its name from its sandy soil which glimmered white at a little distance.

Tuvia and Shimon set up the machine gun on the slopes near the factory and began to fire at the White Hill.

"Ishay, you go up to Post 1", Tuvia ordered. "Tel Sevek that he is to take command there — Hershel was wounded. And keep your head down. The trench is shallow."

"Don't worry, nothing will happen to me," Ishay answered with the confidence of youth. As he came to the top, Motke was offering a bottle of wine to the tired, parched fighters. "Don't swallow any, just wet your lips", he urged. There was a neat, round hole in the neck of the bottle and he was afraid that there were bits of broken glass in the wine. Ishay was too dry to care. He gulped down some of the wine.

The post was now well manned. At the beginning of the first Egyptian advance there had been only two riflemen and one man with grenades to meet it. Just as the Egyptians reached the wire, reinforcements had arrived — a Palmach section in charge of a corporal named Zigi. Its added fire power had sent the Egyptians running back to the shelter of the White Hill. Now four men from the pill box had joined the little force. The position had been further strengthened by the two-inch mortars which had been put in place behind Posts 1 and 2 with their half crews. Everything was ready for another attack.

The Egyptians began a second advance from the White Hill,

dodging into small, irregular wadis that scarred the ground almost to the foot of the little bluff. Again there were about sixty attackers, Sudanese among them, officers with drawn revolvers behind them. Heavy cover fire poured down on Posts 1 and 2. While the men in the trench kept low until it should be their turn to fire, the mortars were sending shells into the enemy ranks. The noise of the battle rose to a higher pitch. On the flank of the hill Tuvia had taken over the Browning and was directing it at the attackers. Zalman and the others near the water tank turned their rifles on the advancing enemy. The setting sun was in their eyes but the helmets of the Egyptians were silhouetted against it.

"Aim just below their helmets!", Zalman yelled. The defenders of Yad Mordechai had no helmets but for the moment this lack was cancelled out by a trick of the sun.

As the Egyptians approached the barbed wire entanglements in front of Post 1, they tripped some of the shoe mines and men fell. The Egyptian cover fire ceased abruptly. Jumping up in the trenches the defenders began to shoot and hurl hand grenades.

"I got one!" screamed Ishay. A minute later he shouted, "I hit that Sudanese!" Again he yelled in triumph, "That's the third one!" Then he threw up his rifle and fell backward. Someone called for first aid and Pola crept up the trench. She crawled past the legs of the fighters as they continued to throw hand grenades at the Egyptians below. "Such a little hole", she said to herself. "How could a man die so quickly from such a little hole?" But there was no pulse, no heartbeat, no life. She covered Ishay's face with a jacket. As she crept away she heard the triumphant shouts of the defenders, "They're retreating! They're running! They're running!"

The commanders of Yad Mordechai had not expected an Egyptian attack on Post 1. They had felt that their most vulnerable side was on the east, facing the road. There had not been time to mine this section in which stood Posts 7, 8, 9 and

10; instead signs had been erected reading "Warning — Mines!" To this day they puzzle as to why the Egyptians chose to concentrate their attacks on Posts 1 and 2. Both were built on top of a small hill. Although they were no more than thirty feet above the wire entanglements below, the sloping height gave the defenders a certain advantage. Furthermore, in order to cut the wire and storm the posts, the attackers had to come within range of hand grenades. Yad Mordechai had began the battle with 400 of these devastating weapons.

After the Egyptians had been beaten back the men sat in the shadow of the trench wall, exhausted from the violent action. They did not talk much. They cleaned and loaded their weapons.

When a half hour had passed, the watch shouted "Another attack!" The men responded slowly. Their lethargy was so great that they scarcely could push their bodies upright. But then the fury of battle took hold of them.

"Grenades! Grenades! Get them with your grenades!" Sevek yelled.

Once again the tired men threw themselves into feverish activity, firing, tossing hand grenades, ducking down, firing again. A few of the Egyptians got to the barbed wire entanglement and began to cut through it. Several men jumped out of the trench, threw themselves on the ground, and took careful aim. One after the other, the Egyptians slumped over the wire. Those coming up behind them threw away their guns and ran back to the protecting wadis.

The sun was setting. Three attacks on the pill box and three on Post 1 had been beaten back. The watch reported that he could see movements of withdrawal on the Egyptian side. Guns were being pulled back, troops were moving off.

"They're through for the day", Zigi said knowledgeably. "If they're like the Arabs we've fought in the Palmach, they won' attack at night. They may send over some shells but they won' attack."

The men began to relax from their tension. "I think I could eat something", Motke said. "Let's open a can of guavas".

"Hey!" Zigi called from an angle of the trench. "Here's somebody wounded!" It was Aba Glinski, a Palmach first aid man. No one had seen him hit nor heard him cry out. Now he was unconscious.

"Get him to Dr. Heller", Sevek ordered. "Don't wait for the stretcher bearers — he's almost gone". Two men laid him in a blanket and carried him to the doctor's shelter but he died on the way.

In headquarters Alex dictated and signed the last message of the day.

> "6:50 The enemy succeeded in cutting the wire and there was a face to face battle. They were repulsed. The Egyptians have entered the pill box area. Our losses are six dead and many wounded. The Egyptians have many dead. Reinforcements can be seen coming into Deir Suneid."

The commanders consulted on the tasks for the night. There was little possibility of rest for the men who had been in the trenches all day; the shelters were filled with women and wounded. The best that could be done was to allow half of the personnel of each post to lie down in the trenches while the other half stood guard. Food and drink must be distributed to the posts, — the women would attend to that. There was a pressing need to re-dig the trenches that had been ruined by shellfire, and to deepen others.

Runners were dispatched with orders for digging crews. Then the commanders took up their most urgent problem — arms. They called in Natek for a report. He came with his lists of the guns and ammunition he had issued to the fighters. Today he no longer remembers exactly how much ammunition remained at the end of the first day's fighting, but then he was able to tell the commanders what supply was on hand down to the last bullet. The situation was not good. Ammunition for all types of weapons was running low. He also had to report a shortage of rifles. Some of the precious Czech rifles had been spoiled in the day's fighting. He had been overjoyed when he had received these guns made in the famous Skoda works, but they had proved to be undependable. They had not been designed for desert heat. With the unreliable Italian guns they made up a third of the available rifles. Henceforth they could be issued only to the quiet posts.

"That means we have only about forty good rifles left, counting what the Palmach has," Alex said, his voice heavy with discouragement.

Salek Bielski, the "Galilee fighter" spoke up confidently. "Let the Egyptians supply us", he suggested. "There's plenty of stuff lying around in front of Post 1. Why not send out a patrol to bring it in? I'll volunteer to go."

"Excellent idea" Tuvia agreed. "Who else should go?"

"Let's ask the boys of the Palmach to take on this job", Alex said.

"Agreed."

Some anti-personnel mines remained which the Palmach squad had not been able to put in place during the frantic night that had preceded the battle. The commanders discussed where to sow them. There were not enough to secure the side of the meshek nearest the road. They would have to trust that their signs and the gossip of the local Arabs would persuade the Egyptian command that it would be unwise to approach the eastern side. They felt that Post 3 might be in danger of an infantry attack since the abandoned Arab house opposite might well be used as a jumping-off place. They decided to concentrate the mines in front of this post. Dani, who had thrown himself down in the headquarters shelter and was fast asleep, would go out with his Palmach boys as soon as the moon had set.

Alex took charge of all these arrangements while Tuvia went

to the factory area to prepare his fighters for the night ahead. He was concerned about the abandoned pill box. The mortars and fire from Post 10 had kept the Egyptians out of it all afternoon, but if they should manage to slip into it during the night, they would be able to do a great deal of damage. From there they could fire directly into the heart of the meshek. They would be able to use it for cover fire for troops attacking Post 1. They could immobilize Post 10. Tuvia decided to try to prevent this with the Browning machine gun. He found Shimon Rosen lying with the Browning near the tank traps that had been set up behind the kibbutz gate. He ordered men to bring spades to dig a hole for better protection. He appointed Zalman as Shimon's second, to feed the belt into the gun and also to advise Shimon when and where to fire.

Shimon was a slight man with a big nose and a look of permanent bewilderment on his narrow face. He had not been a member of the early kibbutz in Poland, but had come to it during the war in extraordinary circumstances. He had been a private in the Polish army when the Nazis invaded Poland. At the defeat he was taken prisoner. Marching toward a prisoner-of-war camp he was singled out for abuse by a Nazi officer — possibly his "Jewish nose" was the reason. Shimon was naive enough, or angry enough, to think that he could trade insults with his tormentor. "You Hitler swine", he cried, whereupon the officer grabbed a bayonet and slashed him in the thigh. For nearly a week Shimon had to march twenty miles or more a day with the column of prisoners. Others fell behind and he saw them shot; he had to keep up or die. His comrades-in-captivity tore off parts of their clothing to bandage his wound. A peasant threw him two branches that he used as canes. Somehow he arrived at the camp. At the end of eight months he was shipped out in a labor battalion; he escaped from the train. His one thought was to go eastward, into the Soviet zone of Poland where his family lived Travelling at night, dodging Germans, half starved, he finally entered the Russian zone only to be arrested as a suspected spy! He was given a sentence of three years at hard labor.

It was much better to be a prisoner of the Russians than to be in a Nazi concentration camp. He received more food and the guards did not abuse the prisoners. He was sent to Murmansk, in Siberia, to work in the nickel mines. After the Soviet Union was invaded, life in the labor camp worsened considerably. Shimon went to help build a railroad in the Ural mountains. There was less and less food, no warm clothing was issued, the cold was intense. Prisoners died from exposure and hardship. Shimon did not believe that he would survive; nevertheless he worked as faithfully as he could and did everything that he was told. Rumors began to circulate in the camp that Poles would be released if they would join the Polish Army-in-Exile then being formed by General Anders. One day Shimon was called into the office and asked if he wished to enlist; he agreed. The army trained in Persia, Iraq and Syria; the warm countries seemed like heaven after Siberia. But there were drawbacks. This army was more fiercely anti-semitic than the regular Polish army had been. The Jews were submitted to endless humiliations. In spite of the prejudice, Shimon became a machine gunner and was raised to the rank of corporal. On the way to the Italian front General Anders' troops stopped off in Palestine. To Shimon, as to many other Jewish soldiers, this was a heaven sent opportunity. They had been longing for years to escape the anti-semitism of Poland; now they had arrived in the Promised Land. Scores deserted. Many joined the Jewish units in the British army, but Shimon had had enough of war. Some of his friends in Poland had belonged to Hashomer Hatzair. He managed to get in touch with that organization and was sent to kibbutz Yad Mordechai. There he was assigned to tend the ducks.

Now, suddenly, Shimon was a soldier again. Partly because of his soft and gentle nature and partly because of his army training, he always waited for orders before he would make the least move. He even had to be told to move to the left or to the right when the enemy felt out his position. But he was a good gunner, he had extraordinary stamina and he stayed with the Browning for three days and nights.

Once the machine gun was secured to his satisfaction, Tuvia visited all of the posts. Mortar fire still was coming over, but the shelling was not as heavy as it had been during the day. Digging was going on in the trenches. A few men were sleeping. A very few were trying to eat, although the violent action and the profound emotions of the day had robbed most men of appetite. Dried out by the hot sun, they begged for something to drink. The warmed over morning coffee was most welcome.

At Post 9 Tuvia found the fighters under Miriam's command lying outside their trenches near the fence. "We heard sounds coming from the vineyards", Miriam explained. "We made a patrol and didn't see anyone, but all the same it's better to be on guard. The Egyptians might try to steal into the meshek during the night."

Knowing what he did about the reluctance of the Egyptians to fight at night, Tuvia may have thought that Miriam's precautions were unnecessary. But he valued the qualities of caution and responsibility that made her a good commander, so he did not countermand her order.

The two mortars had been left in place behind the forward posts and Tuvia found their crews sitting together in a small depression between the two hills. Dina was with them, she had just brought them their supper of sandwiches, oranges, leben* and lukewarm coffee. "What's going on at home?" the men asked. "How are the wounded? How are the women standing

* Artificially soured milk, tastier than yogurt.

it?" Although they were only a few hundred yards from the command shelter, they felt completely isolated. Tuvia gave them news of the activities at the other posts, reassured them about the women and the wounded and told of the heavy casualties inflicted on the Egyptians. "They'll be back for more tomorrow and we'll give them a taste of the same", he said with his belligerent air. "They won't find it so easy to take Yad Mordechai". Wherever he had gone that night he had brought his confident, fighting attitude. It heartened the lonely mortar crews just as it had stiffened the morale of the tired trench diggers.

At eleven o'clock everyone in headquarters stopped whatever they were doing to listen to the news broadcast. What they heard dismayed them all. At many points along her lengthy land frontiers, the Arab armies had invaded Israel or were threatening to invade. Except for a narrow section of the coastal plain, there was fighting almost everywhere. The position of Jerusalem was critical. For two days the Jewish quarters had been shelled by the Arab Legion and now the situation had worsened; the suburb of Sheikh Jarrah had been captured, opening a roadway into the heart of the city. In Northern Galilee there was heavy fighting. The Jordan Valley seemed about to fall into the hands of the Syrians, for on that day the Jewish-occupied Teggart Fort at Zemach, which lay in its path, had been lost after a fierce battle. All of the news told of the successes of the enemy; there was no report of a Jewish victory anywhere.

After Shapta shut off the wireless no one spoke. What was there to say in the face of this desperate situation? Other settlements and other soldiers would meet the enemy on other fronts. Yad Mordechai had her own place on the perimeter of the country, her own battle to fight, her own griefs to bear. Silently men left headquarters to carry out the tasks to which they had been assigned.

When the full moon had set, two parties of the Palmach went outside the wire, one to lay mines and the other to collect arms. Salek Bielski and the Palmach corporal, Zigi, were in charge of the latter detail. The men at Post 2 were alerted to cover the party in case it should be discovered by the Egyptians. Zigi took five of his own men and since another was needed so that they could go out in pairs, Salek asked Yurek, the bee-keeper, to accompany them.

Earlier, by the light of the moon, the Palmach lads had seen a three-inch mortar poking its muzzle out of the banana plantation. What they would give for such a heavy gun! The Palmach had only three like it in the entire Negev. They longed to capture it, but Zigi forbade any such rash venture. He told his men to look for rifles and ammunition, to take no chances and to answer no calls for help. They went outside the wire between Posts 1 and 2 and stole up the little wadis. There were about forty dead and wounded Egyptians lying in the wadis and more on the White Hill. The party began to gather arms and ammunition. Yurek found so many bullets that he had to take off his shirt and use it to carry the booty. When they had been outside the wire for some time the Egyptians must have heard them; they began to fire tracer bullets. Post 2 returned the fire. The men ran back toward the meshek but one was missing. "Dov! Dov!" Zigi called. "Where is the boy? What is he doing?" Everyone was anxious for all of them loved the handsome, spirited lad. They knew that he was only sixteen years old; he had lied about his age in order to join the Palmach. In spite of his youth he was a good, steady machine gunner and one of the best fighters in the platoon. Could a wounded Egyptian have shot him? They dared not wait as the Egyptian fire was heavier now. Someone began to whistle "Hatikvah", the agreed upon signal, and they started climbing through the wire. At the last moment Dov appeared. His explanations for being late were hasty and vague. But after they were safely back in a trench he said excitedly to Yurek,

"I found what I was looking for", and showed his prize — a revolver that he had taken from a dead officer. There were no bullets for it except those in the chamber; Dov wanted it as a souvenir.

"Let's make an agreement, Yurek", he said. "If I live, the revolver will be mine, but if I die then you take it."

There was nothing in the world that Yurek cared so little for as a revolver, but Dov had risked his life to get this one and Yurek did not reprove him. They agreed upon a hiding place in the meshek for the treasure and solemnly shook hands on their bargain. If Dov had been older, Yurek would have hugged him, but he knew better than to insult the soldierly lad with such a caress.

In this night and the next, Zigi's group increased the kibbutz armory by 12 British rifles and much ammunition, a Piat anti-tank gun with twelve shells, and 2 Bren guns with 24 magazines of bullets.

All during the terrible day, Batia, the wife of Shymek, had been in charge of one of the shelters. The lightly wounded had been brought there to take turns lying down on its two bunks. She had tried to keep the other women busy with caring for the men, — wetting their lips with gauze, giving them a drink, or trying to get them to eat. She had made rules for the shelter — so many women could sit, so many others had to stand. The most important rule of all was that nobody was allowed to mention the children.

As night came on and there was no word of her husband, she began to fight down the panic she felt. Other men had come to the shelter after the fighting had stopped, but Shymek had not come. No one whom she asked had seen him. Finally she went out alone into the trenches, thinking that perhaps he was lying wounded somewhere. Whenever a shell came over she froze against the side of the trench. She heard the moaning of the wounded animals. As she walked she thought of her two children, the baby and her six-year-old boy, Abraham. Such a tender love existed between her husband and Abraham! It was as if he were trying to give the lad all of the things he had missed in the stern household in which he had been raised. With her inner eye she saw his gay, laughing face as it always looked when he played with the boy.

Shymek had come late to the kibbutz; he had been trapped in Poland by the war. Like Shimon he had made his way into the Soviet zone. He, also, had been arrested, but on the lesser charge of illegal entry. After a short time in jail he had been put into a factory. Shymek always laughed about the difficulties and privations of those days. "The Soviets were right to be suspicious in wartime", he would say. "When they put me in a munitions plant, a guard watched me but I didn't care. I was a welder making cannons to shoot Hitler. What did I care about a wheezy old man with a gun?" And he would roar with infectious laughter. He also had come to Palestine with General Anders' army, had deserted with Shimon and so had gotten to Yad Mordechai.

Among those whom Batia asked for news of her husband during that lonely night walk there were some who knew what had happened to him after he had been taken out of the smothering sand, but no one had the courage to tell her. Finally she returned to the shelter and lay down, afraid to question more. Some boys from the "Tank Hunters" came into the shelter and one said to another, "You know that comrade who sang so nicely and was always laughing? He was killed this morning and the shell buried him in sand." So then she knew. She did not cry out. She lay by herself and grieved for her husband, for the strong, vital body that would not embrace her again, for his tenderness with his children, for the laughter with which he had met every trouble. The next morning she said to Alex, "You might have told me. It would have spared me half a night of wandering through the trenches." But her voice was more sad than bitter. She knew what burdens Alex was carrying and she understood that it had been hard to tell her loss to the first widow in the meshek.

The kibbutz had been attacked by the First and Second Battalions of the Seventh Brigade of the Egyptian army. In other words, two thousand men were quartered in and around Deir Suneid with the sole purpose of overwhelming Yad Mordechai. The troops had been trained and equipped by the British. Their armament included 24 heavy guns and 8 mediums, a battery of 4.2 mortars, 18 three-inch mortars and 12 medium machine guns. They could count on the support of Spitfire planes.

When the battle began, the defenders numbered 113 men and boys and one woman, of whom 66 had guns. At the end of the day the number of effective fighters had been reduced by fifteen, but since there were more men than arms, others were ready to take their places. The Egyptians had lost about a hundred dead and wounded.

The people of the kibbutz still were confident. They believed that they could hold out until help would come. Surely the Hagana, recognizing the strategic importance of the place, would send reinforcements and arms or would hit the Egyptians on their flank. Shamay had received notice that there would be a bombing raid on the enemy camp. Everyone spoke of "the blow from outside" that would relieve the pressure on the kibbutz. Yet the question was present in everyone's consciousness — which pioneer, which husband, which dear friend, would fall on the day that was dawning?

6

May 20th, 1948

Before dawn a cow wandered near Post 7, bawling as she came. One of the men in this post was Gabriel Ramati who, only a day ago, had been working in the barn.

"It's Tania!" he exclaimed as she came close. "Poor creature, look how her bag is swollen!" He began to talk to her in soothing tones. "So-o bossy, so, bossy, you want to be milked, don't you? There's not much firing now," he said to the others. "I'm going out and milk her."

He climbed out of the trench. As he approached the animal she threw up her head and backed away. Then he saw a terrible, gaping wound in her side.

Sickened, he got back into the trench. The cow moved on, bawling out her pain and fright. Gabriel lay down on the ground and put his jacket over his head. For a long time nobody spoke to him.

In headquarters Alex and Tuvia began to receive reports from the posts as soon as it was light. Post 10 reported that the Egyptians had brought up parts of a Bailey Bridge during the night to replace the weakened bridge on the main road. Persistent fire from the meshek had prevented them from putting it in place, however. The road to the north, to Tel-Aviv, still was closed to them.

141

Runners from several posts came to report that armored cars and tanks were moving out of Deir Suneid. The new tactic soon became clear. The Egyptians posted tanks and guns on the eastern hills above the railroad line, 750 yards distant. Posts 7, 8, 9 and 10 would come under their fire. Other tanks were brought up close to the road facing Post 10. Armored cars advanced to the pill box. Others went down the sandy road toward the sea and took up a position near the Arab house. They could fire at posts 1, 2, 3 and 4. The kibbutz now was encircled on three sides. Actually it was entirely surrounded, but the commanders did not know it. Because of the need to conserve the batteries of the wireless set*, Shamay had not listened to the news broadcast that told of the landing of Egyptian troops at Majdal, less than seven miles north of the kibbutz.

Alex and Tuvia deployed fighters and arms to meet the new threats. Men were called from the northern posts to augment the forces on the east and south. The Bren guns were spread thinly. The mortars were kept in reserve near headquarters to be sent wherever they might be needed. A new position had been prepared for the Browning during the night. It was a mound of earth in front of the eucalyptus grove and near the bottom of the trench that came down the hill from Post 2. From this position the Browning could be used against the new occupants of the pill box. Zalman was sent with the Piat anti-tank gun to Miriam's post, Number 9.

Tuvia went through the shelters, giving new orders to the men who were eating or resting there. In one of the shelters the women pointed out a man hiding under a bunk.

"Get out of there! What are you doing hiding here? We need men at the posts," Tuvia shouted.

"I'm sick — I'm wounded", the man replied.

---

* The battery charger, which had been sent to Tel-Aviv for repairs, had not been returned when the battle began.

"You're not wounded — you're a coward", Tuvia cried furiously. Idiot! Do you want to die here? Go out and kill Egyptians — hat way you'll live." He pulled the frightened man out of his iding place.

The deserter hugged Tuvia around the knees and kissed his irty shoes. "Please sir, don't send me to the trenches", he obbed. "I was in the concentration camps. I only got to Palesine three weeks ago. I want to live a little. I want to see my ister."

Tuvia pushed him off, then dragged him to his feet. The man was tall; quivering and weeping he towered above Tuvia — hat small, energetic man who might be ordering him to his leath.

"I can't! I can't!" he sobbed.

Tuvia let him go. His first furious impulse had been to push he deserter outside the shelter and shoot him. But then he lecided that at least the man could be used for trench digging. As soon as Tuvia loosened his hold, the man scuttled under the unk again.

Tuvia did not say this to me; I do not know whether or not t was a conscious part of his decision, but the fact is that not ll concentration camp survivors emerged stronger than when hey had entered. Scarred and crippled by the privations and humiliations and brutalities to which they had been subjected, some had survived only because they had done some wretched, nhuman wrong to a weaker prisoner. In these people the wounds that they had inflicted on their self respect never stopped bleeding. Still others had borne their sufferings bravely, but only by stretching their powers of endurance to the breaking point; new strains were too much for them. Who knows what miseries had made a coward of this man, who had come illegally to his homeland, who had volunteered to defend it, and who surely must have wanted to do better?

Dr. Heller knew that Hershel was dying. Without operatin facilities, the doctor could not tell how seriously he had bee wounded in the abdomen; perhaps he could not have survived tha wound. What he did know was that Hershel was bleeding t death from his shattered legs. Every time be removed th tourniquets, blood gushed out again. Shamay had sent a messag pleading for plasma, coagulants and surgical instruments bu there had been no reply. From his experience in German arm hospitals, the doctor knew what miracles could be accomplishe by prompt surgery and proper care. He was bitterly resentfu that the commanders could not seem to procure the things h needed.

Dr. Heller was a man who did not give his affections easil but he was fond of Hershel. Perhaps this was because he under stood better than anyone else under what handicaps Hershe lived and worked. Hershel had been born with a deformed foo Until he was thirteen he never took a step alone. After an operatio enabled him to walk, he was left with a limp. One would hav thought that a man with such a handicap would have traine himself for a sedentary job. Instead, Hershel, who had longe to run and jump all during his boyhood, had been determined t learn to do anything that other people could do. He had insiste on joining a kibbutz. In Yad Mordechai he had worked with Fania in the gardens, doing all the heavy spading that was too much for her slender body. What an irony that he should hav been wounded in the legs! His legs had been his life-long weakness; his domination of that weakness had made him into ; rare, sweet human being. Now his life was flowing away through his legs.

Hershel had not complained of his wounds any more than he had complained in the years when heavy work had made his legs ache. Now he was slipping into death. His face was ashen, his hands were cold, his pulse was fluttering feebly

144

Finally the doctor had to tell Leib Dorfman to take the broken body out of the shelter. When it was done he put his head down on his arms and wept.

During the night the fighters had done what they could to make their situation more tolerable. Besides deepening and repairing trenches, they had scooped out protecting cavities from the sides of the trenches and had shored them up with planks. They had furnished these rough bunkers with blankets and pillows taken from their homes. In one of them stood a vase of flowers which had been blown out of someone's room and had been found sitting jauntily on top of a sand bag. In Post 7 Rafael Ruder was shaving. He had crawled through a window to get his shaving things since the door to his room was blocked by the debris inside. When his comrades made fun of him, he said "I hear that the Egyptians have women with them!" So with rough jokes and small human comforts the men tried to establish some thread of normalcy in their nightmarish existence.

The day became stifling. A merciless sun beat down. The men were tortured by swarms of black, stinging flies that seemed to have invaded with the Egyptians. The hot wind blew sand into everything, into food and water, into guns, into throats and nostrils and eyes. And this tormenting wind carried something else, not yet as overpowering as it would be later, the smell of dead animals and dead men. The sickening stench reached everywhere; the people drew it in with every breath.

About nine o'clock there was a flurry of shooting at Post 1. The watch reported that the Egyptians, who now had possession of the pill box, were burying some objects at a little distance, probably mines. Motke crawled out of the trench to get a better view. With him went Efraim who had been Yad Mordechai's Ghaffir when the settlement was founded. He had come only a few minutes before as a reinforcement from Post 6. Motke and Efraim had been friends since the age of seven. They had gone to school together, had suffered the rigors of the training camp together, had shared the hardships and joys of building their kibbutz in the homeland. Their sense of comradeship was strong as they lay on top of the little bluff and fired at the Sudanese who were laying the mines. From the slits in the pill box, their fire was returned. Sevek, who was lying with them, felt a bullet strike his rifle. "Let's get out of here" he exclaimed. "They have our range." He scrambled back into the trench. Motke tumbled after him but Efraim did not move. "Efraim, get down! Efraim, are you hit?" Motke cried and pulled his friend into the trench. "He's hit. He must be hit — but where?" There was no sign of blood, no wound that he could see. Efraim's legs twitched. "Haviva, Haviva come quickly!" Motke called to the nure. "He's still alive. Somebody send for the stretcher bearers." Haviva found the wound. The bullet had entered Efraim's left ear and had coursed downwards. "Take his ammunition", she said to Motke. "There's not much hope." But Motke could not acknowledge the death of his life-long friend by stripping him of his soldier's equipment. He turned away in tears while someone else took the bullets.

When the stretcher bearers brought this first casualty of the day to Dr. Heller, the harassed doctor cried, "Why are there no helmets?" In every war they give helmets to the soldiers. If the Hagana didn't have them, you could have made them in your own foundry. We're losing men for lack of such a simple thing as a helmet." So he mourned the gentle Efraim with an outburst of rage.

Promptly at ten o'clock the spotter plane appeared over Yad Mordechai and a fierce bombardment began. Shells fell everywhere, shells from 2-inch mortars, from 6-pounder cannons. And every few minutes the cannons behind Deir Suneid delivered a twenty-five pound shell. It approached with a special, terrifying scream of its own. The fighters had learned to recognize it; they cringed when the explosion came. Were there new casualties? Had the children's house been hit again? Or their own rooms? Or had the shell only dug a new crater in the destroyed grounds?

Smoke and dust boiled up into the sky. The sun was blotted out, but not the heat. The men lay in the trenches, panting, sweating with fear, nauseous, miserable.

If anything, the shelling was more intense than it had been on the previous day. The Egyptian gunners were not wasting shells on the water tower and other such targets. They were feeling for the trenches, while raking the whole settlement with fire in order to stop all movement. Casualties were inevitable. In Post 9 Miriam was expecting an infantry attack. To her that seemed to be the meaning of the heavy fire coming from the guns placed in front of her position. By her side, Zalman tried to encourage the fighters. "We saw yesterday what poor soldiers the Egyptians are", he said. "As soon as an officer is killed or a few men fall in the front line, they turn and run. We'll be able to beat them back, — you'll see."

No sooner had he said these reassuring words than a mortar shell burst within the trench. When the smoke cleared, Zalman saw three of his comrades lying on the ground. He needed no more than one glance to know that there was nothing to be done for Hilel Glickman. He was one of the early pioneers, much appreciated by his fellows for his knack of coining apt sayings that took the sting out of uncomfortable reality. "Eating is what keeps us poor", he had said when the young kibbutz was suffering from undernourishment and his words are repeated lovingly until this day. Baruch was lying near him. A shrapnel had hit him in the thigh; blood ran from his leg. Zalman leaped for a field bandage; in the meantime someone was throwing water on Miriam's face. She had been knocked unconscious by air concussion.

When Miriam came to, she saw that stretcher bearers were needed. Zalman was busy with Baruch. She called for a messenger but no one answered. She began to crawl along the trench in search of someone to send. When she had gone only a few yards, another shell dropped on the edge of the trench and buried her in sand. She almost lost consciousness again but her

147

starving lungs and the weight on her chest made her claw her way out. When she got to the air, she was dizzy and her head was ringing with the noise·of the shell that had buried her. But she remembered that there was something she had to do — get stretcher bearers. Forgetting all about a messenger she started to run toward shelter number 1, 150 yards away. Running, throwing herself down, running again, she finally reached it. Dr. Heller recognized her state of shock and forced her to lie down.

For some reason that he no longer remembers, Leib Dorfman, the chief stretcher bearer, went alone to aid the man in Post 9. Leib had been in charge of first aid since the early days in Natanya and had been a medical corpsman in World War II. When the "illegals" came in, he had been stationed on the beach to give help to anyone who might need it. He was the man who had received his own brother from an illegal boat and who, instead of welcoming him, had sent him off into the darkness with whispered warnings to keep quiet. When Leib reached the trench, he found that the dressing on Baruch's leg was soaked with blood. He put on a larger dressing and then tried to decide how he could get the wounded man to the shelter. Finally he tied his leg with wire in such a way that it could not move and began to drag Baruch to the doctor's shelter. The shelling was heavy. Baruch was suffering intense pain.

"Please, Leib, let me stay here. You have a larger family than I have... you can't get me to the shelter... we'll both be killed."

Both of them lying flat on the ground, Leib dragged him a little further.

Baruch began to lose consciousness. "Give me your revolver", he mumbled. "Let me do it myself. Please, Leib, I can't stand it," and his voice faded out.

Leib left him then and ran to the shelter for a stretcher. Only one man was available to help him. They ran back to the wounded man but once Baruch was on the stretcher they could not run, his pain was too great. In the midst of the bombardment they walked the last fifty yards to the shelter.

Dr. Heller shook his head when he saw the large wound, blackened and burned by the heat of the exploding shell. Skillfully and tenderly he cut away the dead flesh, bandaged the wound, injected penicillin and morphine. In spite of the loss of blood and the impossibility of giving a transfusion, Baruch survived.

Before the shelling began on this second day of the battle, three men were sitting in an angle of Trench Number 2, having their breakfast. They were eating sandwiches which the women had made the night before and, in place of coffee, of which there was none, were drinking sour milk. One of the three was Meilech, a handsome young man with wavy red hair above his broad forehead. Meilech was one of the earliest pioneers in the kibbutz. He had broken away from a poor, deeply religious home when he was very young and had come to Palestine before Mitzpe Ha'yam was founded. His tasks in the kibbutz had been various. In Natanya he had been a baker. His real interests, however, were intellectual ones. Several times he had been called to Tel-Aviv to write for "Al Hamishmar", the daily newspaper published by the parent movement of the kibbutz. Whenever something fine was needed for a ceremonial occasion, Meilech always was asked to write it. It was he who had composed the scroll which went into the cornerstone of the first permanent building in Yad Mordechai.

Dovik, the second of the three, was a tall, hearty man full of jokes and laughter. With Bizek he had been in charge of the illegal store of arms in the kibbutz. During the war he had managed to increase it by "dating" some of the Jewish girls of the British Auxiliary Territorial Service; instead of more romantic favors the girls had given him stolen grenades and ammunition. Dovik used to joke with his wife about it, "You only grow vegetables in your garden", he would tell her, "but those soldier girls know how to grow bullets." As they ate their meager breakfast, he was laughing with Meilech and a young Palmach lad who was assigned to their post.

149

"I had a fine rest last night", he told them. "After Tuvia relieved me I went to my room to get something to lie down on. The first handy thing was this bedspread. What war does for a man! In peacetime I wasn't even allowed to put my feet on this spread unless I put down a paper first; last night I slept in it on the ground."

Tuvia passed by, inspecting the posts, and laughed at the joke. He told the men not to sit so close together and left to survey the situation at the pill box. From the lower part of the trench that angled down the hill from Post 1 he had a clear view. Three armored cars were stationed around the pill box, their machine guns plainly visible. Tuvia knew that their presence would hamper the defense of the Post.

As he was watching, the bombardment began, the machine guns on the armored cars firing at Post 1. He ducked for cover. When about a half hour had passed, a messenger came crawling toward him, pale and shaking with the horror of the news he had to tell. A shell had fallen in the trench of Post 2; Meilech Dovik, and the boy from the Palmach had been killed instantly.

Under the storm of shells and bullets, coming from three directions, Tuvia ran back to Post 2. There he found a desperate situation. Not only had three men been killed, but the post was virtually destroyed. The lookout had been battered to pieces and a large section of trench had caved in.

"Where shall we go?" one of the fighters shouted.

"How about the Turkish Position?" Salek Bielski yelled. "I'll go and see."

Crawling and jumping over the ground, Salek reached a deep hole a few yards away that had been dug during the First World War when the Turks had defended this little bluff against the British. Underneath a thin layer of sand the earth was packed and hard in this place; the walls had held firm. There was room for two men. Tuvia sent for reinforcements from Post 3 and placed them in what remained of the trench, while

Salek and another veteran occupied the Turkish Position.

Now the Egyptians employed a new weapon — smoke. The shelling on Post 1 and 2 was intensified as smoke bombs burst in the air, blotting out the White Hill, the little wadis, and the approach from the pill box. Knowing that an infantry attack must be preceding under cover of the smoke, Tuvia returned to Post 1, taking the men of the Browning crew with him.

At the top of the little hill the defenders were shooting anxiously into the smoke. Then something happened that the Egyptians had not anticipated. During a *sharav* the wind may make an abrupt change from east to west, and it happens that at Yad Mordechai such a change often occurs at eleven o'clock in the morning. The Egyptians had timed their first infantry attack of the day for eleven o'clock. Suddenly the wind shifted. The smoke thinned out, then was blown away entirely. The defenders saw Egyptian soldiers already at the wire, busy with their wire cutters. Yelling with excitement, they threw hand grenades and poured fire on the enemy. Dani, the young Palmach commander who had spent part of the night placing mines, jumped out of the trench to assist the mortar crew. Heedless of danger he stood fully erect calling out the range, directing the shell bursts upon the attackers who were so close to their objective. The Egyptians, caught without the protection they had counted upon, fled back to the banana plantation.

In Shelter number 2, Bracha was having problems. Before the shelling began, she had allowed the girls to take turns standing in the corridors which connected trenches at either end of the shelter. The air was better there and one could get a glimpse of the sky. But during a bombardment the corridors were dangerous; shell splinters and bits of debris could enter. When the firing started at ten o'clock, Bracha called to the girls to come into the central section. One of them refused. She lay down close to the wall with her head in her arms. "Please, Bracha, don't make me go inside" she begged. "I can't bear it inside."

"My dear child, it's dangerous for you here. You must come now."

"No, no, I can't", the girl sobbed. "I won't lie there on the shelf all day. I'd rather die here. We're all going to die anyway."

"Stop talking nonsense", Bracha said, dragging the girl to her feet. "You can stand in the aisle if you don't want to lie down. I'm responsible for you. Now stop making trouble."

The young girl — she was barely fifteen — was forced to obey. But it was not long until she slipped back to the dangerous corridor. A powerful emotion had taken hold of her. Whatever the cost, she would not endure again the indignities of the concentration camp; she would not lie all day close to another stinking body; she would not suffer the humiliation of soiling another person if fear should loose her bowels; she would not re-live Bergen-Belsen. Bracha brought her back once again but finally she saw that it was no use. The child was determined to have the little bit of freedom that the corridor offered. She lay there all day, her head in her arms, and miraculously no shell splinter found her.

As the day wore on, a terrible apathy took hold of the women and girls in the shelter. They forgot the relief they had felt the evening before when they had been called out into the open air to help carry food to the trenches, when they could feel a part of things at last. It seemed that such another evening never would come. They stood in the aisle, leaning against one another or lay crushed together on the narrow shelves. The air was stifling. Added to the merciless heat of the *sharav* was the body heat of thirty people. Sweat poured from them and wet their clothes. They slept as much as they could or lay in a half-conscious state, trying to feel nothing and to think nothing. They forgot to eat. Even the shelling could not rouse them from their depressed state; they had gotten used to it. There was nothing to do but to endure their misery.

Finally the spell was broken. Someone lying in her bunk began to sing. Others joined her. At first they sang the songs of their native land — all of them were Polish. Then they began to sing the few Hebrew songs they had been taught. One song they sang over and over:

> *"We came up to the land of Israel,*
> *We came up to the land of Israel,*
> *We came up to the land of Israel,*
> *We ploughed and we planted,*
> *We ploughed and we planted,*
> *But we have not reaped.*
> *No, we have not reaped."*

It is one of the mysteries of the battle of Yad Mordechai that, in their heavy bombardments, the Egyptians did not manage to destroy the barbed wire entanglements in front of the posts. In a report, captured later on, an Egyptian officer noted that a lack of Bangalore torpedoes* accounted for the failure to get through the wire. Whatever the reason, the Egyptians made many attempts to cut the wire by hand.

While the defenders had been occupied with beating back the first attack of the day, a group of about fifteen Egyptians had made their way around the foot of the little bluff. Hidden by the smoke, they began to cut the wire near the main gate. If they were to succeed in gaining entrance from this side, they would be able to ascend the trench and take Post 1 from the rear. They were seen as soon as the smoke cleared. Tuvia summoned several men, including the Browning crew, to the lower part of the trench from which they had a straight line of fire toward the Egyptians. As soon as they began to shoot, however, the machine guns on the armored cars in front of the pill box replied. The defenders were in a precarious position; the trench

---

A long pipe filled with explosive. It is set off by a fuse or by an electric battery and is used for blowing up fortifications or barbed wire.

was shallow at this point. The pill box, which had been their strong point yesterday, now menaced their lives. Dani stood highest in the trench and nearest to Post 1. He was a good looking boy, with large, dark eyes in his oval face, heavy black hair and full lips. Although he was only twenty years old he was a veteran in the Palmach. Since he spoke Arabic fluently, having been born in Damascus, he had been sent on many dangerous intelligence missions into Arab territory. Below him in the trench stood Menahem who had fought at the pill box and was one of those who had been unable to shoot the dog. Next came Tuvia and Shimon with the Browning. Below them were two pioneers of the kibbutz, Nahum and Benio, both armed with Sten guns.

"Watch out! Keep down!" Tuvia shouted to the men. But it was impossible to be safe if they were to prevent the Egyptians from cutting the fence. They rose, fired ducked down again. A Vickers machine gun at the pill box raked the trench.

"Oh, I've been hit — my hand is paralysed!" Dani cried.

"Who has a bandage?" called Tuvia.

Benio turned his head, profile to the pill box, to take a bandage out of his shirt pocket. As he did so a bullet creased his forehead and he fell backward. In the same instant there was a loud "A-ah" from Nahum. The two men went down together. Benio was out of action with a fractured skull but Nahum was dead. Shimon caught him as he fell and heard his last whistling breath. He laid him down gently and went back to the Browning.

Benio struggled to his feet with blood streaming down his face. He threw up his arm to wipe it away and tried to fire his Sten gun. Tuvia pulled him down into the trench and bandaged his forehead.

In front of them the Egyptian soldiers were crawling away through the tomato patch and out of sight among the potato plants which had grown unusually tall that year. Half of their number were lying dead by the fence. The danger of a break through had been averted by the last bursts of fire from the defenders.

Dani had been hit in the elbow — it was this wound which had paralysed his hand. As Tuvia wrapped a bandage around it, Dani said, "You take Benio to the doctor. I can go myself. I'll follow you." When he did not arrive at the shelter, Tuvia sent Haviva to look for him. Haviva had seen Dani only a few hours before when he had brushed by her in a trench. As he passed he had brought down a shower of sand. "Oh dear, what have I done to you!" he had exclaimed. "What a big ox I am!" She had laughed at him saying, "Only bend down a little, Dani. You're so tall — the Egyptians can see you for miles." She thought of the little exchange as she ran through the trenches.

She found Dani lying in the open. He had been hit again on his way to the shelter. He could not get up — he had been shot through the lung.

"Help me, Haviva, I want to live!"

They were under fire but she bandaged him and tried to drag him to a trench. With grief she saw him slipping into unconsciousness. Stretcher bearers came and took him to Dr. Heller. As she returned sadly to her post in the eucalyptus grove, Haviva took a piece of gauze out of her kit and wiped Dani's blood off her hands. There was no water to spare.

An hour after the first infantry attack had been beaten back, the wind still was variable and the Egyptians could not use a smoke cover. For their second attack against Post 1, they sent armored cars ahead of their troops, the machine guns firing steadily.

Two men were in the lookout, Sevek, and a newcomer to the kibbutz, Sioma. Although he had joined Yad Mordechai only two years before, Sioma was well-known to some of the members. He had pioneered with them in the training camp back in Poland; in fact he had occupied the important post of work chairman for a time. Part of the war years he had spent in the ghetto of Chenstohova where he had helped to organize groups of fighters against the Nazis. When the ghetto was almost emptied by "selections" of people to make the dreadful trip to the gas chambers at Auschwitz, he had managed to escape and join a group of Jewish guerrillas in the nearby forest.

One of the armored cars was directing fire at the lookout post. The bullets rattled on the twisted iron plates of its roof, coming closer and closer to the firing slots.

"Get down!" Sevek shouted and dropped to the floor. Sioma fell with him, but he was dead.

"His death did not affect me at all", Sevek told me twelve years later. "It seemed very clear that it was a thing that had to happen. It would have happened to me if I hadn't ducked in time. I thought coldly that I would be next. Wasn't that strange? — for I loved Sioma. But my feelings were dead. Yes, I felt cold and dumb and dead."

The firing slackened and Sevek crawled out of the lookout. From Post 2 the mortars were firing at the armored cars, driving them back. Their ranks decimated, the Egyptian foot soldiers already were in flight. The second wave of attackers had been repulsed.

In the middle of the afternoon Menahem was sent to Dr. Heller's shelter with a wounded comrade. There he learned that Dani had died. There had been no news of Dani since he had been wounded and had left the trench as the Egyptians by the fence were crawling away. Menahem was shocked at the death of this gallant young fighter; he had thought that his wound was slight. Saddened and discouraged he went into one of the women's shelters. He lay down on a wooden bunk, stretching his big body for his first real rest in two days. One of the women came to him. She was not a special friend, just one of the women of the kibbutz. She had brought a damp cloth and without saying a word she began to wipe the grime from his face. She passed the cool cloth over his forehead, exposing the mole that grew there, wiped the rest of his face and cleaned his big ears that stood out a little from his head. Menahem was grateful for her motherly attention.

"Won't you clean my teeth, too?" he asked. "My mouth feels as if it were stopped up with mud."

She put her fingers in his mouth and with her finger nails scraped away the caked dirt from his teeth. Then she gave him a little water to rinse his mouth. When he had finished, she pressed him back on the bunk.

"Do you feel better?" she asked. Without waiting for his answer she leaned over and kissed him.

Suddenly the rough bed seemed luxurious to Menahem. The shelter walls contained him in safety and even the foul air seemed good to breathe. The sharp surprise that he had felt when the woman had kissed him gave way to a warm feeling of comfort. "How would we be able to stand it without the women here to help us?" he said to himself. His tired limbs relaxed and he went to sleep.

In headquarters the wireless operator, Shamay, kept close track of what the men in the spotter plane were reporting to the Egyptian command. He was fluent in Arabic.

"They say that there were no more than fifteen men in Posts 1 and 2 before the attacks started", he told the commanders who were having a brief conference in the shelter. "They say that they will fly lower to take another count."

"And at each attack we routed half a company!" Tuvia exulted.

"But we lost almost a third of the men", Alex noted grimly. "It's not the first attacks of the day will count but the last ones."

"Their soldiers are demoralized. They can't send the same men back into action. I'm sure," Tuvia agreed. "We'll chew them up, a company at a time. They won't be able to keep on."

"We must get reinforcements and arms", Alex said. To this Tuvia agreed and they dictated a message to Shamay:

> 13:55 Two infantry attacks have been repelled. We have suffered losses. The posts have been destroyed. We must have reinforcements, arms and ammunition.

There was a change in the roaring orchestra of sound that had been a background to this conversation. Firing continued but it was lighter.

"They're advancing again!" Tuvia yelled and ran out of the shelter.

"Another infantry attack" Shamay added to his message.

It was late afternoon. A haze of dust and smoke lay over the battlefield. The screams and cries of wounded Egyptians could be heard in momentary lulls of the roaring cannonade. In the trench of Post 1, Sevek was talking, loudly and excitedly:

"... aimed right at me ... a mortar shell ... I knew it ... I threw myself down. I felt it pass ... yes, I felt the shell pass right above me and the air pressure flattened me into the ground. Don't you understand? I heard the terrible murmur and when I looked up I didn't know if I was dead or alive ... dead or alive. Bells are ringing inside my head. What are you saying? I can't hear anything ... just the bells ringing. You can still see the shell buried in the trench wall. It's only a few inches above where I was lying. Oh, my head ... " and he clasped it between his hands.

"Be quiet, Sevek", the others tried to tell him. "The Egyptians will hear you and aim at us. Quiet!"

Sevek began to cry. The tears ran down his face as he called the names of his friends, those near him in the trench and those who had been found by other Egyptian shells "I want to hear my voice — my human voice" he sobbed. "My head is exploding and still I can't hear my voice."

For the most part, the men were too weary to deal with Sevek's hysteria. They sat or lay in the trench, half deafened themselves from air concussion, coughing from the acrid powder fumes of their own guns, their bodies aching from the fierce tension of the day. They had beaten off how many attacks? Some thought that there had been three, others were sure that they had withstood five or six. An irritable, aimless discussion began which stopped only when the lookout announced that a new attack was beginning. The men got slowly to their feet and two of those who had been arguing stood in a silent embrace.

This time the firing on their post was so intense that the defenders had to abandon it. They took cover in a little depression in the earth. Lying flat on the ground they fired their rifles or flung their hand grenades. For the fifth time that day the combination of their entrenched position and their determination won over the superior forces of the enemy. It was the last attack.

One man had remained in the trench, Wolf Kriger. He had returned to the kibbutz on the eve of the battle, with his Russian wife who had borne a dead child only a few days before.

"Wolf, come down," the others called. "Get out of there! The trench is too shallow — you can be seen."

"Just a minute more", he called back. "I want to be sure that they are retreating."

It was not the bullet of a sharpshooter that killed him in his exposed position; it was blind chance that a six pound shell from a cannon fell directly on him. With horror they saw his limbs fly up into the air. Where a living, curious man had been a few seconds before there was not even a body left. The shocking contents of every man's skin lay there in a bloody, disordered pile.

During part of the first morning, Vered, Kriger's wife, had insisted on staying in the trench with him; only Tuvia's forceful insistence had made her agree to go to the shelter. After that Wolf had sent her little notes whenever a runner had come to Post 1. The others knew of this couple's troubled history; they did not tease Wolf about his love letters. Wolf had been a soldier in the defeated Polish army. In retreat his unit had reached the Soviet zone and had been taken into the Red Army. He had survived the battle of Stalingrad. Then, as happened to other Poles, he had been put in a labor battalion. In far away Turkestan, where he was working as a mechanic, he had met and married Vered. She was a Russian woman, Jewish, who had fled from the invading Germans. Vered remembers how he showered her with stories of his kibbutz; she felt that she knew its people years before she met them. After the war, Wolf was repatriated to Poland and Vered became a Polish citizen. Determined to get to Palestine, they moved on through Germany and France. After many months of wandering they received certificates and emigrated. Exactly one year before the date of his death, Wolf and Vered had been received into Yad Mordechai.

All during the long day in the stifling shelter Vered had been distraught with anxiety. No message had come from Wolf since the bombardment began. Under the stress of emotion she lost her small knowledge of Hebrew and Polish; she was unable to relieve her feelings in speech. She felt herself a stranger, shut out of the close community of women who had grown up together, had founded the kibbutz, had shared each other's joys and sorrows for so long. She was filled with premonitions of disaster. When the news came, it did not surprise her; it was as if she had known all along that this had to happen. Now she had lost everything, her country, her family, her child, her husband. She was alone in a strange land and among strangers. She began to scream. She let herself go in hysteria, screaming out her grief and frustration. In the small, hot, crowded shelter her screams were more than the women could bear. They tried to soothe her but no one could console Vered whose life had fallen in pieces around her. Finally Dora came and gave her an injection that put her to sleep.

From Nir 'Am, where Palmach headquarters were located,

Gershon had watched the battle anxiously. The kibbutz that he knew so well, and whose children he had rescued, looked like a boiling pot of fire. He could tell from the slackening of the bombardment when an infantry attack must be taking place. The answering fire of the defenders was reassuring; it did not seem to lessen with the successive attacks.

When the Egyptian bombardment began again for the fifth time, Gershon was called to a staff meeting. While the windows rattled from the shelling, the officers tried to decide what could be done to help the beleaguered settlement. Gershon was called on for his estimate of the situation.

"I know their defenses well and I know the people of Yad Mordechai", he said. "We can count on them for a fight to the end. They are better prepared to hold off the Egyptians than any other settlement on the main road. Let's give them everything we have."

Colonel Nahum Sarig, the commander of the Negev forces, agreed as to the strategic importance of Yad Mordechai; at this moment it was holding up the main Egyptian column from marching on Tel-Aviv. But he was short of both men and guns. Half of his 800 men were stationed in the lower Negev. The 400 in this area were split up among fifteen settlements or were engaged in evacuating their children or protecting their communications. He had only two platoons — sixty men — available for reinforcement.

While they were talking, the wireless operator brought in another message from Yad Mordechai.

> 18:30. The fifth attacks, covered by machine guns, mortars and heavy artillery, beaten off. We have sixteen dead and twenty wounded. There is no place to lay them. The doctor is at the end of his strength. We must have help. S.O.S.

"We'll do this", Colonel Sarig decided. "We'll send in one platoon. We can't do more; it would be wrong to send in every man to a surrounded point."

"What about the wounded?" Gershon asked.

"You know as well as I do that every truck is tied up in evacuating the children", the Colonel replied. "Half of Yad Mordechai's children are still in Ruhama; if they had to choose, they'd want us to get them out first. The Egyptians may bomb Ruhama at any moment."

Gershon had to agree.

The platoon chosen to go was made up largely of immigrants who had arrived recently in the country. They had had little training and no experience of war. They had not been toughened in the Battle of the Roads as had the young veterans under Gershon's personal command. They were armed with rifles, Sten guns and light machine guns. They would take with them as much extra ammunition as could be spared. Gershon appointed Yoshke, who knew the terrain well, to lead them through the fields to the kibbutz after moon-set.

At the beginning of the battle, no plans had been made for the burial of the dead or for how to care for their bodies until burial was possible. When Yehudi Rosen, one of the Spandau crew, was killed in the first few minutes of the battle, stretcher bearers had brought him to the doctor's shelter. After he was pronounced dead they had laid him outside and his body had been hit again by splinters from a bomb. Leib Dorfman and Alex then decided to place the dead in the laundry building which was somewhat protected from shelling by a hill.

At nightfall of this second day, Alex and Tuvia called Leib to arrange for burials. They decided to use the small shelter which had been intended for their headquarters and which had been ruined by shell fire on the first morning. They could take off the damaged roof and use the ready made excavation for a mass grave.

Zalman and another man were asked to help Leib and the other stretcher bearers. About twenty men and women, the closest friends of those who had died, were permitted to brave the occasional mortar fire to go to the grave. There were two widows, Batia, who had walked through the trenches seeking her husband, and Aliza, whose husband, Meilech, had been killed that morning in Post Number 2. The other women had persuaded Vered not to go to the grave. They did not want to tell her yet that the only parts of Wolf's body left to bury were one arm and one leg.

Aliza had received the news early in the day that Meilech had been hit and buried in sand. Because of the fierceness of the battle there had been no further word for several hours. During those hours she was the wonder of all the other women. As a few rare people are able to do, she had turned her anxiety, and later her grief, into something positive. Her comrades had not thought of her before as a tender woman, but now she was all tenderness and motherliness. She nursed the wounded, she comforted frightened women, she worried about the messengers running through the trenches under the bombardment.

When she came to her dead husband, she knelt beside him and took off his watch and his blood covered cartridge belt. "He won't need these bullets any more and the kibbutz can use them", she said and handed the belt to a friend. She smoothed his red hair, kissed him on the lips, and helped carry him to the grave. Zalman, standing in the excavation, received his body.

Those who had been terribly mutilated were wrapped in blankets. Others were buried in the stained, dirty work clothes that they had worn in the trenches. Dovik was shrouded in the bedspread that he had joked about a few minutes before his death.

Seven of those who had died were unmarried; six had left widows who were outside the kibbutz with the children. Friends who had come to part from the dead looked at them silently, without tears. But one woman stepped forward and kissed the dirty, uncovered faces of those whose widows did not yet know of this hasty burial. Aliza and Batia cast the traditional handful of earth on the mass grave. The mourners did not wait for the burial party to complete its work. Silently they filed through the trenches. The stench of the unburied Egyptian dead was strong in their nostrils, and in their hearts grief and fear and despair were mingled.

It was ten o'clock at night. The headquarters shelter was crowded. Yesterday's rule that only the commanders, the wireless crew and the men in charge of the store of arms could be present in headquarters had broken down. Lightly wounded men had had to be transferred to this shelter. Now that the bombardment had slackened with the coming of night, women came in to visit the wounded, and men from various posts came to ask for news.

In one corner the Defense Committee was holding a meeting. Zalman, as secretary of the kibbutz, and Dina who had wanted an easy job that year and who had been acting as a nurse or as a messenger all day, joined Ruben, Alex and Tuvia. Trying to keep their discussion private, they spoke in whispers. But the other men and women in the shelter insisted on joining in. They had taken part in every debate on the affairs of the kibbutz since they had come together as youths. They had not given up their democratic rights when the question was whether to build new homes or to buy new agricultural machinery. How much less would they give them up now in a matter of life and death?

One by one the post commanders, who had been summoned to the meeting, came in to report. The casualties were known to all; nevertheless they mentioned them. Not counting the lightly wounded who had bandaged themselves and had gone back into action, twenty men were unable to fight. Sixteen were dead. They had begun the battle with 114 men and boys. Thirty six casualties meant that a third of all of the manpower was out of action; actually, of the effective fighters the figure was nearly half. Natek reported on the armory. There still were plenty of hand grenades but more than half of the kibbutz store of ammunition for various types of guns had been exhausted. The amount remaining was further reduced by the fact that the Italian and Czech rifles were nearly useless. But the great disaster to the arms supply was the loss of one of the two-inch mortars. It had been hit at Post 1 that afternoon in the midst of a heavy bombardment.

After Natek's report the discussion became general, with everyone in the shelter taking part. Many people were deeply discouraged. How can we go on? they asked. What about ammunition? What about water? The water in the storage barrels would not last much longer. No water could be pumped from the well — the half buried generator had been hit in the day's shelling and could not be repaired. Dead animals had fallen into the swimming pool which they had counted on for an emergency supply. Soon it would be contaminated, unfit for use. And what about the women?

During the first day and a half of the battle this question — what about the women? — had gone unvoiced. The men did not want to frighten the women with their secret fears and the women did not want to unnerve the men. But something had happened in the late afternoon that had made it impossible to ignore the question any longer. An hysterical young runner had brought a report that posts 1, 2 and 10 had fallen and that the Egyptians had broken into the meshek. Panic had swept through the shelters. The people of Yad Mordechai believed, and with some reason, that ravishment would be only one of the horrors that conquering Egyptians would inflict upon the women. In the irregular war of the past five months, Arabs had committed dreadful atrocities — the most revolting on women. Some of the women had rushed out of the shelters to find Alex. They had demanded weapons, they were determined to die rather than be captured. Alex, himself deeply anxious for the women, had given them hand grenades. Now the very fact that the women possessed the means of self-destruction was a terrible, unnerving factor. There were bitter words against the Hagana for its refusal to allow the evacuation of the women before the battle began. And, indeed, the Hagana theory that evacuation would undermine the morale of the men now was turned into its opposite. The presence of two score women who had nothing to do, who filled the shelters, leaving no place for the wounded or for exhausted fighters, and for whose ultimate fate the men were in terror, lowered everyone's morale.

There was a stir at the shelter entrance. Nachman Katz burst into the center of the group, waving his rifle.

"I've shot all of the cows", he sobbed. "All of the animals. I've shot them. I couldn't bear to see them suffer. We're all going to die here anyway, why should the animals suffer?"

There was a kind of sigh in the crowded shelter.

"Stop that!" Tuvia commanded severely. "You had no right to use up bullets without an order."

"I shot them all", sobbed the hysterical man. "I found "Atziel" — he was still alive by the swimming pool. I shot "Atziel," I shot one of the mules. I shot the cows."

"Go and lie down — get some rest", Alex said gently, his big, square face full of pity. Someone took Nachman out.

There was a long silence. The loss of their animals was a terrible blow. With what pride and joy they had acquired "Atziel," their famous white riding horse! Their fine cows had represented their growing prosperity. The chickens and ducks had been part of their plan for a diversified farm with many branches. Houses, could be repaired, wounded trees could be restored, but the animals, on whom they had lavished their care and affection, had to be counted as casualties.

"We've got to surrender", one man said suddenly in a high, tense voice. "How can we few men hold up the whole Egyptian army? We haven't got a chance. Why should we die here? I say, surrender!"

"At least if we went as prisoners we could survive to be mothers to our children," one woman said.

"I'll never surrender", cried Dov Livni who had been wounded in the head by a shell splinter that afternoon. He was the sixteen-year-old Palmach lad who had secured the trophy of a revolver the night before. "I'll be all right tomorrow and I'll fight to the end."

Alex began to speak soberly about what surrender might mean. He reminded his hearers of what had happened only a week before at Kfar Etzion. This settlement, on an inner road to Jerusalem, had been under siege for months, it had been attacked by the Arab Legion. After two days of fighting it had been overrun by tanks. The surviving settlers had surrendered; they had been lined up for a photograph; then they had been machine gunned*. Only three had survived the massacre. If Yad Mordechai should surrender, after it had inflicted such heavy casualties on the Egyptians, could it hope for more merciful treatmnt? "We have been promised reinforcements", he finished. "A platoon will come in tonight after the moon sets."

"A platoon!" someone else cried. "What is the use of sending in a handful of men to die with us? And what kind of a platoon? Is Gershon coming with the best men or are we being abandoned here?"

"We all are soldiers of the Hagana", Tuvia said firmly. "We have our orders to stand and fight. We did not choose this war; we did not expect this battle. But we have our duty to do. Let's not hear more talk of surrender."

"When the new platoon gets here, we can relieve the men at

---

* Although the accounts of the survivors of the massacre are unclear, it is probable that Arab irregulars attached to the Arab Legion did the shooting. One of the survivors actually was rescued by an officer of the Legion. However this was not known at the time; the fighters in Yad Mordechai had grounds for their apprehension.

the posts," Alex said. "Everyone needs rest. The fresh men can repair the trenches while you sleep. They will bring their own weapons and ammunition and we will ask the Palmach boys to go outside the fence to gather more."

Shamay, who was monitoring the Egyptian wireless, broke into the meeting. "Egyptian headquarters is reporting to Cairo," he said. "They say that they have two hundred casualties. They say that they are unable to capture the place. They are asking for reinforcements."

"Reinforcements!" someone exclaimed. "They need reinforcements?"

"They don't fight like we do", Zalman explained. "They fight by the book. They were trained by the British, just as we were in the Jewish Brigade. They don't send a platoon back into action when it has just been defeated and cut to pieces."

"They've used up at least two companies already!" Tuvia added. "This will give us time — time for more reinforcements to get here or for the Palmach to hit them from the outside."

On this encouraging note the meeting ended.

At 2 a.m. the expected platoon arrived in command of Yoshke, whom the people of Yad Mordechai knew and trusted. Tuvia used them to relieve posts 1, 2, 3 and 10, and set them to repairing the trenches. Yoshke reported that two battalions of the Palmach were said to be coming down to the Negev from the north. He added that he had heard Colonel Sarig say that the Israeli government had received some Czech planes in the past few days. Yoshke believed that they would be used to bomb the Egyptian headquarters in Gaza. The news ran quickly through the shelters. "We are saved", some people cried. The fact that the platoon had been able to get through to them meant that the kibbutz was not entirely cut off. If there were those who still doubted that victory was possible, at least the somber mood of the meeting had lifted and the fighters were able to face the morrow with more confidence.

7

May 21st — 22nd, 1948

While the battle of Yad Mordechai was going on, the situation in the rest of Israel was no less critical. Although a grand plan for concerted military strategy had failed because of political differences among the Arab nations, their armies were driving into the country at several points. Except for a narrow section of the coastal plain, there was fighting almost everywhere. It divided itself roughly into four fronts.

Whatever the strategic importance of other battle-fronts, Jerusalem was the fulcrum of the war. For how many centuries the exiled Jews had cried, "May my right hand wither if I forget thee, O Jerusalem!" The Israeli leaders could not envisage a new state without David's city as its capitol. But this city is sacred to three religions. It was the prize for which King Abdullah of Trans-Jordan had sabotaged a unified command; to be King of Jerusalem, third holiest city in Islam, was his chief ambition. His Arab Legion, under the command of the former English army officer, Lieutenant General Glubb Pasha, was the best equipped and best led army among the Arab Nations. When it had invaded on May 15th, some units had fanned out to occupy territory assigned to the Arabs by the partition plan, while others cut off from Tel-Aviv and the country for most of the time had moved on to Jerusalem. The city was in chaos. It had been since December. Water and food stocks were low; electricity was intermittent. After the British left on May 14th, there were no administrative services. Fighting broke out all over the city between the Hagana and Arab units as both sides rushed to take over strategic points. The arrival of the Arab Legion on May 17th worsened the situation of the Jews. From the Mount of Olives the Legion's batteries began to bombard the Jewish sections. Two days later (when the Battle of Yad Mordechai was beginning), the Legionnaires captured a northern suburb; then from both north and east they pushed toward the walled Old City in the heart of Jerusalem. All during the days of Yad Mordechai's ordeal, the Hagana High Command feared from hour to hour that Jerusalem would be lost.

In the north the military struggle that had been going on since early May had come to a climax. Upper Galilee is a narrow valley which extends itself like a pointed finger between the hills of Lebanon and of Syria. It is a beautiful valley, watered by many little streams which finally join to form the Jordan River. A rich prize, — this valley — for whoever controlled the head-waters of the Jordan would have much to say about the destiny of water-hungry Israel.

Since early May, Lebanese irregulars had been attacking border settlements on the western side of the "Finger". On the eve of the declaration of the State, the Palmach received reports that Lebanese army units were concentrated near the border and that the Syrians seemed to be preparing to enter from the east. The "Finger" is no more than ten miles across at its widest point and most of it is even narrower; its defense would be difficult once the invaders were inside the borders. Brigade Commander Yigal Alon sent Palmach troops to forestall them. His men captured two Lebanese villages; then lost them again with heavy casualties. However, Palmach units succeeded in blowing up bridges and disrupting communications within Lebanon. They captured the Teggart fortress, occupied by Arab

170

irregulars, which controlled a main road into the "Finger". For the time being, this invasion route was closed to the enemy.

The Syrians chose to invade further south. Just below Lake Kinneret (The Sea of Galilee) they attempted to force their way into the rich Jordan valley, with Haifa, thirty miles away, as their ultimate goal. After overcoming the defenders of the Teggart Fort at Zemach, they approached Degania, the oldest kibbutz in the country. Degania lies on the eastern bank of the Jordan; it would have to be taken before the Syrians could advance. On May 20th they attacked the settlement with cannons, tanks and armored cars. Tanks actually broke into the kibbutz itself; it seemed that it surely must fall in spite of the fierce resistance of the settlers. In the late afternoon, help arrived. Two 65 mm. cannons, which had been unloaded from a boat only a few days before, were put in place on the hill opposite the battlefield. They had been acquired in South America and represented half of the heavy guns then available to the Israelis. Mounted on wheels so as to be horse-drawn, they dated from the last century; they even lacked gun sights. The gunners found the range by firing first into Lake Kinneret and correcting their aim until they were dropping their shells on the attacking troops. The Syrians retreated and never again were able to force their way into that part of the Jordan valley.

In the south, the Egyptians made a three-pronged attack. At Gaza their invading forces had split into two columns. The smaller of the two was advancing on Beersheba, an Arab town, which it would enter without opposition. Moving northeast toward Hebron and Bethlehem, it would be able to shell the outposts of Jerusalem by May 21st.

The larger column which had moved up the coast road and now was pinned down at Yad Mordechai, had planned to besiege Tel-Aviv within a few days. It had allies in the vicinity of the city: the Arab towns of Ramle and Lydda, seven miles to the southeast, were heavily fortified and were garrisoned by Arab irregulars stiffened with small units of the Arab Legion. North of the city, Iraqi irregulars were stationed only three miles from the Tel-Aviv — Haifa road. The Egyptian air force was bombing Tel-Aviv at will. It seemed that the Egyptians had every right to count on an easy victory once they had passed the few settlements that stood in their way.

In the meantime an Egyptian ship had landed troops at the seaside town of Majdal, only a few miles north of Yad Mordechai. They moved inland to occupy a Teggart Fort which had been turned over to the Moslem Brotherhood by the British. Near it was Kibbutz Negba which they would besiege before the battle of Yad Mordechai was over.

This, then, was the situation that confronted the new State when Yad Mordechai began to clamor for reinforcements and arms — a powerful attack on Jerusalem, fighting in Upper Galilee, an invasion in the Jordan Valley, invasion at three points in the Negev and threats and feints in many other places. With an area no greater than that of New Jersey, there was little room for manoeuvre. Any break-through on any front could prove disastrous — could enable the Arab nations to carry out their threat to "drive the Jews into the sea". Every struggle was crucial and there were not enough arms or men for any one of them.

On the third day of the siege of Yad Mordechai, Tuvia roused himself at first light from a short sleep and went to inspect the posts. The men of the Palmach, who had arrived at 2 a.m., had worked all the rest of the night repairing trenches, building more bunkers and adding connecting trenches. Tuvia arranged for changes of shift and sent the diggers to eat and rest. The last posts he visited were 9 and 10 on either side of the main gate. These posts were close to the barnyard area; here the carnage among the animals was concentrated. He saw cows and calves by the scores, bloated and decomposing. Dead chickens and ducks lay about by the hundreds. A calf that had escaped Nachman's bullets came up behind him and nuzzled his hand. The poor creature seemed to be asking for his protection. For the first time since the battle had begun, Tuvia's confidence faltered. He had been living on a plane of high excitement in which he could not admit the possibility of defeat. Now he was overwhelmed with a sense of tragedy and loss. This helpless young creature — the last of all of their animals — would die also. Tears started out of his blue eyes and ran down his brick colored cheeks. He plunged into a trench, hoping that he would not meet anyone on his way to headquarters. When he reached the shelter he lingered outside, struggling for control. Alex and the wireless operators, the women and the wounded in the shelter, must not know of his moment of weakness.

A few minutes later the two commanders were planning how to make further use of the reinforcements. They relieved as many of the tired fighters as they could. Men from Posts 1 and 2, who had borne the brunt of the previous two days' battle, were sent to the quiet positions on the northern side or were told to rest until they should be needed — although there was no place to rest. The houses were unsafe; the occasional shells that were coming over might land on someone's room. The shelters were overcrowded with the wounded and the women; extra people could not be allowed to use up the already fetid air. Most of the men stayed in a trench somewhere, sleeping fitfully in the broiling heat.

As the eleven o'clock deadline approached — the hour in which the kibbutz had been assailed by infantry attacks on the two previous days — Tuvia recalled some of the fighters to Posts 1 and 2. Everyone waited for a renewed attack. But the hour passed with no increase in the shelling. In the banana grove the Egyptians could be seen forming into lines and then dispersing. They did this several times. Alex sent a dispatch to the Palmach, pleading for "the blow from the outside."

11:45. It seems that the enemy is waiting for reinforcements. Their spirit is very low. They prepare for an attack and then disperse. It would be worthwhile to hit them now.

But the Palmach had neither the men nor the arms for a daylight attack. No commander would have said "Yad Mordechai is expendable", yet this was the hard fact. It was more important to prepare strong positions which would prevent the Egyptians from getting to Tel-Aviv than to exhaust the slender resources of the new State in defending an isolated point. All of the border settlements were being asked to hold out, no matter what the odds.

In the middle of the afternoon three planes appeared in the southern sky and circled over the meshek, dropping bombs. It was the first of three raids. Although the planes damaged the already ruined buildings and weakened the roof of one of the shelters, there were no casualties. The men, hugging the walls of their trenches, felt certain that these visits were preliminary to renewed infantry attacks, but the afternoon passed and still no infantry approached.

At dusk armored cars were moved closer to the eastern posts and to Post 7 which stood at the north-eastern corner of the meshek. They began heavy fire. Everyone was on the alert. Did the Egyptians intend to attack the weak eastern side at last? Alex rushed the remaining mortar and additional men to the threatened point. But the Egyptian command had something else in mind. Under cover of their artillery a long line of trucks and armored cars began to move along a field road some hundreds of meters in front of Post 7. They passed rapidly, evidently bound for Hirbya and the Arab town of Majdal. Tuvia, watching this puzzling manoeuvre, gave orders not to waste ammunition on the column; with the few mortar shells that remained, they could not hope to stop it. Later, when the commanders learned that

Cairo had announced a "victory" at Majdal, they understood the meaning of this move. The Egyptians had sent troops — probably their defeated companies — to join the troops that had come by sea. Together they would provide "victories" for the Cairo newspapers which would cover up the failure to take Yad Mordechai.

With evening a heavy fog came down. It made the Egyptians nervous. They kept their guns going, evidently fearing a commando attack. The people in the kibbutz waited and hoped that the Palmach would be able to hit the Egyptians from the rear. During the night, shooting was heard behind the Egyptian lines and some even thought that they had detected the sound of a bombing raid on Gaza. Whether or not this raid took place — the log book of the Israel Air Force says that it did — the kibbutz felt no lessening of the pressure upon it.

Headquarters in Nir 'Am had promised to evacuate the women and the wounded during the night. The commanders sent word around that letters could go out with the convoy. Before writing what might be their last messages to their wives, many men went to their rooms to take a few pictures out of the family albums. Most of them had not visited their rooms since the battle began. Zalman found his untouched. Sand had sifted in on the chintz bedspreads and some of the pictures hung askew; otherwise everything was as he and Chaska had left it on the night before the battle. The quiet order of the room made him furious. It seemed to him that such a perfect room had no place in the ruined meshek. Without taking anything he rushed out and slammed the door. Others found their rooms destroyed and searched in vain for their albums. Still others rescued pictures for their children to remember them by.

Although they were not sent out that night, since the promised convoy failed to arrive, all of these letters were saved. Some were given to the widows of the men who wrote them — men who fell on the last day of the battle. Others were turned over to the archive which the kibbutz began to build as soon as the battle was over.

"The scene which I see around me does not remind me at all of my home and kibbutz", Moshe Kalman wrote to Yael. "I hope that some of our comrades will live to see the victory and rebuild the ruins." Evidently remembering the argument that he and Yael had had as she prepared to leave with the children, he wrote, "You certainly remember what my opinion was as to what lay in store for us. I have been lucky so far and I hope that we will see each other again. But if not — as I told you when we parted — I know that you will be able to carry the burden. If we manage to beat off the enemy and not let them capture this place, we will not have given our lives for nothing... Tell Avi that there are thousands of shell cases here. Kisses to you, to Avi, to Sara and the rest of the family."

Gabriel Ramati's wife was in hospital, awaiting the birth of their first child. She was the Polish girl whom he had found near death in the concentration camp of Bergen-Belsen. After telling her of the bombings, the destruction, the casualties, he wrote, "If reinforcements arrive, perhaps we shall manage to hold out... Maybe this will be my last letter, my heart. When the child is born, take care of him and educate him to be an honorable Jew and an honest man. Don't sorrow, my love, this is our fate. We didn't want this war and we didn't start it. Millions of kisses. Ruined Yad Mordechai, May 22nd, 1948."

Tuvia wrote in a different vein to his wife Raya. They had known each other since their days in the training camp in Poland; she had given him money for his emigration, postponing her own, although they were then only friends. "It is very difficult for me to concentrate, but still I want to send you greetings from our front line," he wrote. "When I see you, I will tell you more about the brave stand of our comrades, but at the moment neither the time nor my nerves will permit it... I think that I am standing it quite well and my spirit and strength do not fail me. I am upset by the deaths, but still I manage to give orders, to guard the lives of the men and to kill the enemy". After asking his wife to leave school where she was studying and go to their children, he appended a note for his older son.

"Dear Shay: After you left I missed you very much. I promised to look after your toys, but you will have to excuse me because perhaps when you return you will not find them. The Egyptians may blow them up. Until now they are safe and there are many rooms where the toys are still safe. I hope that we will be able to get rid of the Egyptians and kill them because of all the bad things that they have done here. Look after Eyal because he is your brother. I send you many kisses and you give them to Eyal."

During the evening many of the fighters came to the headquarters shelter to deliver their letters, or to take off their shoes and rest a little. The women served them coffee and biscuits. "It was tremendous coffee", one of the women told me. "It had taken hours for the water to boil on our broken Primus stove. The coffee was black, for now we had no milk, and instead of cream there floated on top some of that green stuff that collects on stagnant water. But it was all we had and the men drank it with pleasure."

Someone remembered that there were bananas in the children's kitchen. These were rescued and reserved for the wounded. Dov, the sixteen-year-old Palmach lad who had been wounded in the head, was given two. "Eat a lot, you have to grow still," the women joked.

Women went out to the posts with sandwiches, *leben*, and preserves. Even after the "quiet" day some of the men were so exhausted and apathetic that they had to be coaxed to eat; some had to be fed with a spoon like children. Even more important than the food was the fact that the women came to the trenches. This was like a tonic to the weary men.

During this "quiet" day a sense of discouragement and defeat had grown among the people. They were shocked that Egyptian troops were now to the north of them — they felt more cut off than ever. They were disillusioned because the convoy had failed to arrive. On the following day — the fourth of the siege — this feeling increased. Hour after hour went by without a sign of an approach by the Egyptian infantry. The tension was almost unbearable. What were the Egyptians waiting for if not to put into motion some massive attack that would overwhelm the kibbutz and kill everyone in it? It had become obvious that no more help would be sent to Yad Mordechai. Soon it would be impossible even to ask for it, since the batteries of the sending machine were beginning to weaken. The generator that could have recharged them had been smashed by the shelling.

Alex dictated a desperate call for help:

> The spirit of the fighters is going down. They are at the end of their strength. They are worried that it will be a Kfar Etzion all over again. There is no water and no place to put the wounded. We ask for permission to leave the place or else send us help; evacuate the women and the wounded.

In the trenches and in the shelters the people discussed their situation continually. For most of their adult lives they had lived in a perfect democracy in which every man's — and every woman's — opinion on every topic had been considered. The people were not willing to admit that their affairs had passed into a military situation in which military men had to make the vital decisions. They obliged the Defense Committee to listen to their ideas.

No one now discussed surrender, but another plan gained adherents in the kibbutz. Why should they not try to break out of their partial encirclement, while they still had some strength left and the weapons and ammunition to fight? They could carry their wounded with them. True they would be abandoning the meshek to the enemy, but would it not be better for the people to escape than to stay and die when it seemed certain that the place would be captured anyway? The Defense Committee discussed this suggestion and voted against it unanimously. The kibbutz must carry out its responsibility to the Hagana and to the whole country.

Another idea was brought forward. Not realising fully that the nation was besieged on all sides, some people were sure that if only the authorities knew of the desperate position of Yad Mordechai, help would be forthcoming. The suggestion was to send out a committee to explain their situation and demand help. Many high officers of the Palmach were known to the people of Yad Mordechai. The committee would be instructed to seek them out, to force them to acknowledge the strategic importance of Yad Mordechai, to secure arms and men for the beleagured settlement. Tuvia opposed the suggestion. He pointed out that the committee would have to be made up of strong people — strong physically and with the best morale. He could not spare such men from the fighting force.

When the Defense Committee adjourned without coming to a decision on the proposal, there occurred an explosion of despair in one of the men present, Arale Meller. In the light of this man's record in the kibbutz and what he would achieve on the very next day, his outburst was a fascinating illustration of human complexity. Arale had been wounded by shrapnel that afternoon. Physically a small man, like so many who had come out of the ghettos and Jewish villages of Poland, he was running over with energy and determination. During the war he had persisted in trying to join the Jewish Brigade in spite of having been rejected because of his flat feet. He was not daunted by the fact that there were ten times as many Jewish soldiers in the army as could be accepted into the all-Jewish Brigade. Everyone believed that units such as his would be left behind in

Africa to herd prisoners and guard munition dumps while the Brigade would see front line action. Arale was determined to get into it somehow. Learning that chauffeurs were needed, he put in an application as a driver although he never had driven a car. He got a fellow soldier to teach him and demanded a second medical examination. Finally he was accepted.

After the Defense Committee adjourned Arale lay on his bunk for a while; then suddenly he jumped up and seized his rifle. "I won't stay here to die uselessly", he exploded. "All this talk of holding on is nonsense. We are doomed — we are waiting for death here. I'll break out by myself if no one else will go with me. I'll go by myself. I'll fight my way through." He plunged toward the door. One of the women took him by the hand and led him back to the bunk; he submitted with an air of help-lessness. The others in the shelter understood that his outburst was a crisis of nerves. They knew that of all men in the kibbutz, Arale was the least likely to take anarchic, individual action.

Four days had passed since the beginning of the battle. This was the second one without an infantry attack. With the night came another fog and the Egyptians increased the ration of shells. Nevertheless, Tuvia insisted that new posts with con-necting trenches be dug on the northern side. Women were sent out to help. They worked with children's spades and tin cans since most of the digging tools had been scattered or destroyed.

It was a hard and bitter night. The people were worn out, physically and emotionally. They fell asleep with the spades in their hands. After a few hours Tuvia sent the women back to the shelters; it had been a mistake to bring them out to this hard work, exhausted as they were by the anxious, heat-ridden days that had gone before. He visited all of the posts. There were persistent rumors of an attack by the Egyptians, always on some other post. Tuvia recognized that these rumors were signs of demoralization and hysteria.

The rumors reached headquarters. Miriam, who still was confined there since she had been buried in sand two days before, rose from her bunk and went back to her command. "I will not let the Egyptians catch me here in the shelter", she said. "I want to be on the front line." She would not listen to Dr. Heller who declared that she was not fit to leave.

"I'll go after her", Dora, his nurse, offered.

"No, you won't!" the doctor cried. "How will you ever find her? There are no signs on the trenches — there ought to be signs. Why have your commanders been so stupid as to forget to put signs? I forbid you to go out."

"All right, I won't go out", Dora said. "But you lie down and get some rest. And take your shoes off".

"I haven't had my shoes off for days", the doctor replied wearily. "Here, let me take them off myself. My feet must smell."

"All of our feet smell", Dora replied cheerfully. "I'll bathe yours in a little alcohol. Lie down!"

"No, no! No alcohol!" the doctor cried in a hoarse, irascible voice. "Do you think we are swimming in alcohol, woman? No sterile water, no supplies, no plasma! No arms, no drinking water, no place to rest! What am I doing here, anyway?"

"Lie down, lie down", she soothed him, and in spite of his protests she took off his shoes and socks and wiped his feet with alcohol. She did not mind his sudden anger. Perhaps in the next moment she, too, would shout at some small irritation.

Just before dawn the fog was dispersed by a wind from the sea. Shamay roused Alex, who had been sleeping, with the suggestion that the women who knew Morse should be sent out to signal Nir 'Am. The sending set was now so weak that he knew that his messages could not get through. For months Fania and Raya, one of the messengers, had practiced sending signals from the hill on which the water tower stood. Although it was too dangerous to go there now, they could try sending from one of the low hills. The women were ready to go, but there was no torch. It had been lost in the bombing of the original headquarters.

When Arale Meller heard this, he made a suggestion. "I brought my daughter a little flashlight from Italy", he said. "It has a button that's very easy to operate; it will make fine signals. Wait for me — it must be among the children's toys somewhere. I'll see if I can find it."

He went out of the shelter. In a few minutes he came back with the toy flashlight.

"I'll go with you", he said. "You women will do the sending and I can help you read the answers."

The man who, only a few hours before, had declared that he would leave the kibbutz by himself, went with the women to a little rise behind the headquarters shelter. As soon as they began to blink their light, Egyptian snipers fired at them. They fell to the earth, jumped up again to send, flattened themselves on the earth again. "S.O.S. S.O.S. Take out the wounded. S.O.S."

Finally Arale caught an answering signal. "It's moving", he exclaimed. "They must be under fire, too. Probably they're sending from a jeep. I can't read them. Try again."

Over and over the women sent the same signal. "Take out the wounded. S.O.S. S.O.S." Although they could see answering flashes from the moving vehicle, there was no coherent reply.

Meanwhile, in nearby Ruhama, Yad Mordechai's older children still had not been evacuated. The little ones had been sent north on the first night of the battle, together with small children from Ruhama. Now the Palmach was carrying out "Operation Baby" to evacuate all of the children from this part of the Negev; the Yad Mordechai children had to wait their turn. For three days they remained in the "kibbutz of the sirens", sleeping on the factory floor, hearing the thunder of the bombardment, rushing to the trenches whenever the alarm sounded. Although the kibbutz was not bombed, the frequent alerts kept them nervous and frightened.

"What do the Egyptians think they are doing with all that noise and shooting?" the children would ask. "Maybe my house has been burned up." "Maybe we have lost all our toys", one or another would speculate. The nurses, struggling with their own anxiety, tried to reassure them. But the children were restless and quarrelsome, they could not sit still for stories, they soon lost interest in games. The one activity that seemed to relieve them was playing ball. Hour after hour the women threw and jumped for the ball while a question hammered inside their heads — "What is happening? What is happening in Yad Mordechai?"

At the end of the first day, when the children were asleep at last, some of the women went to the shelter where a young girl soldier of the Palmach was operating the wireless set. She was in touch with Palmach headquarters in Nir 'Am. At first the girl was deaf to their pleas for news. "Military secrets", she said brusquely. But finally, touched by their tragedy, she gave them a brief bulletin. "There are dead and wounded. The battle was very fierce. The pill box has been captured."

Each woman tried to smother the fear that her husband was among the dead. But there was one who felt that she knew. She was Chaska, the wife of Zalman. If the pill box had fallen — that little fort — Zalman surely must be dead.

If ever two people deserved a calm and uneventful life together they were Chaska and Zalman; almost a decade of their youth had been spent apart from each other. Since their training camp days in Poland they had been sweethearts. When Zalman got his chance to emigrate in 1938, he had to leave Chaska behind. Then the war had cut her off from him. But she was not one to wait tamely for the invading Nazis. With Miriam and a few other friends from Hashomer Hatzair she fled to Lithuania. In those early days the occupying Soviet army had no fixed policy as to what to do with the thousands of refugees. They arrested some but let others pass. Chaska and Miriam were among the lucky ones who were allowed to proceed. The country was in turmoil. They travelled at night through forests; half frozen they took refuge in peasant huts; finally they reached Vilna where they found other members of their Movement For nine months they stayed on in Vilna supported by what they familiarly called "The Joint."* There were thousands of Jews in Vilna who wanted to get to Palestine, but Soviet policy was anti-Zionist and very few exit visas were granted. Nevertheless Chaska persisted in going every day to the government offices. At 4 a.m. she would get on the queue; by noon she would be turned away again. But one gray morning, for no reason that she could comprehend, she and Miriam were given the precious visas. They crossed the Black Sea, crossed all of Turkey and arrived at last in Jerusalem. There, in the home of her sister, Chaska learned that Zalman had enlisted in the British army. After more than two years of separation and a journey of twelve thousand miles she was not to see him for six more years except for hurried furloughs. Not until 1946 did he return to the kibbutz. Not until then did their married life really begin.

As she went about her duties with the children, Chaska forced herself to thrust her feelings into some corner of herself. Outwardly she was calm but deep inside she felt the trembling of her grief. All day long she controlled herself, but when night came she felt that she must scream, must shout her despair and rage. She tried to find some isolated spot where she could let herself go, but there was none in the crowded kibbutz. Finally she crept into the darkness behind the factory, where the children were sleeping, and cried quietly to herself. She brought Zalman's face before her, his narrow face with the close-set eyes that

* The American Joint Distribution Committee which tried to ameliorate the condition of Jewish Refugees throughout Europe.

184

always seemed to be twinkling. She remembered how he had greeted her that day in Jerusalem. Unable to get a furlough when he learned that she had arrived, he had reported on sick call with a "toothache". There was no dentist in his camp at Jericho; he knew that he would be sent to an army clinic in Jerusalem. Once there, with a two hour leave, he waited nervously while the waiting room slowly emptied. Finally, with only forty minutes to go, he was ushered to the dentist's chair.

"Which tooth is it?" the dentist asked.

"This one", Zalman replied, pointing at random.

Without further examination the dentist pulled it. When Zalman finally got to Chaska, bloody handkerchief pressed to his mouth, he had only ten minutes left of his leave.

The other women were reacting in much the same way as Chaska. With the thundering noise of the guns always in their ears, they were reviewing their own intimate memories, fearing the loss of their husbands, struggling for control in front of the children. They went apart to mourn; then, feeling the need to share their anxiety and grief, they sought the group again. They had been so used to sharing everything.

In spite of all precautions the children got to know that there were casualties. "Who knows how children learn these things? — they seem to pick them out of the air." One four-year-old girl expressed her anxiety to her mother, a nurse in another group. "Father's very sick", she told her mother. "He has a very high fever. Tomorrow I'll go to visit him. Oh, I won't wake him, I'll just peep through the door. But if he is awake already, then I'll go in and kiss him." And she tiptoed back and forth in front of her mother, acting out this comforting fantasy.

A little boy remembered the preparations for defense. "The machine gun was always in our room and I covered it with a blanket so that dust would not get on it. Amran would come our room to see it being loaded and unloaded and all of the children wanted to help clean the bullets. That machine gun will get rid of those terrible Egyptians. They will run away with fright. And my daddy will be a hero."

The wireless brought the news of the second day's battle. Sixteen dead and many wounded, the meshek destroyed, the defenders calling for re-inforcements and ammunition. But still no names. "If you find out anything please tell me", one woman would say to another.

Finally, on the third day of their stay in Ruhama, the nurses were told to get ready to move. They travelled all night and were met in Tel-Aviv by Naftali Gross, the kibbutz treasurer, who had been sent out with the children so that he could arrange for their care in other settlements. The women besieged him for news, but he knew no more then they. It seemed strange to be in a nearly normal city. Tired and depressed, the women could not answer when passersby asked them where they had come from with their charges. They could not utter the words "Yad Mordechai" lest they break down in front of the children. The drivers answered "These are children from the Negev who have had to be evacuated." As if they were in the presence of death the questioners would lower their voices and slip away quietly.

Finally the younger children were settled in a Kibbutz near Haifa while the older children went to that same cement house in Natanya where they had lived as babies. In these two places they and their nurses waited out the days of the battle.

A few years after the battle, when Yad Mordechai was blooming again, an American army officer visited the kibbutz. Alex and Tuvia showed him over the battleground and told him the story of the resistance. "I can't understand it", the officer said. "I could have taken this place in an hour."

It does not detract from the heroism of the defenders to inquire why the Egyptians, with their superior numbers and fire power, had been unable to capture it in two days of heavy fighting. So far as I have been able to learn there were three reasons, all stemming from the harsh realities of Egyptian society. The first was the army's unpreparedness for war; the second was the poor physical condition of the troops; the third was their low morale.

No less a person than the Egyptian Minister of Defense had warned his government that the army was not in a fit state to go to war. When the invading force was assembled on the borders, the soldiers were given to understand that they would move into Palestine in order to prevent King Abdullah of Trans-Jordan from taking over more than his share. They did not expect serious opposition. Those officers who had a clearer view of the possibilities were dismayed when they were ordered to advance on Jerusalem and Tel-Aviv. Some of them protested, among them Colonel Mohammed Neguib who commanded the forces in front of Yad Mordechai, and who later was to lead the revolt against King Farouk.

There is clear evidence that the inexperience of the officers was an important factor in the failure. In their Officer's School they had studied the classical British books on strategy but never before had they faced an actual battle situation. They made mistakes. The soldiers among Yad Mordechai's defenders knew that the kibbutz could be overwhelmed if the enemy were to attack several sides at once. The Egyptians did not do this; instead the officers sent eight waves of infantry against Post 1 which was well protected by barbed wire entanglements and had the advantage of 30 feet of height. On the second day they varied their tactics only by bringing up more artillery; they did not try another approach for the infantry. They had tanks but they did not use them in these first two days as anything more than gun emplacements.

In the diary of an Egyptian officer, which was captured later the war, there is a series of explanations of the failures at Yad Mordechai which reflect the confusion and indecision in the command.

1) The officer of the front line was given his commands from the rear, and this made it impossible to fulfill his function.

2) The officer in command of the infantry interfered in the selection of targets for the artillery although this is the task of the artillery officer alone.

3) The lateness of the infantry in attacking on the first day was caused by special reasons. The artillery was forced to continue shelling which caused an unaccountable waste of ammunition.

4) More time was needed for the preparation of the artillery before opening fire.

As the battle progressed, the Egyptians would make other mistakes. But these would be compensated for by their sheer weight in men and arms and by another factor as well. They could impose exhaustion and thirst on the defenders. However poor was the planning and leadership of the invaders, the advantages were all on their side.

The second reason for the initial failure of the Egyptians was the poor physical condition of the rank and file soldiers. War is the supreme test of a society; the calibre of a soldier is determined in great part by what his life has been as a civilian. In 1948 Egypt was a land of unbelievable misery for the great mass of the people. In the countryside, 75 per cent of the population was affected by Bilharzia, a form of hook worm, which is contracted from the infected water of the irrigation ditches. While the victim lives he is lethargic and lacking in energy; eventually he dies an early death when the parasite lodges in his liver or in other organs. The life expectancy of an Egyptian boy of 10 was 38 years before World War II and had not gone much higher by 1948. Trachoma was so omnipresent that there were more blind people in Egypt than in India — almost four times as many. Tuberculosis, malaria and venereal disease were rampant. Formerly the *fellah** made extensive use of hashish to increase his physical energy, but since that traffic had been controlled, he had resorted to a black brew of tea taken in such quantities as to have a narcotic effect on the nervous and digestive systems. From this disease ridden population the Army drew its conscripted rank and file. In a debate in the Egyptian Senate in 1943, General Alouwa Pasha declared that in his experience ninety per cent of those called up for the army were physically unfit.

The soldier who was ordered to advance against the hand grenades and accurate rifle and machine gun fire of Yad Mordechai had other disabilities. He was illiterate as a matter of course. He was superstitious; his fear of demons made it impossible to send him on night patrols, much less into night attacks.

Perhaps the most important factor of all was the low morale of the invading army. This was due, basically, to its structure which accurately reflected the relationships of civilian life. While the rank and file soldiers were drawn from the countryside for the most part, the non-commissioned officers came from the towns and cities; they had been selected, not for any qualities of leadership, but for the simple reason that they could read and write. Miserable as their lives may have been in the slums of Alexandria and Cairo, they still were not as wretched as the *fellah* and they despised him.

Also they exploited him mercilessly. A young Egyptian Jew, who was a teacher in Yad Mordechai and who had been imprisoned in an Egyptian concentration camp, told me the following story of petty tyranny: the Egyptian soldiers who were guarding his camp were forced to give up half of the cigarettes issued to them to their sergeant; presumably he sold them. Some of the prisoners interested themselves in the matter and offered

* The Egyptian peasant.

to help the soldiers write out a complaint to a higher officer. The soldiers refused. They felt fortunate to have been left any cigarettes at all. They always had been abused by the non-commissioned officers and they felt powerless to change the situation and fearful to even make the attempt.

The gap between the commissioned officers and the rank and file was even wider. The Egyptian officer came of a good family with money and influence. He had at least a high school education plus his three years in Officer's School. His tastes were sophisticated. He had no connection with the countryside and no liking for it. With the aristocrat's contempt for the uneducated, backward, superstitious *fellah,* he despised the men under his command. His every action in the barracks or on the battlefield emphasized his superiority. He commanded his troops; he did not lead them. When he ordered them to advance, he followed them with a drawn revolver pointed at their backs. However much he might be fired with national pride and a martial spirit, he was unable to communicate these sentiments to his men. They had no stake and no future in conquering Israel. If every inch of the new State should fall into Arab hands, it would not benefit them. It was no wonder that Colonel Neguib found it necessary to ask for reinforcements at the end of the second day. He could not send these demoralized men into battle a second time.

In contrast to this was the exceedingly high morale of the defenders of Yad Mordechai. Their officers had been elected by themselves and were ready to share the hazards of the trenches. They were fighting for the land they had enriched and the homes they had built with so much labor. They were imbued with patriotism and love of their new country. They had an unusually high sense of responsibility toward each other, developed in the years of building and sharing. Not all of them were heroes. The threshold of endurance is not the same for everyone and there were some members of the kibbutz who fell short of full participation in the battle. Yet they all held on in spite of the odds. "The inner struggle of each of us was bitter", one of the veterans wrote after the battle. "Innocent is the wish to hold in your arms a woman, to take into your hands the babe that was born in the time of siege and whose face you have not yet seen. There is the simple longing for your wife and children whom you may never see again; there is the simple and strong will to live. Yes, there were fears and doubts in our hearts. Yet we knew how to get rid of our weaknesses and in the end the struggle strengthened us. It made the man pure, strong, self-sacrificing. It strengthened the woman and made her, in spite of her disaster when her man was killed, the source of comfort and courage to us all. It brought us close to one another so that when we thought we were about to die, we men parted from each other with embraces and kisses."

This was the spirit that equalized, somewhat, the fight between two thousand Egyptians and 144 men and boys of Israel.

8

May 23rd, 194

Sunday was a beautiful Spring day. The *sharav* had ended and the wind blew from the sea. But though the sky was blue and birds flew over, on the ground there was desolation, and the stench of the dead was overpowering. It was worse than a nauseating smell, it invaded the mouth as well as the nostrils so that people felt that they actually were tasting the corruption. The men in the trenches were grateful for a half cupful of water — the morning ration — but few could eat.

There was very little firing. Alex and Tuvia called a meeting of the post commanders for noon. In the meantime the Defense Committee discussed the situation. Over the objections of Tuvia it finally approved the proposal of the previous evening that a delegation be sent out to ask for help. At nightfall, three veterans of the kibbutz would steal through the Egyptian lines and go to Palmach headquarters in Nir 'Am. Moshe Kalman was summoned from Post 1 to formulate the demands.

When this decision was announced at the meeting of the commanders of the posts, everyone felt renewed optimism. There was an immediate assumption that the mere sending of the delegation would guarantee reinforcements. The tired fighters had to believe this. Their wishful thinking was a measure of their desperation. When Natek reported that there was enough ammunition remaining to defend the meshek for another day, even if there should be a strong infantry attack, all agreed that this would allow time for new arms and reinforcements to arrive. A plan was presented for the better utilization of the shelters once the women and the wounded had been evacuated. The post commanders were promised that their men would be relieved every twenty-four hours and allowed to rest in the shelters.

About two o'clock, just as the meeting was breaking up, a heavy barrage descended on the meshek. Nothing before had equalled the fury of this bombardment. It seemed that the Egyptians were pouring fire on the meshek from every gun they had. Those fighters who had not yet left the shelter for their posts, agreed with the commanders on the meaning of this sudden bombardment. They believed that it was a repetition of the previous day's shelling; the Egyptians must intend to pass more troops to the north. Perhaps they were going to leave a small force to keep the settlement under siege, as they had done at Nirim and at Kfar Darom, farther to the south, while the main body by-passed the kibbutz. This theory was a contradiction of their belief that their position on the main road made their capture imperative for the Egyptians. However, to add substance to the idea, there was yesterday's manoeuvre. No one thought that the bombardment might be the prelude to a new infantry attack; the Egyptians had mounted such attacks in the morning, not late in the day when darkness might overtake them.

When almost an hour had passed, two runners burst into headquarters. They were from Post 2 on the south and Post 10 on the southeast, yet both brought the same message. "Tanks are advancing from the pill box."

Tuvia and Alex held a hurried consultation. They agreed that the Egyptians probably were going to attack the eastern side at last. It was decided that Tuvia should go to Post 2 to make sure that the situation there was secure while all available reinforcements were sent to Post 10. Alex instructed the runners to go to the northern posts to summon extra men. Dina, the only woman member of the Defense Committee, volunteered to go too. "Everybody to Post 10!" Tuvia cried. There was a surge toward the exit. Just then the shelling was intensified. The first men to go out dodged back into the shelter. "It's hell out there!" they cried. Dina pushed her way through the group of men at the exit. She cast one glance behind her and then disappeared into the entry way. Inspired by her example, the men followed her into the storm.

Tuvia dodged through the trenches toward Post 2. With him went the Palmach corporal, Yoske, and two Palmach lads who were in charge of a Piat. Shells were raining down on the trenches. At the first close explosion the two boys with the Piat hugged the earth and refused to go further.

"You can die here, too!" Yoske screamed and threatened them with his rifle. They jumped up and ran forward. Finally the group reached the shelter of the eucalyptus wood and ascended the zig-zag trench that led from the grove to Post 2.

In the meantime, the defenders of this post, with Zalman in temporary command, had been crouching in their trenches under the bombardment. The sky was darkened with smoke; the ground trembled. Some huts at the foot of the hill were hit and began to burn fiercely. Chemicals and mines belonging to the Palmach had been stored in them; the explosions made it seem as if the enemy were right inside the meshek. The men in the trenches scarcely dared to lift their heads. Suddenly the experienced Zalman detected a new note in the dreadful cacaphony: it sounded as if a machine gun had been brought up close.

During other bombardments the men in the trenches had taken turns in the lookout, but so far no one had gone on watch. Zalman decided that someone must find out what was happening. He called to the man whose turn it was — one of the new immigrants who had come in on the second night.

"Go to the post and see what's going on."

The lookout post — the Turkish position — was only about five yards away but it had no connection with the trench. In order to reach it a scout had to expose himself to the hail of bullets.

The man who had been summoned slowly shook his head.

"I give you an order", Zalman shouted.

As if he were speaking to an enemy, the man answered curtly "You go first."

Zalman fought down his resentment. He remembered the Palmach concept that an officer must not send his men where he would not go himself. Perhaps he had been wrong to order the other man into the post. He got out of the trench, wriggled over the open ground and jumped into the Turkish position.

What he saw filled him with horror. While the defenders had been crouching in their trenches waiting out the bombardment, the enemy had advanced upon them. Tanks and armored cars were standing about 30 yards away between Posts 1 and 2. Zalman could see squads of soldiers behind every vehicle and more troops were being brought up in a large green bus. But this was not all. While fire from the tanks was immobilizing the post, a half-dozen Bren carriers were moving out in front of it near the White Hill. This group, firing as it went, seemed to be headed for a point between Posts 2 and 3. Apparently it intended to penetrate the meshek between the two hills on which these posts stood. The Egyptians must have committed at least a company (120 men) to this manoeuvre and Zalman guessed that attacks on other posts must be going on at the same time. In the few seconds that it took him to realize all this, the tanks advanced further and the firing became even heavier.

He jumped back into the trench to rally the men.

"Tanks are almost on the position", he screamed. "Everybody up! Hand grenades! Bren guns!"

He posted two riflemen in the Turkish position and distributed four others so that they could fire and throw hand grenades at the soldiers behind the tanks. The two machine guns also were directed at the tanks.

Just then Tuvia arrived. "What's happened here? Is everybody all right?" he shouted.

Zalman told him what he had seen.

"I've brought a Piat", Tuvia said. "Tell the boys where to set it up and I'll send for the mortar."

The Piat was in charge of a young Palmach fighter named Ovadia Cohen. He put the Piat in place and lay down behind it. "Shoot calmly", Zalman said. "You only have three shells."

The first shell missed. The second shell missed. The third shell hit a tank but did not explode. Ovadia threw the Piat to one side, in despair at his failure.

In spite of his own consternation, it was in Zalman's nature to try to comfort the lad. "Never mind", he said. "They know now that we have a Piat. Maybe it will scare them off."

Suddenly a machine gun ceased firing. One of the men sat down with it on the floor of the trench. "Don't be nervous — don't be nervous", he reassured the gunner. "I know how to fix it. I'll repair it". As if he were in a machine shop in Tel-Aviv instead of in a front line trench under heavy fire, he worked calmly and methodically until the gun was ready for use again. This was his one contribution to the battle. All during the fighting he had been too frightened to raise himself out of the trench far enough to shoot.

Moritz, the commander of the post, returned and conferred with Tuvia and Zalman. "Where is that mortar?" Zalman exclaimed. "It's been a half hour since we sent for it."

"I saw Motes running through the trenches with a rifle", Moritz said. "Maybe the mortar was hit?"

"You've got to have the mortar," Tuvia said, refusing the suggestion that it was out of action. "Find a messenger and send for it again. Maybe the first one was killed on the way. Keep firing with all you've got. I'm going to see what's happening at the other posts."

He went down the trench in the direction of the eucalyptus grove. As he came to the machine gun post at the foot of the trench, he found Shimon almost wild with despair. "The Browning is gone", Shimon shouted. "Everything is gone. The ammunition box is gone. The Browning has disappeared. Nothing is left of it."

Tuvia rushed to the position. It was true. The only heavy machine gun in Yad Mordechai's armory had been destroyed by a direct hit. Later he wrote that he felt "as if a knife had been struck into his heart" when he realized the loss of the Browning.

"Come along with me" he said to Shimon. "There's nothing for you to do here. We'll go to Post 10".

They ran into the grove. From there they saw the new disaster that had overtaken them. An Egyptian tank was standing inside the meshek between the chicken houses and the factory, about seventy yards from the wood. There was a frozen moment when Tuvia looked unbelieving at the scene in front of him — sheets of flame from the burning huts, clouds of black smoke overhead, guns roaring everywhere, and in the midst of it all the steel monster spitting fire. He saw three Egyptian soldiers dodge out from behind the tank and run toward the trench leading to Post 1. He grabbed up a rifle that someone had dropped and fired at them. They took cover in the trench.

"The Piat — the Piat!" he cried. "Let's get the Piat crew." Just then Maks appeared at his side and he sent him back to Post 2 to bring the anti-tank weapon and its crew.

While he waited for the Piat he tried to see what else was happening. What was the fate of Post 1 which the tank had outflanked? Nothing could be seen of the Egyptians who had entered the trench. From the chicken houses people were firing at the tank. He heard the peculiar plut-plut of the German Spandau — Hertzl must be there. Someone rushed out from behind a shed and threw a "fortified" grenade — a Palmach device of two grenades tied together with a bag of TNT. It burst but was not effective against the steel wall of the tank. Outside the broken fence stood another tank and some Bren carriers. Tuvia had time to wonder why the Egyptians had not sent in both tanks at once and why the one inside was standing still, a target for grenades. More of their hesitant tactics, he guessed. But the intention was clear — to capture the south-eastern corner of the meshek in a pincer movement. Once in command of the two hill top posts the Egyptians could fire at will into the heart of the meshek. It would be the end. Further resistance would be impossible. Maks came running down the trench carrying the Piat. He was alone. The two-man crew had not come with him nor had he brought any shells. They had been expended against the tanks.

In this emergency, Tuvia decided to send for Alex. He himself was not familiar with the Piat nor was anyone else nearby. He sent Shimon to headquarters to inform Alex that he was needed on the firing line and to bring back shells from the reserve supply. Five minutes later he sent Maks with the same message. Every movement of a messenger put him in danger of death. The Egyptian gunners had perfected their knowledge of the targets within the meshek. While lifting the barrage on Post 2 so that their tanks could approach, they were keeping the rest of the meshek under heavy fire. If Shimon should be killed on the way, perhaps Maks would get through.

Tuvia then realized that headquarters, the nerve center of the battle, could not be left without a commander. He would have to relieve Alex. Reluctantly he followed his messengers.

Slowly, despite the fierce bombardment, the news of the tank and infantry attacks on Posts 2 and 10 was carried to the other posts. Leika, who had dashed out of the shelter at Alex's command, jumped into Post , her thin body shaken by her panting breath, her face wearing its usual anxious frown. As always she told her news without exaggeration or dramatics. The orders were to leave two men in the post; all others were to go to Post 10. Four or five men went out at intervals, running through the trenches when they could, leaping over open ground where the trenches were ruined. Among them were Gabriel Ramati and Pinek. Before they reached Post 10 another messenger intercepted them, shouting that a tank had broken into the meshek. "The Egyptians put up a smoke cloud and it got through. It's right at the bottom of Post 1. Everybody to the tank!"

The men ran toward the chicken houses where the tank was still standing. About fifteen fighters, Miriam among them, had thrown themselves down behind whatever cover they could find and were firing whatever weapon they had. Hertzl was directing the Spandau machine gun toward the opening in the fence in order to prevent the entrance of infantry. Some of the Palmach boys were dodging out from behind the chicken houses to throw their "fortified" grenades at the treads of the tank.

In front of the eucalyptus grove, seventy yards away, Alex was lying behind the Piat. The tank's machine gun was shooting directly at him; nevertheless with great deliberation he fired the anti-tank gun — once — twice. The fighters at the chicken houses saw that the shells had fallen short. They watched while he ran with the heavy gun in his arms to the hill. Perhaps he was going to try to fire from the side? But he disappeared into the gully between Posts 1 and 2.

"Where are the Molotov cocktails?" someone yelled. These weapons, which had been made with such care by Sevek's "Tank Hunters", could have been decisive in this moment. But they were not on hand. There was no plan for this battle, no coordination amongst the desperate defenders, no commander of the people by the chicken houses. In the confusion and disorganization that had followed the breakthrough, each man felt that he was fighting the tank by himself.

Sevek, hiding behind the shelter of a small mound near the chicken houses, was worrying about how to get back to Post 1. When the meeting in the shelter had broken up, he had lingered to talk to Tuvia and so had been pinned down there by the bombardment. Along with the others he had rushed to Post 10 when news came of the new attack. Soon it became clear that the firing on Post 10 was diversionary; the main blow would fall somewhere else. With the entrance of the tank, he had come to this spot.

Sevek did not want to believe that Post 1 had fallen. Yet there was logic to the rumor. Given the Egyptians' failure to capture the post by frontal attacks, it was possible that they had tried to take it from the rear. He had come too late to see the three enemy soldiers run into the trench that led up to the post. But he knew what he would have done in the Egyptian commander's place. He would have sent men up the trench to surprise the defenders. Then he saw something that settled his doubts. A man was crawling along the hill toward Post 2. He was not in uniform — therefore he belonged to the kibbutz. His scurrying retreat could mean only one thing — the post had been captured. Sevek hoped that this small, crawling figure was not the only survivor. The man disappeared into the little hollow that lay between the two posts.

Sevek told his conclusions to the two men who lay near him. "We can't let them keep Post 1, we can take it from the rear just like they did. All we have to do is to cross in front of the tank — close — so its machine gun will be firing over us. Then we'll go up the trench and throw grenades." This desperate plan seemed quite logical to Sevek. He did not stop to think that the three of them might meet opposition on the way. It did not occur to him that they might be outnumbered if they did succeed in reaching Post 1. Nor did he think of danger. In this roaring catastrophe, he acted as other men have acted in such moments, with a convulsive impetus to do what had to be done without counting the cost. His comrades agreed with him. Warning the men nearest to them what to expect, the three dashed into the open and ran at a crouch in front of the tank. Another few jumps and they were in the opening of the trench. Sevek saw a dead man lying face downwards, but there was no time to find out who he was.

"Look! Egyptians!" someone screamed.

On the near side of the tank four Sudanese soldiers were sheltering themselves from the fire from the chicken houses. They were no more than ten yards away. Sevek raised his rifle and fired. A red stain appeared on the khaki uniform of one of the men and he cried out as he fell. Sevek pressed the trigger again. Nothing happened. Frantically he tried again. The gun was jammed. "Hands up!" he cried in Arabic, threatening the three remaining Sudanese with his useless rifle. They did not move nor did they return his fire. They seemed to be paralysed with fear. Still in the grip of his compulsion and defying all military sense, Sevek grabbed the barrel of his gun and rushed upon them, beating at them with the stock. Just then something exploded in the air above him and threw him to the ground. He fell on his back and his gun flew out of his hand. Half stunned, he saw an amazing vision in front of him — a vision of his aged grandfather wrapped in his prayer shawl and saying the prayers for the dead — for the grandson who had died defending the homeland. He knew that he should do something, should get up and run or should roll away from his enemies. But in that agonized moment his legs were paralysed, they would not respond to his will. He lay helpless, waiting for the shot that would kill him. But the Sudanese soldiers did not fire. Instead, out of the dislocated psychology of men new to war, they also reversed their guns and advanced on Sevek with the stocks raised. An instant change flashed over the man on the ground. He felt powerful, suddenly, and cunning and cold. As the Egyptians swung their rifles back and then forward again, intending to beat him to death, he kicked out at their faces. There was a wild scramble and somehow he got away. As he ran for safety he heard the clatter of the tank's gears. It was backing up. Apparently fearful that they would be left behind, the Sudanese soldiers left off their pursuit of him and ran back to the protection of the tank.

All of this had taken only a few minutes, or perhaps only seconds. As he lay gasping for breath in the shelter of a ruined building, Sevek wondered what had happened to the two men who had been with him. Actually they had pursued the fleeing Sudanese almost to the fence. Now that the fantastic struggle was over, Sevek felt fear — he was weak with fear. He was a sensitive man and his imagination plucked at his nerves. He could see himself being beaten to death by three gigantic enemy soldiers. He became more and more frightened. Soon he must get back to his comrades, get another weapon, make another try to reach Post 1. But now he had to rest until he could stop trembling.

Time is not measured by the clock in such a battle. It stands still while shocking sights and unbearable noise batter a man's senses. It ceases to exist as men gamble their frail mortality in order to gain a yard of ground. The realization of a narrow escape from an enemy bullet marks a moment of time. So also is time marked off by a deed that transcends courage when a man becomes a willing martyr for the sake of his fellows.

When time had passed — two minutes? five minutes? the tank, which had retreated for a few yards, moved forward again and its gun began to fire. No one knew why it had remained stationary for so long, but its movement had an instant effect on Arale Meller.

"We've got to stop it!" he cried. Only the night before this man's despair had made him want to desert; now that the enemy was within the gates even his wound had not kept him in the shelter. He grabbed up a fortified grenade in each hand. "I'm going to stop it", he yelled.

He ran directly toward the tank. As he ran there was a quick movement of the machine gun as the gunner inside depressed its barrel to take aim. At the climax everything happened at once. Arale ran toward the tank and threw his grenades. They exploded directly in front of the machine gun slit. At the same moment he fell, his belly stitched from side to side with bullets. The tank stopped and three Egyptians jumped out of the turret and ran to hide. Arale lay on the ground, screaming.

Thirteen men of the kibbutz had died since the battle began, most of them old comrades and friends. Those who were watching the agonized figures on the ground had grieved for them. Especially they had grieved for Hershel whose life had bled away from his amputated legs. But the sight of Arale, who had earned a special place in their affections, was more than they could bear.

"Oh, we can't let him suffer like that!" cried Hertzl. "He's a dead man already — maybe I should give him a round and help him to go."

"Look out! Look who's coming against you!" Gabriel Ramati exclaimed.

Egyptian soldiers had passed through the break in the fence. Hertzl turned the Spandau on them. Two men fell and they retreated.

"We're holding them. We're holding them", Pinek shouted between bursts of the machine gun.

"Pinek, if there's another attack like this one we'll be finished", Hertzl answered.

They were his last words. A bullet hit him in the forehead and he died without another sound.

From the opposite side of the tank, Shimon appeared. He had no weapon since the loss of the Browning and had been following

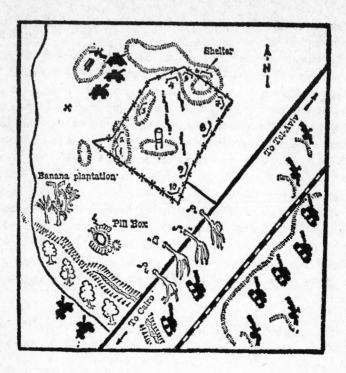

The Egyptian tank breaks into Yad Mordechai

Alex with the shells of the Piat. He went close to Arale and saw his fatal wounds.

"Kill me! Kill me!" Arale begged.

But Shimon turned away. Even if he had had a gun, he could not have given the death shot to his friend.

In their accounts of Arale's heroic deed, several of the survivors told me painfully that they could not bring themselves to help their beloved friend to die. But it seems certain that someone did put an end to his agony.

Arale's sacrifice stopped the tank and stopped the forward

drive of the enemy from the southern side. To the people of Yad Mordechai, he is the supreme hero of the battle.

At Post 2 the mortar had failed to arrive. A third messenger had returned to report that he could not find it. Alex had left headquarters to go to the Piat and no one knew where the mortar had been stationed or whether it had been sent to some other post. The messenger brought the news that Post 1 had fallen.

"Shut up!" roared Moritz. "Don't bring us such news when we are almost overrun ourselves. Go back to headquarters. Ask everyone where the mortar is. And bring us another Bren gun — this one is broken. And shut up with your rumors."

No sooner the messenger had left than Mates appeared in the trench, with a rifle in his hand.

"Where is the mortar?" Moritz cried.

"Back there", gasped Mates.

"What do you mean 'back there'?" Moritz yelled. "We need it — we've got to have it. What are you doing here without it?"

Mates could not give a coherent answer. "Egyptians! Inside the meshek! Everybody — everybody ran!" he stammered. He never was able to explain, even to himself, the powerful yet confused emotions that had led him to abandon the mortar, grab a rifle and run toward the Egyptian threat when he had heard the awful news. He should have known that he would be sent for, but lacking orders, his one instinct had been to throw himself into the hand-to-hand conflict that he had assumed was taking place.

Moritz sent him to bring the mortar. On the way he met Yanek, the only other surviving member of his team. Yanek was marching through the trenches fully erect. He suffered from severe arthritis, a heritage of the damp, cold training camps in Poland. Not if his life depended upon it could he run in a crouch.

"Get down!" Mates exclaimed. "I'm going for the mortar. They need it in Post 2. Wait for me."

"You can't carry the mortar by yourself and the shells too", Yanek protested.

"Never mind, I'll find somebody. It won't help any if you get killed carrying them."

Finally the mortar was set up in the protection of the little hill. Zalman acted as observer, directing its fire to the Bren carriers. "Closer! Closer! Now fifty yards to the right!" Mates was afraid to fire in the close trajectory that Zalman was demanding for fear the shells would hit the Turkish Position or other forward points. However his shots came near enough to discourage the Egyptians, who halted the Bren carriers before they could penetrate between the two hills.

When Sevek had rested awhile in the ruined building he began to feel that he must get back to his comrades. His lack of a weapon worried him, but at least someone would give him grenades. He stood up and moved cautiously around some piles of potatoes that had been stored there.

Suddenly he came face to face with another Sudanese. He saw the whites of the man's eyes; in his dark face they looked enormous. He saw the rifle pointed toward him. Instinctively he twisted his body to one side. There was a roar and Sevek fell to the ground. For a few moments he lay still. Then he touched his side and his fingers came away bloody. Half unconscious from shock, he knew that he ought to try to crawl away to safety, but his body felt heavy and tired. He wanted to sleep. Finally he roused himself and looked around. The Egyptian was nowhere in sight. He did not dare to call out for aid in case his enemy was hiding somewhere near. He crawled along slowly, stopping often to peer through the gathering darkness.

"What, you are alive still?" someone said in a normal voice. Two first aid men had seen him fall and had come to rescue him. They took him to Dr. Heller who probed the wound for bits of lead and bandaged him. With the sour humor of a Jew who had been abandoned by all of his colleagues in his home town in Nazi Germany, the doctor prodded Sevek in the chest and said, "You are very lucky. The bullet only sliced off some of your fat." It had not entered the abdominal cavity.

Sevek lay in the shelter, in the immense luxury of safety and rest. He was grateful for a sip of apricot juice, he was grateful when Fania came and caressed his face and his hair. He felt like a child who is happy to be kissed and tucked into bed at nightfall.

Post 1 was held by only four men when the battle started. Although Moshe Kalman had come back early from the meeting, bringing a boy from the Palmach with him, Sevek had not returned nor had several other men. The Iraqi corporal, Zigi, was in command. Since this post had borne the brunt of previous attacks, Zigi kept someone in the lookout constantly. Yurek, the beekeeper, and Kalman took turns. They saw the tanks approaching them from the pill box, saw them pass the post and direct their fire on Post 2. The Palmach lad kept the Bren gun firing at the Egyptian soldiers behind the tanks. The range was good and he saw men fall under his fire. Suddenly the gun jammed. Zigi worked with it frantically but could not repair it.

"Kalman has been hit", Yurek cried. He ran to pull him out of the lookout post but Kalman was already dead.

A moment later a grenade exploded in the trench, killing the boy from the Palmach. It had been thrown from their rear by the Egyptians whom Tuvia had seen enter the trench. Yurek and Zigi, protected by the angle of the zig-zag, were the only defenders left.

"Run!" cried Zigi. "Run toward Post 2." They abandoned the position, running at a crouch. Bullets whizzed past them; they dropped to the ground and crawled. In the little depression between the two posts they met Alex and told him that Post 1 had fallen.

"We'll get it back later", Alex said confidently "Right now we've got to hit the Egyptians below us. They're trying to get into Post 2. Go up there with your grenades, Yurek. Zigi, put the Bren gun on that little hillock."

"It's jammed."

"Well, get it going. We've got to have it."

Zigi sat down in the hollow with the gun in his lap and began to tinker with it. Alex found a place at the top of the hill from which he could fire the Piat. Soon the Bren gun was in action, too.

Between this small task force and Post 2, reinforcements appeared, summoned from the "quiet" posts by Tuvia. The seven men were armed only with rifles. Trying to make the enemy believe that another heavy gun had been brought up, they all fired together, as one. They were charmed by their idea. Who knows whether it fooled the Egyptians? But to these men, who had had to sit in the northern posts and watch the battles from a distance, it gave a sense of extraordinary satisfaction. They fought with a kind of fierce joy.

Late in the afternoon, Alex decided that the time had come to take back Post 1. He could not know, but he had to assume that it was strongly held. A counter attack was risky, of course, but beyond recognising its dangers, he refused to take them into account. The Egyptians had to be thrown out of the meshek, therefore he must organize the attempt. The tank was silent now so that it was possible to send to the chicken houses to get men and arms. Zigi volunteered to go. Finally six or seven men gathered in the hollow between the two hill-top posts. They were armed with a Bren gun, a Tommy gun, the Schmeiser, rifles and grenades. Alex had one shell left for the Piat. They moved as close as they dared and Alex fired into the trench. He knew that a Piat was not an effective weapon against anything but armor, but he hoped that the noise it made would demoralize the Egyptians. As he expected, the shell buried itself in the sand and did not explode. The men ran forward, shooting and throwing grenades. As they got to the top of the trench an Egyptian aimed his rifle at Alex whose face was turned the other way. "Down!" screamed Pinek. He grabbed at his comrade's legs and toppled him into the trench. Someone else shot the Egyptian. He was the only enemy soldier in sight — others must be hiding in the zig-zags. Throwing grenades before them, the men went cautiously down the trench. There was no answering fire. As they advanced they came upon the corpses of two more Egyptians. These three, whom Tuvia had seen from the eucalyptus grove, were the only ones who had succeeded in reaching the post. The fire from the chicken houses had been accurate and deadly and had prevented the enemy from sending reinforcements to this all-important point. Nine or ten Egyptians had died near the foot of the trench.

Once the post had been secured, Alex went back to headquarters. There was none of the jubilance of victory among the men he left behind. It did not occur to them that the energy and daring of their counter-attack had been a high point of the battle. They felt that their success was only temporary. Enemy tanks stood just beyond the wire. Surely the Egyptians would follow up their advantage and send tanks in force that would overwhelm the kibbutz. The men made a count of their ammunition. Almost everything had been spent in recapturing the post. All that they had left to defend it were a few bullets and some hand grenades.

Three men were standing close together in an angle of the trench near the top of the hill. In their discouragement and despair they had become heedless of the endless injunction to stay well spread out. Suddenly they heard a tank in motion and saw a smoke cloud puff out over the broken wire. Perhaps they would not have reacted as they did a day before or even an hour before.

"They're coming in! They're coming in!" cried Rafael.

"Oh, what will become of the women?"

The savagery of the Arabs toward Jewish women was a bitter fact that was known to all. One of the men gave a hysterical sob.

"They won't treat us as prisoners of war — not after this battle", Menahem said. "It will be a massacre like Kfar Etzion".

"Better to end it ourselves", Pinek cried and took the pin out of a hand grenade, holding down the handle.

The three men threw their arms around each other. They embraced and kissed. Sorrow filled their hearts. This was the end of all their youthful dreams, all their toil, all their shared experience.

"Wait! Wait!" cried Menahem. "They're not attacking. Look, they're pulling out the other tank. Not yet, Pinek! Oh where is the pin, where is the pin?"

Pinek could have thrown the grenade but if they were to live, a grenade was precious. Menahem scrabbled frantically in the sand and found the pin.

"Put it back! Put it back! We can't die yet!"

Pinek put the pin into the grenade. Laughing and crying the three men threw their arms around each other again but this time it was an embrace of life.

Finally the sudden dusk dropped over the land. The shelling slackened. Through the thinning smoke the men could see that the Egyptians had coupled the two tanks with a chain and were pulling it beyond the broken fence.

In front of Post 2 the Bren carriers wheeled about and went back behind the White Hill. The tanks that had threatened the post retreated also. Zalman and Moritz climbed out of the Turkish position from which they had been firing a Bren gun. Just as they wriggled over the open ground and dropped into the trench, a shell fell directly into the position. "Sorry, you came too late!" Moritz exclaimed. "Everything could have been finished but you came too late." He flung himself full length on the ground. "I'm so tired I almost wish it had come on time", he murmured.

"That was close", Zalman said, shaken by their narrow escape. "But we've been lucky". All during the long, tense afternoon, he had marvelled that there had been so few casualties in the post in spite of the fearful shelling. The man who had refused to go into the Turkish position had received a flesh wound while hiding "in safety" in the trench. Another man had a broken leg; he had been attended in a nearby trench by Haviva. Other wounds were minor. He himself was without a scratch.

No one knew how many had lost their lives in the wild, disorganized battle. Men went out to search for the dead. A new grave had to be dug. A spot was chosen near the ruined shelter which had been used for those who had died in the first two days. Exhausted men took turns in digging.

From Post 1 they brought Moshe Kalman to the mass grave. Moshe had not believed that he would survive the battle. From the night when he and Yael had packed their children's things for the evacuation, he had tried to prepare her for his death. He left her a legacy of trust. "You will be able to carry the burden."

The boy from the Palmach who had been killed in Post 1 was brought in. For several years he was listed as an "unknown" among Yad Mordechai's dead. Finally his name was furnished from records of the Palmach. He was called Peretz Rabinov. Nothing more is known of him except that he had arrived in the country only a few weeks before his death.

Nothing was known either of Mark Schneider, another Palmach boy, not even how he died. Today the kibbutz has his photograph and it is shown lovingly with the rest on the anniversary of the battle. Perhaps it was taken for his high school graduation. It is the only photograph in the collection that shows a buttoned-up collar and a tie.

No one remembers when Ovadia Cohen left Post 2 after his failure with the Piat. His body was found near the chicken houses. When he had arrived with the Palmach reinforcements, he had said jubilantly, "I didn't tell my mother that I was going to the Negev. She thinks I'm in Tel-Aviv. She wouldn't have let me come if she had known."

When Shimon had come to headquarters to summon Alex to fire the Piat, young Dov had jumped down from his bunk: "I'll go — I can fire a Piat!"

"No, no!" the nurse had exclaimed. "You're wounded. You can't go."

But in spite of his head wound Dov ran out of the shelter. He did not even get to the scene of the battle, he was hit on the way to the eucalyptus grove. Two days after his death, the Palmach received orders for his demobilization. Since he was only sixteen, his mother had moved to get him released. No one claimed the revolver that he had taken such pleasure in finding among the Egyptian dead.

Hertzl was brought in. On his sensitive face his brows were drawn together in the slight frown that he had worn so often in life. He had had many problems and frustrations. Because he was one of the principle leaders in Hashomer Hatzair, his emigration had been postponed until he was caught by the war. He had escaped to Vilna and there had carried on his work. About to emigrate with Miriam and Chaska, his documents had been stolen. He had retreated with the Red Army, had worked on a Russian collective farm, and, after the war, had organized illegal immigration from Italy. There had been little time for him to put his energies and his love to the service of the kibbutz.

Arale Meller was the last to be brought to the grave. The chief stretcher bearer, Leib Dorfman, could not bring himself to go to his body. They had been born in the same little Polish town;

they had been friends since childhood. Leib could not even face the fact that Arale was dead. But finally, when the stretcher bearers had searched all the battleground, he sent them for the shattered body.

Zalman, standing in the mass grave, received it. At first he did not recognize Arale for his face had changed in death. It was marked by the agony that he had suffered. Then Zalman saw the familiar wrist watch, a twin to his own. The two men had worn them through the Italian campaign. Memories of Arale overwhelmed him — Arale demanding to become a driver in the Jewish Brigade so as not to be left behind in Africa; Arale's gaiety in the furloughs that they had spent together; the shared yearning for their kibbutz, for their wives and their mutual friends. They had been home from the army for only two years. The others said that Arale had saved the meshek by his gallant death, but as he helped to cover the grave Zalman could only think that his dearest friend was dead. He wept.

The kibbutz now had lost twenty three of its defenders. There were forty wounded. More than a third of all of the available man power had been put out of action and part of those who remained were demoralized by exhaustion and by fear. How could they go on? Alex dictated a last desperate message. Fania and Raya sent it with their toy flashlight.

> "We are at the end of our strength. We have no more ammunition. Give us permission to release our surviving members."

9

The Retreat

About ten o'clock that night a messenger ran into headquarters with the news that blinker signals could be seen coming from Nir 'Am. Fania and Rachel went to the hill behind the shelters to receive them. There was rejoicing in headquarters when the message was decoded. The Palmach was sending reinforcements and armored trucks to take out the wounded. They should arrive within the hour.

Arrangements already existed for the approach of any aid coming from the outside. Entrance would be through Post 7 on the northeastern corner of the meshek. The Palmach platoon that had reinforced Yad Mordechai on the second night of the battle had come to this post by way of a side road which ran for about three miles to an abandoned British army camp. The route had been free of the enemy at that time. In the last days, however, the Egyptians had placed mortars and machine guns on some low hills overlooking the road.

Gabriel Ramati and Benio were sent outside the fence to wait for the arrival of scouts. The agreed-upon signal was a flashlight held inside a sleeve, so that its light would not attract Egyptian fire. The men crawled away from the meshek to a point where they could see the juncture of the side road with the main highway. There they waited, showing their light at intervals. Both men had taken part in the battle of the tank; they were exhausted but their prickling nerves kept them awake. Every now and then the Egyptians sent up flares. The two men took advantage of a little hollow in the sand so as to remain unseen.

When an hour had gone by with no sign of an answering flashlight, mortar and machine gun fire started up from the hills overlooking the road. "They're going to have to fight their way through", Benio said. In spite of the risk the men moved from the hollow to some rocks, then on to another hollow, crawling in a wide arc so that they would not miss the answering flashlight. Finally they saw a weak spot of light. Two men from the Palmach crawled into sight. They were Gershon, the commander who had evacuated the children, and another man.

"We've been looking for you!" Gershon exclaimed. "We thought you must not have caught our signals or that you were all dead."

He told them that three armored trucks were waiting in a wadi on the other side of the railroad tracks, about four hundred yards from the fence. Five additional trucks carrying reinforcements and arms had not been able to get through.

The four made their way through the wire, entered Post 7 and went on to headquarters. The commanders called the Defense Committee together and led it outside. They said that the shelter was too hot and crowded, but their actual reason was that they wanted privacy for the meeting with Gershon. The decisions that were to be made must be made by military minds and there was no time to hear the opinions of the kibbutz members. As they settled down in a trench near the ruined children's house, Dina pointed to two dark shapes on the roof. "Look!" she said in amazement. "Our peacocks! Where have they been all this time? What did they eat? Where did they hide?" It was one of those weird accidents of war, that out of all of the animals and fowls in the meshek only the peacocks should have survived.

Gershon asked questions and Tuvia told the story of the tank battle. Then he reported on the general situation. In regard to arms and ammunition it was most serious. The Browning and one mortar had been destroyed by direct hits. The English ammunition was exhausted. Many Bren guns and rifles were out of commission.

"How long could you hold out in case of another infantry attack?" Gershon asked.

"Natek says not more than two hours, and then every bullet would be gone."

As to manpower, Tuvia listed the losses and pointed out that some of the new immigrants, who had arrived on the second night, were demoralized and could not be counted on in the firing line. The dozen teen-age students could not be used for anything more than messengers or trench diggers. There were perhaps sixty real fighters left to spread over the ten posts and they were exhausted. Nevertheless, he believed that the kibbutz could hold out indefinitely with the proper reinforcements and supplies.

"I have brought one platoon, if it manages to get through", Gershon said.

"Thirty men are not enough", Tuvia objected. "We must have at least two platoons. We need a three-inch mortar. And there must be attacks from outside." He went on to list other needs — more arms and ammunition shovels, medical supplies.

"We will need other things as well", Dina said. "Our Primus stoves are broken — we can't even boil instruments for the doctor. We'll have to have stoves. We must be able to give the fighters something hot to drink, at least. There is food enough. And what about a doctor? Ours is worn out. We must have another doctor."

"We also demand that you evacuate the women", Tuvia said.

"They take up shelter space that we must have for the wounded and for our men to rest."

"I only have orders to evacuate the wounded" Gershon replied.

"Yes, but you are here on the spot and you see the condition we're in", Tuvia argued. "We're a front line point and we have received orders to hold it. We *will* hold it if you will give us the necessary help. The Egyptians have greater losses than we and after today's battle they will be demoralized."

Alex did not agree altogether with Tuvia's estimate of their position. "It is true that the Egyptians have bigger losses than we, but they can afford them", he said. "Look at our real situation. Today's shelling has destroyed the wire in several places. Our fighters are tired out, yet they cannot rest. They are working now to repair the trenches. We have no water. Even if the Palmach can send two platoons, which I doubt, can it send water for a long siege? It is impossible to repair the pump — it is under fire from the pill box day and night. My opinion is that we should retreat while there is time."

"We will be false to our name, to Mordechai Anilevicz, to the fighters of the Warsaw Ghetto, unless we do everything possible to stay and hold this place", Tuvia exclaimed passionately.

"But what if the Palmach cannot send us help?" Alex argued. "We have been begging for it all these days it has not come."

"I think of it this way," Ruben said thoughtfully. "Our meshek is like a pill box standing far out in front of the State's defenses. Such a pill box can hold out for a time, but if it does not get help, it will be captured. We must think what it will mean to the rest of the country if we should be wiped out. Won't other front line posts get the feeling that resistance is useless? It seems to me that the duty of the fighters in such a pill box is to escape, as our men did. We have hit the enemy and ruined his plans. We have done our duty."

As they argued back and forth the feeling grew that their situation was indeed hopeless, that the Palmach would not be able to supply their many needs, that only two alternatives confronted them, certain death or retreat. Zalman summed it up. "I do not believe that in the few hours that remain, help can be brought in to us", he said. "We must make a Dunkirk. We must leave here, so that we can fight again somewhere else."

Gershon was shocked by the situation — the losses, the condition of the survivors, the destruction. However, he was a military man with his orders to carry out. "I cannot give you permission to leave," he told the committee. "The orders are that you are to keep standing. I will take out as many of the women as I can. I will report what I have seen here. We will let you know by flashlight signals or by runner what help can be given you."

"We will prepare to stay," Alex replied. "But we also must prepare to go. If we do not get an answer by three o'clock, we will start the retreat."

Since Gershon had agreed to evacuate some of the women, the Defense Committee was faced with the decision as to which women were necessary to continued defense and which should go out. They decided that nine women were indispensable; Miriam, Dina, the three runners, the two first-aid nurses, Lea who was in charge of food, and Rachel, the Palmach wireless operator. But the trucks could not possibly carry all the rest of the women as well as the wounded. How to make a choice when at the back of everyone's mind was the grim question, "Will any of those who stay here now remain alive?" Finally the Committee decided that eight girls of the youth group, who had been studying in Yad Mordechai, would have to stay behind. The women of the kibbutz, most of them mothers, would leave.

In the meantime, while the meeting still was going on, Leib Dorfman had organized the evacuation of the wounded. There were sixteen stretcher cases; he had only seven stretchers. The bearers would have to make three trips. Men and women were taken from other tasks to carry the wounded to the waiting trucks. The moon was still up — it was necessary to proceed cautiously through the network of trenches to avoid being fired upon.

When the stretcher bearers came for one of the wounded, he begged to be left behind. He was Leon Blau, who was suffering greatly from the wound in his lung. He had been hit in the first bombardment and for two days had remained standing in the shelter because the pain was worse when he tried to lie down. Finally he had escaped Dr. Heller's vigilance and had gone outside. He wanted to die; he hoped that an Egyptian bullet would finish his suffering. A friend had found him and had forced him back to the shelter.

"Don't take me", he begged the stretcher bearers. "It's no use. I can't stand the jolting and it's no use anyway. Don't take me — I'm finished."

"Yes, you must go", Dr. Heller insisted. "They'll operate on you* — you'll be all right."

Many of the wounded were apprehensive about the journey. As they passed through Post 7, Rafael Ruder felt one of them take a hand grenade from his belt. "What do you want with that?" he demanded. "Give it to me We might be needing that grenade."

"If we're caught on the way, I'd rather use it than fall into the hands of the Egyptians," the wounded man replied.

"Stop worrying", Rafael told his friend. "You mustn't think of going like that. Your family needs you and so does Yad Mordechai. I'll walk with you as far as the trucks and Gershon will look after you from there on."

The wounded man began to cry, but he gave back the hand grenade.

---

* Six months after the battle, the bullet was removed in a delicate operation. It had broken a rib, the splintered ends of which were piercing the lung. When I asked Leon how he felt now, he replied, "I try to be healthy."

When it became known which women would leave the meshek, there were hasty partings. Wives whose husbands could not leave their posts sent messages with friends. A few of the women ran to their destroyed homes to rescue their family albums, but most arrived at the armored trucks with nothing more than the clothes they were wearing.

Although the moon was up, the Egyptians did not detect the movements within the meshek. But while the stretcher bearers still were loading the wounded onto the trucks, something alerted them. The mortars and machine guns on the hills above began to fire. Two of the wounded were hit again; fortunately their wounds were minor. Two trucks started off. The firing increased.

Leib Dorfman and his helpers were bringing the fourteenth man — Sevek — to the last truck when the driver started his engine.

"Wait! Wait!" Leib called. "There are three more."

"Can't wait; it's too dangerous", the driver said. "Another ambulance will have to come."

"You take this man", Leib shouted. "He's right here. Don't you dare to leave him behind!"

Sevek was shoved into the crowded truck and the driver raced away. Between him and Gvar 'Am, five miles away, firing began. The Egyptians were shooting at the trucks that had left and the Palmach armored cars, which had not been able to reach Yad Mordechai, were returning their fire. All of the trucks got through, but the last one reached Gvar 'Am with one of its tires burning.

In the meantime the bearers brought the last two wounded men, both members of the Palmach, to the rendez-vous only to find that the truck had gone. They could hear the humming of its tires on the road.

"He has to come back!" one of the bearers exclaimed and ran after the truck. Forgetting all danger he whistled and called

The truck went on and the Egyptians began to fire at him. He jumped into the ditch that paralleled the road and pursued the truck all the way to Gvar 'Am.

Leib and the bearers tried to decide what to do. "He said that another ambulance would come", Leib told them. "Let's wait." They settled down in the protection of the wadi.

While Tuvia remained at Post 7 to supervise the evacuation of the wounded and the women, Alex returned to headquarters to organize the night's work. All of the men who were resting in the shelters were sent to the posts to re-dig the shattered trenches. Natek was summoned and told to distribute the remaining weapons and ammunition. If the decision were to stay and fight, they would need every bullet; if they were to retreat they must not let a single gun fall into the hands of the enemy.

When Zalman left the meeting of the Defense Committee, he did not go directly to his post, but made his way to the wooden hut in the eucalyptus grove which had been the secretary's office in the days of peace. Although its walls were askew and the door had been blown out, the building still stood. He turned on his flashlight. It was as if the world of yesterday were recreated. Everything was in its place. On top of his roll top desk stood the kibbutz flag which he had come to get. The folder of papers with which he had been working when the first air raid came, was still open. With a stab of pain he remembered that Arale had visited him that day to talk over some problem of the carpenter shop. He heard a sound and turned to see Ruben in the doorway. "I thought of the flag", Ruben said. "We can't leave it behind for the Egyptians." Zalman already was taking the flag off its standard. "Yes, I thought of it too", he replied. Then, as he began to wrap it around his waist for easier carrying, he added with a touch of poetry, "When the Jews were taken as prisoners to Rome, they carried the Menorah with them. I saw it in Rome on the Arch of Titus. We'll take our flag."

As they turned to go, Leika appeared in the broken doorway. "I've come for the kibbutz stamp", she said. "We mustn't leave it. The Egyptians might use it for something and besides we'll need it. And there are twenty pounds of petty cash. I'd better take the money along; if we go out it will come in handy."

So they prepared to leave, if they had to, not by collecting their personal possessions but by rescuing the funds and the symbols of their collective life.

A few minutes before three o'clock, Tuvia came back to headquarters with the news that a messenger had arrived from the Palmach. No help could be sent. The commanders ordered the retreat.

In spite of all that they had endured, many people were dismayed to receive the order. In Post 4 Dina found Natan digging furiously. He was a veteran of World War II and had an amputated leg. Alex had kept him in a quiet post, but during the night he had outdone everyone else in repairing trenches. Because he was one of the few who still had a shovel, he threw his powerful back and arms into the work as if he were struggling with the enemy.

"Leave? Leave here?" he cried when Dina told him the news. "Leave when we're beating them? I won't go. I can't go. How am I going to march all the way to Gvar 'Am?"

"You can't stay here", Dina told him. "Come along with me — I'll help you."

"I'll never make it", Natan said despairingly, but he threw down his shovel and limped after her through the trenches.

Miriam's post was one of the last to be cleared. The messenger found her helping to drag a sand bag into place. She was shocked at the order. In her post everything was ready for the next day's attack — trenches re-dug, look-out post repaired, ammunition counted. She was too good a soldier not to know that she was preparing for a last stand, but she had gathered all regrets, all fears, all thoughts of her husband and her little son, and had put them behind her. "We must fight like the Jews who defended the ruined walls of the Temple", she had told herself. "We must make a second *Masada** in Yad Mordechai." Now it seemed that this was not to be. She did not feel any sense of relief although she realized that the order might give her a chance at life. She felt only the sorrow of defeat. To have endured so much, to have lost so many dear friends, only to let the Egyptians capture the meshek! She gave quiet commands to her men. "Take all of the weapons and ammunition. Take water if you have any. Go out one by one." Twelve years later she could not speak of this moment without tears.

As the people assembled near Post 7, all turned for a last look at their destroyed home. The moon was low in the sky and its level rays cast dramatic shadows over the strange, unreal scene. The familiar buildings in which they had lived and worked had become alien; roofs and windows were gone and doors hung crazily ajar. Piles of junk marked the places where wooden buildings had been. The carefully. nurtured trees were ruined, their tops sheared off or their branches dragging on the ground. Only the Chinese Bohinia tree had escaped. Sheltered behind a hill, its white blossoms glimmered in the fading moonlight. Above the desolation stood the water tower, symbol to these pioneers of their struggle to make the desert green. It stood on three legs, the holes in its sides like great, black wounds. How bitter it was to leave this place, even this nightmare of a place! Most of the people reacted with wrenching grief.

This daring retreat of tired fighting men, women and walking

---

* *Masada* was a nearly impregnable fort, carved out of a mountain not far west of the Dead Sea. For three years after they had conquered Jerusalem, the Romans held it under siege. When they finally succeeded in battering their way into the fort, they found that all of the defenders had killed themselves rather than surrender. Only two old women and a few children were left.

wounded had been planned carefully. Alex and Tuvia had consulted with the two Palmach commanders, with Salek Bielski and others who knew the terrain well. There were two possible routes, each with its own dangers. They could use the road to the abandoned British camp and go through the fields, from there to the safety of some low hills behind which lay Gvar 'Am. This was the route Yoshke had used when he had led the Palmach platoon to the kibbutz on the second night of the battle. The danger here was that the Egyptians could open fire from the hills above the road. The other possibility was to lead the people through the fields and vineyards somewhat farther north. In this case they would have to skirt two orange groves and pass by an abandoned Arab house. The Palmach commanders felt that the grove and the house probably were occupied by Egyptians. After considering the dangers, Alex and Tuvia decided to risk going by the road. It was the shorter way and every yard would count for the exhausted people.

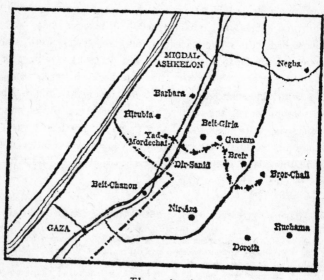

The retreat

The order of the retreat had been organized as follows: Tuvia and Salek went ahead as scouts. Zigi followed with ten of the best fighters, behind them the men and women were divided in groups of ten, each in charge of a captain; a squad of the Palmach brought up the rear, under command of Alex and Yoshke. Altogether there were 110 people. Twenty-five of these were walking wounded; there were seventeen women and a dozen young boys.

Although they had taken no personal possessions from their shattered kibbutz, the fighters carried what arms they had left; 35 rifles, the Schmeiser, the Spandau, those Sten and Bren guns that still were usable, fifty hand grenades, and 100 rounds of rifle ammunition. Most of the ammunition did not fit the rifles they were carrying; it was Italian ammo for the old rifles which they had discarded. In spite of its weight, they also took the remaining two-inch mortar although its ammunition was exhausted. Shamay and Rachel carried the wireless receiver and transmitter. They had smashed an old transmitter and had torn the code into tiny pieces and scattered them to the wind.

Just after the point-men crossed the main road they encountered the two stretchers that had been left behind. Leib Dorfman explained that he and his men were waiting for another armored car to come for them.

"Fall in behind the first squad", Tuvia ordered. "There's no help for it now. We'll have to carry them. When you need relief, call on those behind you."

Tuvia and Salek waited at the wadi in order to direct the people over the improvised passage that had been made after the Arabs had blown up the bridge during the days of siege.

"We'll have to get them off the road," Salek said. "They make too much noise on the asphalt."

They turned the column into a shallow ditch at the side of the road. The people tried to move quietly, holding on to one another. The moon had set and the rough ground was obscured in darkness. Leib Dorfman stumbled and fell and the Palmach man he was helping to carry almost slipped off the stretcher. Leika rushed forward to take Leib's place.

"Don't leave me! Oh, please don't leave me!" cried the wounded man.

Raya stepped up and took his hand in hers. "Don't worry, we'll bring you in safe," she soothed him. "You'll go to the hospital and have your leg set and after a bit you can go home to your own kibbutz. Don't worry, everything's going to be all right."

"We'll soon be safe, Naftali," Leika said cheerfully. "We all thought we would die there in the meshek. But now, you see, we are saved."

"Don't be happy too soon", Dora whispered from behind.

"We know the Egyptians", Leika said confidently. "They won't come out to fight us in the dark. We'll be in Gvar 'Am in no time."

At the head of the column, Tuvia and Salek* were going forward cautiously, scouting the ground ahead, then waiting for Zigi's party to catch up so that they could maintain contact. They estimated that it would take about a half hour to reach the hills which lay between them and Gvar 'Am. When they had gone a third of the way, with the column stretching five hundred yards behind them, the Egyptians discovered the movement and opened fire. Mortar shells screamed overhead and exploded with terrifying thuds. There was the tac-tac-tac of machine guns; tracer bullets arched down from the hills. Actually the Egyptian

---

* It was a sad irony of fate that Salek should have survived his service in Galilee under Orde Wingate, should have survived the battle and the retreat, only to fall victim to a sniper's bullet. In 1955 he was in charge of defense in Yad Mordechai. He went out one night to investigate a rumor that Arab infiltrators were in the neighborhood and was shot from ambush. A half hour after his death, a truckload of children from a neighboring kibbutz passed that way. It may be that his timely intervention saved many lives.

226

gunners were overshooting the road but the people did not realize this. Each person felt exposed, helpless, alone. There was no possibility of fighting back and this increased the panic. Everyone felt that there must be casualties either in front or behind and that he would be next. The well planned retreat turned into a rout. Some people flung themselves down behind heaps of rubble left in the dismantled army camp; they crouched there, afraid to go forward. Others struggled through the sand, threw themselves to the ground, got up and ran again. The more experienced waited for a shell burst and then ran, sometimes falling into the hole the shell had made. Some fled north through a vineyard to the protection of the orange groves. Here and there small groups stayed together but most people had a sense of running alone through the darkness with disaster behind and unknown dangers ahead.

There was one man who could not run — Natan, the one-legged veteran. He hopped along as best he could; then he got down and tried to crawl, dragging his artificial limb behind him. "Better leave me," he cried hoarsely to Dina and Lea, "I'll never make it."

"Yes you will", Lea replied. "Lean on us". Natan was six feet tall and both of the women were tiny. He made up for the disproportion by resting his great hands on their shoulders. With their support he managed to stumble along a little faster. Occasionally they all fell to the ground in a heap. But the women stayed with the crippled man and finally brought him safely to Gvar 'Am.

Soon after the firing began, Rachel lost her shoes. She ran on with Shamay for a few hundred yards and then sat down suddenly. While shells fell all around she began to take a thorn out of her bare foot.

"Come on!", Shamay yelled. "We can't stay here."

"It hurts too much", Rachel said calmly and began to examine the other foot.

"We'll get killed! I'll leave you!" Shamay threatened. Rachel got up and ran again, but every little while she sat down to take care of her feet. When they were safe from the shells, she refused to go any further until she had bound them with strips torn from her clothing.

When they had run about three quarters of a mile, the people got out of range. Tuvia and Salek, who had stayed in the field to direct them, showed the way to the check point behind the hills. As people passed them they asked, "What has become of the two wounded? Where did you see the stretcher bearers last?"

"I was carrying for awhile and then I was relieved." "I didn't see the stretcher after the firing started", one or another would answer. No one seemed to know.

It was almost dawn. Finally a group of people appeared carrying a stretcher. As they stumbled toward him Tuvia saw that they were at the end of their strength. He relieved two men and a Palmach man took hold of the other end. "Where is the other stretcher?", he demanded. The bearers did not know; in the confusion they had separated. "It must be with Alex and the rear guard", they said. Leaving Salek in the field, Tuvia went with the stretcher to the armored cars behind the hills. They put the wounded man in one of them — he was a Palmach fighter whose name has been lost.

A little while later, Alex appeared with the rear guard marching in good order. He had come around the north side of the orange groves. The missing stretcher was not with the party.

"What happened? Why did you come by the south side?" Alex asked.

"Isn't that what we agreed?" Tuvia answered. "Zigi said it was the safest way."

Somehow the two commanders had misunderstood each other; in the pell mell flight they had led groups by different routes while many people had fled in any direction that seemed safest.

228

"One stretcher is missing", Tuvia said anxiously. "I thought it was with you. Didn't you see it?"

"No, it never was with us", Alex answered. "Maybe the bearers went some other way and are already in Gvar 'Am. Let's hope so."

It was full daylight now and dangerous to stay any longer in the open The commanders hurried toward Gvar 'Am. When they arrived, they found a scene of unutterable grief and despair. Groups of people were gesticulating and shouting. Some women, and men too, lay on the ground, sobbing. Before they could ask questions the news burst upon them from a dozen mouths. The other stretcher and its bearers had been captured by the Egyptians.

Salek Bielski told the story. After Tuvia had left him to go to the armored car, the missing stretcher had appeared. Only two people were carrying it, Jacob and the woman runner, Leika. They were staggering with fatigue. Salek had run to get help. He had gone only part way when he heard shouts behind him in English and Arabic, "Who's there? Hands up!" Rifle shots rang out. With dismay he realized that the Egyptians must have sent out a patrol with the first light. He was cut off from the stretcher. He ran to the armored car; some of the Palmach joined him and they went back to try to recover their people. When they got to the spot where it had been, the stretcher was gone. Sometime later, on a distant ridge, Salek had seen a pitiful sight — the silhouettes of the girl and the man still carrying the wounded fighter. They were surrounded by the Egyptian patrol.

"We are to blame for losing them! We are to blame!" Tuvia shouted, half sobbing with grief and rage.

Others took up his self-accusing cry. "Why didn't we stay together?", they sobbed. "Why were they left all alone with only two to carry?" "Did they lose their way?" "Were they too tired to go faster?"

Three people had been lost, Jacob Yahalom and Leika Shapir from the kibbutz and Naftali Holtzman from the Palmach. But they were only captured; they were not dead. Friends began to reassure Shifra, Jacob's wife.

"He's a prisoner of war, that's all. Carrying a stretcher like that — it's the same as if he were in the Red Cross. You'll see, in a few months he'll be exchanged."

"He came to tell me goodbye when I got into the truck and he said 'shalom'," Shifra said. "He said 'Take care of our daughter' as if he already expected something to happen to him. Oh, I wish I had stayed with him! I could have helped carry the stretcher and I never would have left it."

Shifra and Jacob had been married for a little more than four years. They had met when he was sent from another kibbutz to a police unit that was guarding the shores at Natanya. For love of her he had left his own kibbutz and had joined Yad Mordechai. Like so many of these farmers he was a cultured man; he spoke four languages and was studying a fifth. His work was in the vegetable gardens; in the worst days of the siege he had had to water at night when electricity could be used for the pump. Since he was the political chairman of the kibbutz, it was natural that he should have asked for permission to use a little more electricity so that he could listen to the late news broadcast. Every night he stayed up an extra hour or two to make a wall newspaper. When the people came to breakfast, it was neatly spread out on the bulletin board.

Naftali Holtzman was a big, powerful man; he had been hard to carry. A member of Kibbutz Dalia, he had been called to active duty in the Palmach and had been sent in to help defend besieged Yad Mordechai.

Leika, the second bearer, had carried the stretcher most of the way. Leika had been a fighter all her life and her sense of duty was profound. Orphaned when she was only a few months old, she had been raised by a strict grandfather and three maiden aunts. They had not approved of her desire to be a scout, to go to a training camp, to emigrate to Palestine. But she had fought and disobeyed and persisted until finally the aunts had gone to ask the advice of a rabbi. "Let her go — it's better than if she wanted to change her religion", had been his advice. So she had won permission to emigrate, but she had to do so by her own efforts. She became a bookkeeper and worked for years to save money to go to the homeland. But it was not to be easy for her — nothing in her life ever came to her easily. Her only sister was arrested — she was a member of the illegal Communist party. Leika had to decide whether to realize her dream or whether to give money for her sister's defense. She postponed her emigration. A few years later, when one of her aunts fell ill, she had to make the same choice. Finally her chance came and she arrived in Palestine on the day that the Second World War began.

For months the people of Yad Mordechai hoped for the return of the three. Inquiries were made through the Red Cross and the United Nations. Although news of their capture had been announced on the Cairo radio, the Egyptians denied all knowledge of them. They must have been killed, how or when will never be known. Their deaths brought to twenty six the number of people who perished in the battle — eight from the Palmach and eighteen from the kibbutz.

10

Exile and Return

The refugees stayed only half a day in Gvar 'Am. Some of them showered and ate breakfast before dropping down to sleep, but others were too tired to do either. One man pulled up an onion in the field, but fell asleep before he could finish it. Twice their rest was interrupted by Egyptian planes and they had to rouse themselves to go to the shelters. The planes dropped their morning ration of bombs on Gvar 'Am, but their main objective was Yad Mordechai. When the refugees were evacuated by the Palmach at noon, heavy shelling and bombing of their old home was still going on. Clearly the enemy was not yet sure that they had left the meshek — the three captives had kept the secret. It would be another twenty-four hours before the Egyptians would enter the undefended settlement.

The refugees were taken first to Kibbutz Brur Ha'yil, near the abandoned Arab village of Breir. Although still within sight of their home, it was some miles further inland. The settlers welcomed their Yad Mordechai neighbors whose ordeal they had watched for five days. They gave them their first hot dinner. It was cooked and eaten in the open, since this new kibbutz had not yet had time to build a dining hall. The wounded had passed through Brur Ha'yil in the early morning, bound for

Nir 'Am where there was a deep shelter and a doctor. It was good to have news of their safe passage and to know that they would be taken on to Tel-Aviv that night.

After dinner the refugees sat and lay behind an embankment and talked over their situation. There was not one who did not feel shattered by the defeat. Their hearts were still in the meshek. Their nerves quivered with the Egyptian bombardment which they could hear and see. It seemed incredible to them that they were exiles from the home they had built with such effort and toil. Some began to talk about going back. They were sure that with proper reinforcements they could recapture the meshek. Although there were many who had deep reservations as to the practicality of the idea, they did not express them. The fervor of those who wanted to return overwhelmed their doubts. No formal decision was taken since everything would depend upon the attitude of the Palmach.

Alex and Tuvia set out for Palmach headquarters which had moved back to Dorot during the bombardment on the previous day. They found Colonel Sarig sitting with an American, Colonel David Marcus, who later became commander of the Jerusalem front and was killed there.

"It's good to see you", Colonel Sarig said. "We didn't believe that any of you would escape alive from yesterday's bombardment." Alex and Tuvia told the story of the five day battle, of their strategy, of their day-to-day tactics. It was not the kind of report that would be given to commanders of a regular army. The Palmach was an unorthodox fighting force; its officers wore no insignias of rank; its morale was built on a spirit of equality. Consequently Alex and Tuvia felt free to express their feelings. Tuvia, who had been in the firing line, told of the Egyptian attacks with passionate intensity. Alex, who usually kept a tight rein on his emotions, almost broke down as he described the destruction of the meshek, the deaths of wounded men, who might have survived if they could have been evacuated, the despair of the fighters as they saw their arms diminishing, the gradual weakening of morale. Nor did the two men feel hesitant about offering criticism of their superiors.

"We could have held out if you had fulfilled your promises to us," Alex said severely. "We were told that a column was marching south to relieve us. We were told that Gaza would be bombed, that you would attack the Egyptians from the rear. What happened? Why weren't we given more help?"

"I sent you the assurances that I received from the High Command," Colonel Sarig replied patiently. "You were not the only isolated point in Israel that was under attack. The situation was changing from hour to hour. You didn't get more help because it just wasn't available."

Alex and Tuvia were not satisfied.

Colonel Sarig went on to explain further. "There was a column marching south — the Givati Brigade. It is preparing a defense line fifteen miles north of you. I know that it has plenty of problems — the brigade has been in action ever since December. It had no men to spare for reinforcements."

"And what about *you?*" Tuvia demanded. "You couldn't send us more than that one platoon because you were going to deliver a 'blow from outside'. What became of that?"

"I don't have a division under my command," Colonel Sarig replied, "and I have all of the Northern Negev to defend. We did what we could to harass the enemy."

"Let me tell you what has been happening in the rest of the country", Colonel Marcus said and went on to describe the desperate situation of Jerusalem, the fighting in the Jordan Valley, the position in Galilee. "We are besieged on all sides," he told them, "and there are not enough guns nor men for any front."

"But Yad Mordechai is a strategic point", Tuvia argued. "The Egyptians will never get further north if we stop them there. We can re-take it tonight if you will give us the help we need. The people have talked it over and they are willing. The Egyptians are tired, too, and they don't like night fighting. Now is the time to hit them before they can consolidate their position."

"No," Alex contradicted his companion. "Our men are too tired. They can't go back, not right away. It would be suicide."

"They said they would go back!" Tuvia cried.

"I know what they said and what they would like to do", Alex replied. "But we have the responsibility of deciding what is possible. I say that it is not possible."

They argued back and forth, Tuvia with single minded determination to recapture the meshek immediately, Alex with earnest opposition to what he termed an adventure. Finally he made a proposal. If the people of Yad Mordechai insisted on going back, in spite of their weakened condition, they could not be used for the bulk of the fighting. The Palmach must commit at least a company — 120 men. It would be reckless to assume that a smaller number could wrest the meshek from a whole brigade of Egyptians.

"With two commanders like you, I believe that the point could be taken with one platoon", Colonel Marcus said, in genuine admiration.

"No," Alex insisted, not in the least afraid of contradicting a Colonel who had been one of General Eisenhower's staff officers. "The Egyptians have tremendous fire power. It will take a company at least. A company and a half would be better."

Colonel Sarig came to a decision. He would lay the matter before the High Command. He would report that the fighters of Yad Mordechai were willing to try to recapture the meshek if their conditions could be met. The necessary arms and reinforcements would have to be supplied from Headquarters. "If the answer is negative and your people are sent north, you can leave your arms in Gvar 'Am," he added.

"Give up our arms?" cried Tuvia in dismay.

"We need every gun here in the south", Colonel Sarig replied. "If you go back into action we will supply you with arms."

Alex was as shocked as was Tuvia by this demand. Yad Mordechai had been building its armory for years. How much risk and how much monetary sacrifice had gone into it! The thought of giving up the weapons was unmanning; it emphasized their defeat.

"The weapons belong to the kibbutz," Alex said. "We ourselves cannot agree to turn them over. The kibbutz will have to vote on it."

Colonel Sarig accepted this with good grace. He was aware of the democratic procedures within a kibbutz.

"One of you must go to Tel-Aviv tonight and report to the High Command," he said. "You can explain your point of view about the recapture of the meshek." He suggested that Alex be sent.

As Tuvia turned to Colonel Sarig with a question in Hebrew, Colonel Marcus spoke in English to Alex. "Where did you get your military training?" he asked curiously.

"I was in the British army during the war," Alex said.

"Yes? And what was your rank, may I ask?"

"I was a sergeant," Alex replied.

Colonel Marcus laughed extravagantly. "If we had had more sergeants like you in the Allied armies, we wouldn't have needed so many Colonels", he exclaimed.

Alex flushed. He was feeling deeply unhappy and the American Colonel's praise did nothing to comfort him. All during the journey to Tel-Aviv he was agitated. Had he been right in pressing for evacuation? Had he been too easily discouraged? Even in this last discussion he had opposed Tuvia's plan for recapture of the meshek. Was he lacking in courage and determination? A conscientious man, he went over the arguments again and again.

The first person to interview him in Tel-Aviv was Israel Galili, Commander-in-Chief of the Hagana and later Deputy Defense Minister. Alex had known Galili for a long time —

both had been involved in the adventure of stealing the blue prints of mortars and Bren guns during the war. Alex related the events of the battle and the retreat. Then he put his self-doubts before his old comrade.

"You did the right thing", Galili reassured him. "I don't know where your people found the strength to hold out as long as they did. We don't like to surrender any point, of course. But don't worry any more. Yad Mordechai did its duty and retreat was the only course open to you."

For the first time in two days, Alex felt at peace with himself. A little later he was called into a meeting of the High Command. There he was able to give useful information as to the strength, tactics, fighting ability and arms of the Egyptians. In his earnest, serious way he pled for the recapture of strategic Yad Mordechai by a force adequate to the task. He was dismissed with thanks and the promise that the kibbutz would be informed soon as to what could be done.

On Tuesday morning, Kibbutz Yad Mordechai held a general membership meeting. Tuvia reported on the discussion with Nachum Sarig and the proposal to try to take back their home. The meeting was stormy. Now those who had reserved judgement of the plan brought forward their doubts. They pointed out an undeniable fact, that people were feeling even more exhausted after a day and a half of rest than they had felt during the retreat. The tension of the past week was taking a belated toll of their physical and nervous energy. Would the advantage of a night attack overcome the superior weapons and numbers of the Egyptians? And if it did succeed, how could people so depleted hold out under a new siege? Finally they decided that if the Palmach should mount an attack, the kibbutz would contribute ten men to act as scouts and guides. Although by this decision, they tacitly admitted that the majority of the members would not take part in the fighting, there was fierce resistance to Colonel Sarig's request that they give up their arms. Not until the moment of their evacuation did they consent to "loan" their weapons to the Palmach and then they demanded and received a receipt for them.

In the meantime, Tuvia and a delegation of three members had been sent to Dorot. Perhaps they still hoped to impress Colonel Sarig with the importance of recapturing the home that they had lost. To their dismay they learned that the High Command had decided against it. The decisive effort to stop the Egyptians would have to be made further north. Colonel Sarig, preoccupied with his maps, looked up briefly as he made the announcement and said, "Go and rest. You all deserve it."

At nightfall the refugees left for Dorot where they joined a convoy of trucks evacuating children from other settlements in the Negev. At sunrise they came to Rehovot where the trucks took on gasoline. Across the street from the filling station was a bakery. Tantalizing odors of fresh bread filled the air. But no one had any money. They had come from a moneyless society; the kibbutz petty cash fund which could have been used in this emergency, had been lost with Leika. Finally one man had an idea; he pulled a gold watch out of his pocket. "Here, this will buy bread for all of us", he exclaimed.

"Who are these people?" the bakers asked when they were offered payment in kind. One of the chauffeurs volunteered the information that they were the survivors of the battle of Yad Mordechai. After that there was no question of payment. The refugees had all the bread they could eat, while Giora Biber put his father-in-law's gift back in his pocket. The incident still is referred to in the kibbutz. Whenever someone complains that he cannot afford some little luxury out of his cash allowance, one of his fellows is sure to quip, "Haven't you got a gold watch?"

At seven o'clock they arrived in Tel-Aviv. Naftali, the kibbutz treasurer who had been sent out with the children, was there to meet them. He had arranged for them to go to the two places where their children were. Before they left, most of them went to the communal "store" of Hashomer Hatzair to obtain a change of clothing. The group of youngsters who were students at Yad Mordechai, had to get clean clothing from a different source — from Youth Aliya which had arranged their emigration. Raya was responsible for their physical needs. Exhausted as she was from her five days as a headquarters runner, she went to the clothing depot and made her request.

"You received clothes only six months ago", the woman in charge said sharply. "And now you come again! Don't you know how many thousands of children we have to provide for?"

Raya had only to say "These are survivors of the battle of Yad Mordechai" to enlist sympathy and help. But somehow she could not bring herself to explain. Her feelings were so raw that she felt she would burst into tears if she said another word. Completely defeated, she turned away. She went outside and sat down on a bench to collect herself and decide what to do. The next thing she knew she was being roughly shaken awake. A well dressed woman was standing over her. "You're in the city", she said. "Can't you put on a dress? That's no way to appear in the city streets — you're not on the farm." Raya still was wearing the same stained pants and dirty white shirt that she had not taken off during the days of battle. She looked down at herself and realized for the first time how dirty and unkempt she was. "Yes, yes, I'll try" she answered humbly. "You see, I've had no time".

"It doesn't take much time to at least wash your face", the meddler said unkindly and went away.

After this second rebuff, Raya felt completely unable to face the woman in the clothing depot again. She took a bus and went back to Hashomer Hatzair headquarters. Next day an official of the organization obtained the needed clothing.

While he was waiting in the communal "store", Gabriel Ramati was approached by Naftali.

"What are you doing standing around here?" Naftali demanded. "Hasn't anybody told you yet that your son has been born? Go and get a shave and wash yourself. Buy some flowers and go to your wife."

Without doing any of these things, Gabriel rushed to the hospital. He came into Mati's room in a blood stained shirt. She burst into tears.

"So why are you crying now?" the nurse admonished her. "She has been crying ever since her baby was born and she wouldn't tell us why," the nurse told Gabriel.

"I was sure you were dead", Mati sobbed. "My sister heard on the radio that there were sixteen dead in Yad Mordechai and then she said, 'You must be brave and go and bear your child'. I thought she knew that you were dead and didn't want to tell me."

"I'm here, I'm alive, though I'll never know why", Gabriel told her. "I want to see my son."

The small children could not understand why their mothers and fathers wept when they were reunited. Nor could they understand why some fathers did not come at all. There were twelve widows; twenty-two children had been orphaned. The problem of how to break the news to the children occupied the whole kibbutz. A psychologist from their Movement came to advise them; he suggested that the children be told gradually. So the mothers said to the orphans that their fathers had been wounded and were in a hospital. They planned to tell them later that the wounded men had gotten worse and possibly would not survive at all. In the meantime these absent fathers were made the heroes of the battle to the orphaned children. But too many people knew the truth and before long it slipped out. Moshe Kalman's six-year-old son came to his mother one day and said in a quiet, matter-of-fact voice, "Today Jacob and Ada and I sat and cried because our fathers are dead."

The children reacted to their loss in various ways. For half a year one child would imitate a dying man. His head would fall forward on his chest, or jerk backward as if his body had dining room, anywhere at all, apparently in an unconscious effort been hit by a shell. He would do this in his classroom, in the to understand what had befallen his father.

A few became behaviour problems. Some mothers noticed that older children competed with younger ones for attention in a way that had not seemed necessary to them before. One five-year-old who became especially aggressive toward his baby sister was "talked to" by his mother at bed time. (They do not believe in scolding children in Yad Mordechai.) "You know, if you keep on being so bothersome, they might send us out of the kibbutz."

"No, no, they can't do that!" the child exclaimed. "My father was killed there; that means we belong there. If they tell us to go away, we'll sleep outside the fence until they let us come back."

Before the battle the children had played war games, but afterwards they no longer did so. The gun had lost its charm. Instead they were preoccupied with shelters. For months they built shelters in the sand and hid their dolls or their pets in them. But they did make drawings and paintings of war, especially of threatening planes.

The time of day when every one of the orphans missed the absent parent most acutely was the afternoon play period. "I want a father in my room, like everyone else", a child would wail. To fill this gap, some of the men of the kibbutz dedicated their late afternoons to playing with one or another of the orphaned children.

As those who had been babies at the time of the battle grew to the age of understanding, they also grieved for their lost fathers. "I've never even met him", one little boy sobbed as he looked at the framed photograph in his mother's room. "My sister met him — she has a picture taken with him. But he's my father too and I never knew him — I never even met him". His mother gathered him up in her arms and told him how the man in the photograph had walked with him all night when he had colic — how he had loved to play with his little son by throwing him up in the air and catching him again. But no stories of his father's love in his forgotten infancy could comfort his child who was deprived even of a memory.

However, mothers and teachers and nurses all told me that the adjustment of the children to their loss had been made easier by the fact that so many children were bereaved in the same short period and that the grief was generally shared. Yet, as one of them said sadly, "This was the first time in our experience when we saw that such a grief could not be distributed to the whole kibbutz. As much as we all felt it, really each widow and orphan had to bear the tragedy alone."

There was not enough room in Natanya for the children and their parents too. Consequently the adults went to kibbutz Gan Shmuel which was a kind of mother to Yad Mordechai, since half of its members had lived there when they first came to Palestine. The other half remained at Kibbutz Ma'barot. In both places they were beset with difficulties. Wrenched from their homes, they felt nervous and disoriented. Although their bodies needed rest, idleness was intolerable to them. After a few days they asked for and received work. In theory any member of a kibbutz is willing to do any task assigned to him, but in actuality there were many specialists among the Yad Mordechai people who were used to work in the dairy, in the poultry yard, in the orchards, on tractors. All such posts were filled in the host settlements, naturally, and the visitors were assigned to the general labor pool to be called upon for digging a ditch, out in the laundry, etc., as they might be needed. At another time they could have made an easier adjustment. But now they were feeling a natural reaction to the strains that they had endured. Their nerves were raw. Little things irritated them. Gusts of anger blew up from nowhere. In spite of their efforts at self-control, they found themselves involved in unhappy disputes with their hosts.

The makeshift housing arrangements were particularly difficult. Neither kibbutz had extra living space; the guests were taken into the members' small rooms where they felt like intruders. Couples could not be together, just when husband and wife needed the comfort of physical nearness. Some took to sleeping on the lawn.

Worst of all were the arrangements for the children. The younger children were in Ma'barot with their nurses, the older ones in Natanya, ten miles away. Many parents had children in both places. There was no possibility of uniting them by families. According to the kibbutz system, the children had been cared for from infancy by their nurses. Some had been with the same nurses since the day they had come home from the hospital. The attachment was very strong; to take them away from their nurses was unthinkable in this time of general uprooting. The children needed and missed their parents, but they needed the security of their little groups and their familiar routine even more. The parents understood this and did not even suggest other arrangements. Much of their free time was spent travelling between one place and the other in order to visit an absent child.

To add to the unhappiness of this time, the people felt grieved and sore and half ashamed of their defeat. Although they had obeyed their orders and had fought as long as they could, it was hard for them to accept that it had been necessary to abandon the kibbutz. Instead of realizing the audacity and courage of their retreat, many felt that there had been something ignominious in their flight to safety. When their northern neighbor, Kibbutz Nitzanim, was captured and its survivors taken into captivity they said, "We could have saved Nitzanim. If only we had gotten reinforcements the Egyptians never could have passed us." What remained in their emotions were feelings of loss and defeat. They were in no position to assess what they had accomplished by their gallant stand. But it had meant more than they realized for the defense of Israel.

The Egyptian command had based its battle plans on a fundamental error — an error peculiar to the military mind when it is faced with a civilian army fighting for home and freedom. Considering that the "Jewish rabble" would offer little resistance, the commanders had expected to overwhelm Yad Mordechai within a few hours. Instead they had been held up for six days. They had suffered heavy casualties — about three hundred dead and wounded. They also had suffered a set-back in their time-table; they had lost the momentum of their drive on Tel-Aviv. The quick, triumphant march they had planned was out of the question if every Jewish settlement on the way was going to offer the same stiff resistance as had been encountered at Yad Mordechai. They could not afford more victories like that one. It soon became evident that the battle had forced them to reconsider their situation and to revise their strategy.

On May 25th, after it had occupied the abandoned kibbutz, the Egyptian army began to move north. But now it no longer marched in one column on the macadam road. In order to gain room for manoeuvre and to protect itself from Palmach harassment, it fanned out toward the east. While some units kept to the coast road, others advanced along an interior road and a third military road was constructed between the other two.

It will be remembered that the Egyptians had landed troops at the Arab port of Majdal about six miles north of Yad Mordechai and that these had been joined by a column which had bypassed the kibbutz on the third day of the battle. On

May 21st these combined forces, together with units of the Moslem Brothers, had attacked Kibbutz Negba which lay on an important east-west road. This road afforded a connection with the Egyptian brigades which had invested Beersheba and had moved north toward Jerusalem. If they could dominate it, the Egyptians would be able to seal off the northern Negev from the rest of the country. For this it was important to subdue Negba*. While the main Egyptian forces proceeded north along their three-pronged route, some units were left behind to reinforce the besiegers.

In the meantime, during those six precious days that Yad Mordechai had given to the new State, the Givati Brigade had moved into the area and prepared to meet the enemy. It had built fortifications and tank traps and had blown up important bridges on the main road. A number of hostile Arab villages which might be expected to provide the Egyptians with aid, had been subdued.

It took the Egyptians four days to reach Isdud, which was only fifteen miles north of Yad Mordechai. There they were stopped by the lack of a bridge. Before they had time to construct a Bailey bridge so as to move their mechanized equipment, they were attacked from the air. On that very day the infant Israeli Air Force had assembled four *Messerchmit* at a nearby airfield — the first to be received. Although they were urgently needed on other fronts, the Commander of the Givati Brigade, Shimon Avidan, rushed to the field to demand that they be used to stop the Egyptians. The surprise attack did not do as much damage as had been hoped and one of the *Messerchmits* was shot down by anti-aircraft fire, but the psychological effect seemed to have been great. The Egyptians began to dig in for a prolonged stay. That was the end of Egypt's proud boast that her armies would be in Tel-Aviv within a week after the

---

* Kibbutz Negba, which was so placed that it could receive reinforcements and supplies, never was captured although it was under siege during the whole war.

invasion began. Her commanders had to content themselves with dominating the lateral road and sealing off the Negev. They never got farther north than Isdud.

For a little while the refugees from Yad Mordechai hoped that their old home would be recaptured and that they could return there to build and plant anew. But then came the first truce, on June 11th arranged by the United Nations after twenty-eight days of fighting. It was to last for an equal length of time. By its terms, each side was allowed to retain whatever territory it had occupied.

Early in July, Count Folke Bernadotte, the United Nations Mediator, made his proposals for final boundary lines. His plan assigned the whole of the Negev to the Arabs. Taken together with the fact that the original U.N. boundaries had excluded Yad Mordechai from the Jewish State, the dreams of those who longed to go back seemed Utopian indeed.

As if to emphasize the hopelessness of a return, the Cairo Radio announced that King Farouk had paid a visit to the "Maginot Line of the Jews" — Yad Mordechai. His Majesty had seen for himself, the radio reported, "one of the fiercest and most powerful strongholds of the Zionist settlements, built according to the most modern defense plans. It contained lookout posts two stories high in each of its four corners, one for heavy guns and the others for light guns and observers. It was surrounded by a trench three feet deep — after ten steps there was another trench five feet deep and still further on one of six feet in depth. The final defense line was electrified barbed wire." Remembering how they had dug night after night in the shifting sand to repair their inadequate trenches, the survivors smiled wryly at one another. They knew King Farouk needed victories to prop up his shaky throne — therefore they understood the exaggerations of the report. What really wounded and infuriated them was the statement that the Egyptian flag "was fluttering proudly" over the ruined water tower.

Finally, with heavy hearts, the refugees came to a terrible decision. They would have to start all over again in a new place. Lands offered by the Jewish Agency were investigated. They decided to move temporarily to a farm between Tel-Aviv and Natanya, which had been abandoned by its owner, an Arab Sheikh. The farm lay on the slope of a hill with the Sheikh's stone house at the bottom. The refugees left the house intact, for they had rented these lands with the understanding that they would have to give them up if Ali Cassem should return. They went back to the tents and wooden barracks of their pioneering days. There was an orange grove on the property, a wheat field and a vegetable garden. The settlers built a stable and bought thirty cows. They invested in two tractors and machinery for a carpentry shop. To supplement their depleted manpower, the central organization sent in a group of fifty young Rumanians who had gotten to their homeland after a period of detention in the British camps on Cyprus. All were under 18 — the call-up age to the army. Eventually these boys and girls would leave to found their own kibbutz; in the meantime they would help to build the new meshek.

The refugees settled in Ali Cassem's abandoned farm late in July. In September they observed the Jewish New Year in their improvised dining room. It was a somber occasion. No one felt like saying "Happy New Year". Although the kitchen staff had done its best, the dinner was skimpy — the war had imposed austerity rations. Nor was there the feeling of being one big family, which always had animated their festivals. The presence of the strangers, who had not known Yad Mordechai or suffered their losses, emphasized the depression and grief of the survivors of the battle. In this, the first of their traditional holidays since they had lost their home, they felt like exiles. Their hearts cried out with the Psalmist, "By the rivers of Babylon, there we sat down, yea, we wept when we remembered Zion."

247

There were fifteen Jewish settlements within the great square of the northern Negev which was surrounded by the Egyptian troops. They had continued to hold out against constant bombing from the air and occasional shelling. One of the provisions of the truce was that the Egyptians must permit Jewish convoys to cross the east-west road which they now dominated, in order to supply these settlements. From the beginning the Egyptians refused to open the "Faluja crossroads" to Jewish traffic. Repeated attempts by the United Nations Mediator to secure their compliance were futile. Finally the Israeli High Command decided upon military action to free the road. It also had the frank hope that the planned operation would drive the Egyptians out of the Negev, since it was possible that the final boundary lines would be determined by actual occupation of territory. The fate of Yad Mordechai was about to be decided.

The High Command planned to attack the Egyptians from both outside and from within their lines. More men and arms would be needed inside; they would have to be supplied by airlift. In the course of the war, Israel had received planes, as well as arms, from Czechoslovakia. She no longer had to rely on two-seater sport planes for transport and bombing missions. An air field was constructed near Ruhama, the kibbutz which had sheltered Yad Mordechai's children. The first plane landed there on August 22nd. Thereafter, in more than four hundred two-way flights, two thousand tons of equipment were flown into the Negev.

The High Command envisaged a big operation. The young State now had tanks and armored vehicles. Eight batteries of guns as well as canons and heavy mortars were available. A newly formed armored battalion would join the fight. Two infantry brigades and half of another were assigned to it. In manpower the two sides would about equal each other in this sector, with the Egyptians having superiority in fire power. Yigal Alon, who formerly had commanded the troops in upper

Galilee, was put in charge of the operation.

The Israel build-up of forces and arms did not escape the Intelligence of the Egyptians. The truce became no more than a fiction as the Israelis moved troops and arms into the area and the Egyptians bombed settlements and the airplane base at Ruhama. For a week before the formal ending of the truce, there were stiff engagements as the Israelis took over strategic hills and the Egyptians counterattacked.

On October 15th the Israelis informed the Truce Supervision headquarters of the United Nations that it intended to send a convoy past the Faluja crossroads. As expected, it was fired upon. One of the trucks was left burning, blocking the road, and the others returned to their base. This was the signal for the beginning of the Israeli offensive.

The main thrusts were directed at points near the crossroads. In order to confuse the enemy, however, wedges were driven into the Egyptian lines along the coastal strip in order to threaten communications. One of these was at Beit Hanun, about four miles south of Yad Mordechai. While some of the heaviest battles of the war were being fought further north, the Israelis drove this wedge deeper and deeper until they could shell both the railroad and the main road between Cairo and Tel-Aviv. Although they were bombarded from positions near Yad Mordechai, they dug in and held on. The Egyptians were alarmed. Their headquarter at Majdal was about to be cut off. On October 17th they began to evacuate. Their convoys had to pass under the heavy fire of the Israelis who occupied the hills above the road. In order to avoid casualties, Egyptian engineers built an alternate road out of range of the Israeli guns. Working against time and with great ingenuity, they laid wire nettings, boards and logs along the sea shore. Streams of army vehicles passed over this track and mixed in with them was the fleeing Arab population. All but a few of Yad Mordechai's neighbors left with the troops.

When a new cease-fire was decreed on October 22nd, the Israelis had won an important victory. The road to the Negev was open, Beersheba had been captured, the threat of an Egyptian advance on Tel-Aviv had been liquidated. The only Egyptian force remaining in the north was the Fourth Brigade, in which Gamal Abdel Nasser was an officer, and it was trapped in the "Faluja pocket". Despite the cease-fire, the Israelis continued mopping-up operations for some days. On November 5th they liberated Yad Mordechai.

For days the people in Ali Cassem had been at a high pitch of excitement as the radio reported the Israeli advances. When they learned of the wedge at Beit Hanun and the fighting around Majdal they felt sure that their kibbutz would be freed. On the afternoon of November 6th a man appeared on a bicycle, shouting as he came. He was a special messenger sent by General Yigal Alon to bring the news of Yad Mordechai's liberation. There was no question as to what the people would do. The joy that they felt could be compared only to their emotions when they first had stepped ashore in the Homeland. As many as could be spared from the tasks of the farm began running down the sandy road that led to the main highway. Their two trucks were expected back from Natanya but they could not wait calmly for them to arrive. So great was their excitement that they forgot that the November night would be chilly — they went without jackets or blankets. On the main road they met the trucks. "We haven't got enough gasoline to get to Yad Mordechai", the drivers said. "Never mind, the gas station will lend us some". The gas station attendant, happy at the news, contributed the gas. Palmach patrols opened the road blocks for the two truckloads of singing people.

When they came near the meshek their excitement increased. Those who had gone with the convoys during the time of the siege pointed out landmarks. "Here there were mines! Here we were shot at! Here a truck overturned and burned!" When the water tower came into view, they cried out in happiness. How had it stood so long on only three legs?* Ruined as it was, it was a symbol of their old life, and they rejoiced to see it. But as they passed the site of their orchards they fell silent. "The trees!" Zalman said and began to weep. "They cut down all the trees!" The vineyards had been destroyed also — the deeply rooted vines had been torn out of the ground. The fields that had been green when they left were bare and brown; sheep and cattle had been pastured in the most productive areas. These casualties of the earth had to be added to the many losses that they had sustained.

When the returning refugees got down from the trucks, the first thing they saw was a crudely lettered sign, "Welcome to the Heroes of Yad Mordechai". It had been prepared by the young soldiers stationed there. These were not men of the "Kilometer Platoon" nor any from among the familiar soldiers of Gershon's* command. But the homecoming pioneers felt such joy and gratitude that they embraced and kissed the strange soldiers. They received from their hands a memento of the Egyptian occupation — the Egyptian flag which had been left flying from the water tower

Warned against walking around the meshek because of the possibility of mines, the refugees decided to spend the night in their old dining room. As they entered, they passed the Bulletin Board still in place. One sheet of paper, tattered and stained, was fastened there. It was a news bulletin. "The U.N. Assembly discussed the invasion of Palestine and President Truman said that the United States will do everything in its power to avoid bloodshed" the first item read. It was the last bulletin that Jacob

---

* When the settlers had been back in Yad Mordechai for several months, the legs of the water tower collapsed and it fell to the ground. Several men who were working near it narrowly escaped being killed.

* Gershon had lost his life in the battle of Beersheba.

Yahalom had posted — Jacob who had been lost in the retreat.

Early in the morning the people went to visit their rooms. They were unrecognizable. Only the walls and broken roofs remained. Furniture, pictures, personal possessions of every kind had been carried away. The survivors had few regrets for lost clothes and furniture; after a year or two the kibbutz would be able to provide these. It would be a long time before they would own radios again, but they had done without them before. What they grieved for were their photograph albums. With the birth of each child an album had been presented by the kibbutz to its parents. Although few families owned cameras, they had managed to keep a treasured record of their children's growth. All of the albums were gone. Gone, too, were pictures of their early training years in Poland. And gone were the portraits of parents and of brothers and sisters in Poland who never had been heard from since the Nazi invasion. Only one album ever was returned to its owner. It was found later in the quarters of an Egyptian soldier in captured Beersheba. From this the pioneers could guess that their family mementoes had been carried away as souvenirs.

Toward noon more people arrived. They brought the kibbutz flag and arm loads of flowers. From Tel-Aviv came Israel Galili, "the father of the Palmach" who was an old friend of the kibbutz, and Abraham Hartzfeld, a beloved leader of the agricultural settlements. He had brought wine to celebrate the return. Zalman, as secretary of the kibbutz, called the members together. They sat down on the bare earth which once had been green with grass. Galili repeated to them what he had told Alex on the night following the retreat. "Your battle gave the whole south six precious days for fortification, for organization, for the securing of additional arms", he said. "The Egyptians learned here the valor and the obstinacy of the Jewish fighter. They recognized how much they would have to pay in lives and material if they were to go forward. The nation owes much to Yad Mordechai. Its battle will always be remembered as the battle of Tel Hai is remembered — as a glorious episode in the history of our defense." Hartzfeld, with the optimism and good humor which were characteristic of him, spoke of a matter which the members had been discussing for months. "Turn your faces toward the future", he said. "Decide here and now that you will wipe out this destruction, that you will come back and build again. Let's drink to it — L'chaim!" and he took the first sip. Bottles of wine passed from hand to hand; the teen-agers who had endured the battle drank to their future; the pioneers who had seen so much death, drank "to life"; even Dr. Heller unbent from his severity to join in the toast.

It was in a mood of mingled sadness and hope that the meeting adjourned to pay a visit to the mass graves. During their months of exile, the refugees had wondered often whether the Egyptians had discovered and desecrated them. But the graves were untouched. A bit of iron roof protruded at an angle over the abandoned shelter where the first dead had been buried. The Egyptians had found it a convenient place to throw trash. They had not discovered what lay below.

The people laid flowers on the graves of their old friends, thinking of them as they had been in life. They shed tears, of course. They remembered the fearful effort and danger of the battle in which they might have died instead of those who were beneath the ground. Later on, when they came back for good, they felt the need of individual graves so that the children, and they themselves, could pay homage to each fighter who had lost his life in the battle. The bodies were moved to the hill-top opposite the water tower. Beside a curving walk, twenty-three simple stones mark the graves; three others are set apart in memory of those who were lost in the retreat. Most communities bury their dead at a distance, but these rest in the heart of the meshek. A child may slip away at play time to sit by his father's grave. The widows go often. Old friends climb the hill on their way to do an errand. And every Spring, when Israel's school children are taken to visit historic places, hundreds stand by the graves and hear the story of the battle. The guide may point to the spot below the water tower which was the first resting place of those who died. The survivors have marked that place of the dead with life: 26 cyprus trees cluster together there a tall, green, monument.

II

Afterword

The decision which Abraham Hartzfeld urged upon the kibbutz was not an easy one to make. The war was not yet over; no one knew what the final outcome would be nor where the final borders would be drawn. It was possible that they would be determined by military occupation, but there also was a chance that inhabited places would be taken into account. Territory in which no Jews lived might with justice be assigned to the Arabs. If Yad Mordechai were to remain a wasteland, there was every prospect that it would be excluded from the Jewish State as it had been in the original partition.

The survivors could stay where they were, safe in the center of the country, and build up a farm on Ali Cassem's more fertile ground. But if they did so, would they not be failing their duty as pioneers? They had gone to the Negev in the first place in order to help open up more land for Jewish settlement. They felt a responsibility toward the fields which they had reclaimed from the desert and which they had fought so hard to defend. They could not say, "We have done enough, now let us live in peace."

No one doubted the difficulties and dangers of the return. If their gamble were to succeed, the new border would have to be drawn between them and Gaza. Theirs would be a border settlement, subject to harassment (although they could not have foreseen how much.) If there should be another invasion, they would stand in its path and again would sacrifice lives and property. Nevertheless, after long and serious debate, the pioneers decided to go back, hoping that by re-settling Yad Mordechai they could reclaim it for Israel.

Apparently not everyone agreed with the decision; twenty members left the kibbutz that year. Although they would not say that they could not bear to return to the ruins, those who stayed feel sure that this was their reason. Together with the seventeen men and one woman who had died in the battle and the retreat, this represented a loss to the kibbutz of nearly a third of its manpower. Of the present members, only about half are the Polish pioneers who founded it. The newcomers are Bulgarians and people from Latin America; many of the latter are of Polish extraction.

Today Yad Mordechai is a tree shaded community of nearly five hundred people. At the foot of the hill where the fallen water tower lies tipped over on its side, the Bohinia tree puts out its pale blossoms, and across a wide expanse of lawn stands the grove of cypress trees. A rose garden, a little pool and benches set under flowering oleanders, contribute to the sense of restfulness and peace. Except for the marks of bullets in some cement buildings, all signs of the battle's destruction have been erased.

In these fourteen years, an enterprise worth a million and a half dollars has been built. This does not include the land itself which the kibbutz holds on lease. The farm is almost three times as big as it was before. As has happened all over Israel, the lands of the Arabs who left were taken over by the Jewish National Fund and leased to Jewish farmers. The farm is fully mechanized; the kibbutz owns 60 agricultural machines and others are rented in season from a local cooperative. Two hundred and fifty acres are planted with cotton. Other crops are grain, vegetables and a variety of fruits. There is a herd of 200 beef cattle and 100 cows. Eight thousand white leghorn chickens have taken the place of those that were killed. The bee-hives produce from twenty to thirty tons of honey a year and the bee-keeper raises queen bees which are exported to European countries.

In keeping with the kibbutz ideal of combining agriculture with small industry, Yad Mordechai re-established its canning factory. Part of the raw materials come from the farm; the rest is purchased. In 1960 the factory produced a million cans of peas; jams and orange juice. In order to run this enterprise, the pioneers have had to compromise with one of their ideals. When they came to Palestine, it was with the intention of working the land with their own hands; they did not want to become employers and therefore "exploiters of labor" in their way of thinking. But the chronic manpower shortage in the kibbutz forced them to violate this principle in the factory. Forty-five workers from Ashkelon are employed there. In time, the kibbutz hopes to supplant them with its own members. As younger people join the kibbutz and take over the heavy work of the farm, the veterans expect to enter the factory. Since they can make their own labor policies, they will be able to reduce the work-day to whatever number of hours an older person can manage.

The social organization of the kibbutz remains much as it was when the youthful pioneers began. A weekly assembly decides all major questions. The officers are a Secretary*, a Treasurer, and a Farm Manager. These managerial functions do not carry any special privileges nor confer status. A man who agrees to serve a second year in the onerous job of Secretary is con-

* In 1961 a woman was elected to serve as secretary. As had been done occasionally in the past, an assistant was designated to share the burdens — also a woman.

sidered to have made a sacrifice for the kibbutz. He would prefer to spend his days in the wheat fields and to have time for tea with his wife and a two or three-hour playtime with his children. The Secretary is assisted by a Secretariat and by a number of Commissions: Social, Cultural, Political, Educational, Economic, Building, Financial, Sport.

Although Zalman used to say to me, with a twinkle in his eye, "We're only simple peasants," the cultural interests of the kibbutz belie his words. He himself is at home in nine languages and most of the Polish people speak four or five. The study of English is popular. Classes in Literature and Current Events are well attended. The kibbutz issues a weekly mimeographed Bulletin, attractively illustrated by a boy who lost his father in the battle. It varies from twelve to twenty pages. The Library, which was completely destroyed by the occupying Egyptians, has been re-established; it contains 20,300 volumes in six languages. One section is an archive of photographs and written materials relating to the battle. Especially, interesting are brief accounts on scraps of paper, which the commanders of the posts wrote while they waited in Brur Ma'yil to be evacuated.

Entertainment is not lacking in Yad Mordechai. Each room now has a radio; movies are shown once a week. During the nine weeks that I spent in the kibbutz in 1960, there was a special event every week. Four were ceremonial occasions, Passover, Independence Day, Remembrance Day, in which the whole nation mourns the six million Jews who died in the holocaust in Europe, and Yad Mordechai's own memorial for those who died in the battle. Guests from outside were present at all of these functions.

Cultural evenings included a lecture on literature by a critic — a member of another kibbutz — two theatrical performances, and two discussions of the writing of this book.

The veterans showed keen interest in my work and were generous with criticism and advice. In an initial meeting some of

258

them took exception to my reference to their heroism. They warned me against glorifying their deeds; they made me understand that they do not think of the battle as an example of man's courage in the face of great odds — they think of it as a tragedy. They pointed out that they became front line soldiers by an accident of geography. They did their duty and killed when they had to, but they are men of peace. "Tell how we fought but let every page call out for peace," they demanded at our final meeting.

The theatrical performances were presented by professional companies from Tel-Aviv. The members of three kibbutzim gathered in Yad Mordechai's social hall for a bill of one-act plays. I was especially interested in one of them which dealt with the conflict between personal desires and the kibbutz ideal. The laughter and applause of the audience indicated keen awareness of the problems of fitting contrary human beings into an idealistic society.

The other theatrical function was held in an outdoor theatre in Gvar 'Am. Everyone else rode in trucks but I was conveyed in style in a bouncing jeep. The theatre seats three thousand people and was built by the Area Council, comprising seventeen agricultural settlements. On this evening, Yad Mordechai's chorus of 110 voices sang under the direction of its professional conductor. A theatrical troupe of talented young people from Tel-Aviv performed what obviously were amusing skits, some of them highly political. During a summer series, the best theatrical and musical organizations in Israel come to play in this outdoor theatre, which is one in a chain of twenty similar theatres throughout the country.

Besides these local functions, Yad Mordechai people take advantage of what Tel-Aviv has to offer. Each member receives money for four theatre tickets a year besides his cash allowance of twenty five dollars*. Many people spend a large part of this

---

* Each child receives his own yearly allowance of five dollars which is administered by his parents.

259

allowance on their cultural interests. They attend symphony concerts or plays, subscribe to newspapers, buy prints for their rooms or books in which they are especially interested. I noticed fine china tea services in a number of rooms, a pleasant change from the plastic dishes of the communal dining room.

The way of life of the kibbutz allows for few vacations. People may be excused from work in order to attend a wedding of a relative or close friend in another town, or in case of illness or death in the family. Once in two years each couple enjoys a week's vacation in one of the two seaside resorts maintained by Hashomer Hatzair. Children have more frequent vacations. From the age of seven they belong to the same Scouting movement that brought their parents to Zionism. It arranges hikes, camping trips and visits to other communities during the summer.

The physical conditions of living in the kibbutz have improved with its prosperity. There are three types of housing in use — the wooden houses that were transferred from Ali Cassem, the cement houses that were repaired after the battle, and new houses. These reflect the changes in thinking that have taken place in Hashomer Hatzair since the austerity of the early days. The first houses were built without toilets or showers. This was only partly the result of the need for economy as became clear when a fierce debate raged in the kibbutz, and in the whole movement, as to whether or not private bathrooms were appropriate to its socialist ideals. A compromise was reached with the building of a bathroom for each two rooms in the cement houses. According to the people who used them, these facilities were less satisfactory than the old system of communal showers and toilets. It seemed that the other family always was in the bathroom! Now the desire for privacy no longer is suspect; New rooms have their own bathrooms. The increase in living space is another sign of the times; each successive type of housing has been built with larger rooms. The newest living quarters are 102 feet square. Beautifully designed, with plenty of storage space (always a problem in the older rooms) and furnished in modern style with pieces bought from the furniture factory of another kibbutz, they compare favorably with a nice one-room apartment in Tel-Aviv or New York.

All rooms are furnished comfortably with single beds, an easy chair, a table and straight chairs and a large chest of drawers. There are rugs on the floors and pictures on the walls — Chinese prints are popular. The sewing room provides matching bedspreads and window drapes. Apparently the women may choose the material for these, since I did not see the same design in any two rooms. The kitchenettes contain an electric tea kettle and a hot plate. Many of the women have learned to bake cakes for tea-time in a "top-of-the-stove" oven. The teen-agers who come from their dormitories on the High School grounds enjoy their mothers' cakes and the comparative comfort of their rooms, but like teen-agers everywhere, they are inclined to be critical. Full of youthful idealism, they feel that their parents live too comfortably!

The old egalitarian custom of changing quarters each half year in order to equalize the differences in housing, has given way to a system of seniority. There was an exception to this rule after World War II when the kibbutz took its part in receiving refugees. Newly arrived survivors were put into the best rooms while their original occupants moved back into tents.

Everyone in the village above grammar school age* eats in the communal dining hall. The new dining room, with the adjoining social hall, was erected in 1959 at a cost of $175,000. Food is prepared by a crew of twenty women in a fully electrified kitchen. All of the men and women of the kibbutz take their

---

* The younger children eat in their school-houses. Food for children up to three years old is especially prepared; the others eat the same food as their elders with some additional provision of milk and eggs.

turn at setting the tables and serving. Nowadays, food is plentiful. On the breakfast table there always was white cheese, jelly, herring, a piled-up breadbasket and coffee with milk. The steam table offered hot cereal, an egg, and *leben*. Potatoes are a staple of the Polish diet, they usually appeared twice a day in Yad Mordechai. A typical dinner menu included besides boiled potatoes, soup, a piece of meat or fish, a vegetable, a mixed green salad and a fruit juice drink. On ordinary evenings there was a fried egg, yellow cheese, fried potatoes, herring, and either tea or cocoa. The Friday night supper retained some of the festive nature of Jewish tradition. Although there were no candles lit to welcome the Sabbath, there were flowers on the table and tiny napkins — the only meal of the week in which napkins appeared. A typical menu on that night was *humus,* an Arab appetizer made of ground chick peas, fried potatoes, small frankfurters, egg salad, mixed green salad, fruit compote, cake and coffee. On Saturday mornings, a delicious cinnamon bread was substituted for cereal.

For the most part, meals in Yad Mordechai are not social occasions. People take any vacant seat at the tables and husbands and wives often eat separately according to the demands of their work. Even the evening meals are not leisurely since there are three sittings and the serving and dish-washing crews are anxious to finish their work. In former days, all meals were taken together in the common dining room; it would have been unthinkable that any person should prefer to eat apart from his fellows. As the pioneers have grown older, they have begun to crave for privacy. More than half of the members now eat their Saturday morning breakfast in their rooms, taking supplies from the kitchen or sending to the dining room for what they want. The need for privacy is recognized also in the monthly distribution of coffee, tea, sugar and cookies so that those who wish may have tea in their own rooms rather than in the dining room. Private parties occur more frequently than they did in pioneer days and for these the hostess may obtain a bottle of wine, extra cookies, candies and sometimes a cake.

The physical well-being of the founders of Yad Mordechai is a matter of concern to them "since we all are growing older". The health of the settlers is looked after by a resident doctor, who serves another kibbutz as well, a visiting dentist, a Physical Therapy Department and the Health Committee. There are yearly-X-rays for tuberculosis and periodic inspection for cancer. I asked Nomi, one of the widows, who with the kibbutz nurse comprises the Health Committee, why a committee was needed when there was a doctor on the premises. "To organize everything", she replied. By this she meant that there is much more to health than visits to a doctor. Arrangements must be made to carry out his orders. If he puts the patient on a diet, the Health Committee informs the kitchen. Forty people were receiving special diets when I was there. If someone is ill in his room, the Health Committee sees to it that he gets his food and medicine and if he wants a book from the library, it brings that, too. Special treatments in Tel-Aviv, hospital stays, operations, are arranged by the Committee. Out of its special fund comes the money for visits to relatives hospitalized in Tel-Aviv. And since no one wants to come empty handed into a sick person's room, this fund also supplies money for gifts.

The Health Committee exercises general supervision over the Physical Therapy Department which is run by a woman especially trained for this work. She gives gym classes to children from the age of three, corrective exercises to those who need them, and classes for men and women in the evenings. Rheumatism is a major health problem for the pioneers who now are between forty-five and fifty years of age. They contracted it in their cold, damp training quarters back in Poland and have suffered from it ever since. Besides corrective exercises, the Department administers mud packs. Since it is thought that mud from the Sea of Galilee has special healing properties, the Health Committee imports a supply.

The care and education of their children is one of the main preoccupations of the kibbutz. Originally it established its system of handing over its children to nurses in order to free the rest of the women for work in the fields. Today only a handful do any sort of farm work; fully fifty percent are busy with the children as nurses or teachers; most of the rest are in services — the kitchen, the laundry, the sewing room, etc.

The educational system is "modern". As the children enter school, nursery groups are put together in groups of ten and later on of twenty — the largest teaching unit in the system. No grades, report cards or graduation certificates are given; the children are supposed to learn to evaluate their own efforts. They elect their officers and govern themselves; their Assemblies take care of most disciplinary problems. The educators in the kibbutz say that the system pays off in interested and alert children who seek knowledge for its own sake. To illustrate the point, they told of an elementary class that carried on its own studies for several days when its teacher was called away by illness in her family.

The kibbutz frankly is training its children to stay on the land. From their earliest school years, they have manual tasks to do. They must help to keep their living quarters clean. The smaller children have their own little farm with plants and animals to care for. From the time they are in the seventh grade, they begin to work on the real farm. At first they work for an hour and a half a day; from the tenth grade on they give three hours of labor to the kibbutz.

The curriculum of the High School is divided into two blocks of subjects — Science and the Humanities. The latter course includes intensive study of the Bible (as history), Languages, Sociology, History and Literature. Only in exceptional cases would a child be sent on to the University. It is expected that the graduates will pursue their intellectual interests as the leisure-time activities of farmers, as their parents have done.

All adults in the kibbutz may avail themselves of the extensive cultural and technical courses offered by Givat Haviva, the Educational Institute conducted by Hashomer Hatzair.

Yad Mordechai is proud of its educational establishment; twenty five per cent of its budget goes for educating its children from kindergarten through High School. The school buildings represent an investment of $ 124,000. There is a small but splendidly equipped science laboratory, the gift of a friend in the United States. The art department, under the direction of a talented member of the kibbutz, teaches drawing, painting, sculpture, and a variety of handicrafts — ceramics, jewelry making, mosaics, etc. Exhibitions of paintings are presented regularly in the Social Hall and the several that I saw were more than creditable. The art department also offers classes to adults. There is not a room in the meshek that has not been beautified by something made by children or members.

In addition to their own children, the kibbutz is caring for, and educating, forty five others, orphans or half orphans who need a home. A number of these are Jewish children from Arab countries. Part of their upkeep is paid for by Youth Aliya, but since the kibbutz does not care to establish separate standards for the outsiders, they receive the same housing, clothing, food and education as do the teen-agers of the kibbutz. In addition, each one is "adopted" into a family and spends some time every day in the room of his kibbutz parents.

When I was living in Yad Mordechai in 1960, its oldest boys and girls were in the army, doing their service of two and a half years, and their elders were speculating as to what they would decide about their future once they had finished their training. "After all, they have had a chance to see the cities and to see how other people live", they would worry. "Perhaps they won't want to live in the kibbutz." Their preoccupation was deeper than the normal interest of parents in seeing their children well settled in life. What if, after their years of physical toil and austere living, after the sacrifice and sorrow of the battle and the struggle to build the kibbutz again, their children should reject Yad Mordechai? It would be a crushing defeat. Yet the children had been raised in an atmosphere of freedom to make their own decisions and their elders knew that they must stand apart and wait. Only those who come with a willing heart may join a kibbutz. It would have to be the same with their children.

When I returned in 1962, I found that all of the young people but one had chosen the kibbutz way of life. (The exception was a girl who had married a boy in Beersheba.) Four of the girls had come home with men whom they wished to marry and who were willing to live and work in Yad Mordechai. The wedding must have been a heart-warming occasion as the young people joined their personal futures to that of the kibbutz. It was no casual affair such as the pioneers had known. After the couples had been privately married by a rabbi, the whole kibbutz and many outside guests sat down to a wedding feast at improvised tables on the lawn. There were places for a thousand people. On a decorated and flood lit platform the kibbutz ceremony was held. The brides wore white and carried flowers; the boys were dressed in grey trousers and open necked white shirts. They passed to the platform beneath green arches held by their younger brothers and sisters and were received there by their parents. The ceremony itself was simple. Gideon read a portion of the Talmud and the newlyweds signed the kibbutz register of marriage and toasted each other in wine. As the people danced and sang and feasted in their honor, it must have been more than marriage that they celebrated, it must also have been the justification and the reward for all their efforts.

When people live for an ideal outside themselves, they are marked by it. The people of Yad Mordechai have been molded by the values which they set for themselves early in life. They wanted to be farmers in the homeland and they are successful farmers. Although they gave up school to go to their training camps, they did not give up learning. Their passion for self-improvement has made them into cultured, knowledgeable people who discuss art, or literature, or politics, with keen appreciation. The discipline of living in a co-operative society has made them sensitive and kind. "We understood — it was human", they said in speaking of men whose courage had failed them during the battle. "In kibbutz life, one has to learn to forgive", one of them explained. Whatever may be the jealousies, frustrations or hidden angers beneath the calm surface, the kibbutz members try consciously to be thoughtful of the needs of others. There are many little examples of this in the daily organization of their lives. The men take their turn equally with the women in serving the dining rooms, although it might be argued that the work in the fields is harder than women's work in nursery or laundry. Husbands may be seen shaking out the rugs as they relieve their wives of the task of cleaning their room. Young, unmarried people must live with a room-mate, but adult bachelors are given a room by themselves on the theory that "they must suffer" — lacking the consolations of family life, they are thought to merit extra consideration. Children who need special attention and training receive it. The tenderness with which the kibbutz regards the widows and orphans is another example of this thoughtfulness in human relations. I could cite other kindnesses and courtesies that I observed, but I was requested by members not to do so, lest the recipients of special attention feel hurt by having their private troubles revealed.

The pioneers of Yad Mordechai, and others like them, have contributed a great deal to their Homeland. They renewed ruined lands and laid the basis for the scientific agriculture of modern Israel. Probably it could have been done in no other way. As to their hopes that by living Socialism they would point a way to the future, only the future can tell. Today the kibbutz is a little island of cooperative living in a society that is capitalist in nature. Its products must compete in the capitalist market; it must obtain money for expansion by paying high interest. Its early values of plain living and high thinking are eroded constantly by the affluence of the society that surrounds it. The pioneers are frank about their anxiety for the future. They, themselves would not want any other life, but now they are uncertain as to whether later generations will see the beauty of their dream. Although their first children came back to the kibbutz, others may not, and the manpower requirements of the farm and factory cannot be fulfilled by their children alone.

Nor is their immediate future a certain one. In spite of the peace and charm of the home they have built for themselves, there are signs that all is not peaceful. From the hill where the fallen water tower lies, one can look at the sand dunes that mark the border only three quarters of a mile away. One can see the high fence that surrounds the meshek; at dusk its gate is locked. Armed guards patrol it all night long and a searchlight sweeps over the countryside. In spite of the fourteen-year-long truce, this border never has been peaceful. Spies and marauders from the Gaza Strip come over the sand dunes to do whatever damage they can. Several were caught during the time that I lived in Yad Mordechai. One had fired at a passing ambulance; another had murdered a man in nearby Ashkelon. No one talks of preparations to defend the kibbutz in case the Egyptian Army should cross the border again, but it is obvious that they have been made. The water supply and the pump are underground. Large shelters have been built of which one sees only the air vents and the descending steps. The trenches at Posts 1 and 2 are maintained. Somewhere there must be a store of arms, but I was not told of it. Israel has a strong army now and this border settlement would not be left to fight alone if war should come. Whatever tension they may feel in their hearts, the people of Yad Mordechai never speak of such a possibility.

The heroic bronze statue of Mordechai Anilevicz, standing in front of the broken water tower, can be seen from all but the newest sections of the pleasant meshek. He holds a grenade in his right hand. In the last days of the Warsaw Ghetto he wrote*, "I am proud that I came to this moment and that my eyes see a grenade and a pistol in the hands of the Jew... I am ready to die. It seems to me that only to such an end was I born. To this task I grew up and with the conclusion of this battle I must cease."

His comrades, who named their kibbutz in his honor, have known the feel of a live grenade in their hands. But those hands also have guided the plow and the tractor, have worked with the hoe and the pruning shears, have mastered the delicate intricacies of machinery. For Mordechai Anilevicz there was no future — only the grenade. Yet in a sense his life did not cease in the ghetto's flames. It goes on as the turning year brings the seeding, the growing time, and the harvest.

---

* Part of a note sent to Anteck Zuckerman, who was in another bunker. He was one of the few who escaped through the sewers and survived.